RELIGION AND POLITICS IN COMPARATIVE PERSPECTIVE

Religion and Politics in Comparative Perspective

REVIVAL OF RELIGIOUS FUNDAMENTALISM IN EAST AND WEST

EDITED BY
Bronislaw Misztal
AND
Anson Shupe

Westport, Connecticut
London

Library of Congress Cataloging-in-Publication Data

Religion and politics in comparative perspective : revival of
   religious fundamentalism in East and West / edited by Bronislaw
   Misztal and Anson Shupe.
       p.   cm.
   Includes bibliographical references and index.
   ISBN 0–275–94218–X (alk. paper)
       1. Fundamentalism.   2. Christianity and politics.   3. Sociology,
Christian.   I. Misztal, Bronislaw, 1946–   .   II. Shupe, Anson D.
BT82.2.R44   1992
270.8′25—dc20   92–12120

British Library Cataloguing in Publication Data is available.

Library of Congress Catalog Card Number: 92–12120
ISBN: 0–275–94218–X

First published in 1992

Praeger Publishers, 88 Post Road West, Westport, CT 06881
An imprint of Greenwood Publishing Group, Inc.

Printed in the United States of America

The paper used in this book complies with the
Permanent Paper Standard issued by the National
Information Standards Organization (Z39.48–1984).

10   9   8   7   6   5   4   3   2   1

CONTENTS

ACKNOWLEDGMENTS

This book has been a collective endeavor from the start, and we have found this collaboration to be rewarding and stimulating. However, we bear intellectual responsibility for the overall idea of the volume and for the clarity of the message we wanted to send to the sociological "globological" community. We would like to express our thanks to the contributors who accepted our frequent editorial intrusions into their creative writings.

Although this book has been partially expedited through use of the technological advances of the communications media, we do owe particular thanks to Mrs. Marci Irey for her patient assistance in putting together the manuscript; for compiling the otherwise incompatible electronic versions of particular chapters; for typing, retyping, and copyediting those texts for clarity of style; and for her good-tempered tolerance of our characters.

INTRODUCTION

This volume sprang from an idea that inspired the two of us sometime between the end of 1988 and early 1989. Being peripatetic scholars, we encountered each other while working in the same university department. As we discovered one day amid an intensive debate, we, who came from completely different worlds, shared the same trait: a mixture of intellectual loneliness and a craving to comprehend the fast-paced world around us. And so we continued to meet as friends and scholars, in an attempt to find out to what limits we could expand our academic and professional knowledge about global events.

One of us is a sociologist of religion who for several years has reflected on conservative religious movements in the western hemisphere and East Asia. His ruminations prompted him to articulate some historical generalizations about capitalist culture and its impact on social consciousness. The other is an East European student of social movements who, as many of his kind have done over the past fifty or a hundred years, became an intellectual immigrant to the United States. During the last twenty years he has chronicled the processes involved in the breakdown of the Communist empire, specializing in social change and political sociology. When the two of us started spelling out our predictive hypotheses about what we believed would take place on the face of this planet by the end of the twentieth century, we realized that we spoke *unisono*. We agreed that the two hemispheres of Eastern totalitarian Europe and Western liberal democratic America, which used to be as much different as fire and water, are now converging to form a pool of potentially similar conservative and religiously fundamentalist values.

The late 1980s constituted an era of intense debate about the nature of modernity (Harvey 1989; Feher, 1991) and of democracy (Harrington, 1989; Held 1987) that was meant to be a positive, and indeed constructive and optimistic, remedy to the Rousseauian dilemma of the state of nature. Our own ruminations negated the linear model of progress that was developed by many. In our opinion, an era of fundamentalist beliefs was fast approaching. Unsure as to whether we were the only ones who saw this handwriting on the wall, we turned to several of our colleagues with an invitation to contribute to the debate and to test a hypothesis that we put to them: Are the structural, political, and cultural conditions for the resurgence of fundamentalism present, even in seed form, in the world around us?

We took advantage of the 12th World Congress of Sociology in July 1990, drawing on the broadest international pool of participants and contributors we could find. In special sessions we arranged, we invited scholars from East and West to discuss the issue of conservative fundamentalism. While some accepted the invitation, for others the very idea of approaching the issue of a potential regress during the high tide of progressive hopes seemed too daunting. Nevertheless, very heated discussions took place one hot afternoon on the lawn of the Universidad Complutense in Madrid, Spain.

Following the congress we knew that we had tapped a good deal of interest on this comparative subject, so we began to formalize our assumptions and asked various respected scholars to address specific issues that we believed needed to be dealt with in a more systematic way. Since summer 1990 we have worked with this group of authors, shuffling ideas, concepts, and suggestions worldwide over electronic networks. We also continued our own comparative readings of the political, religious, and cultural scenes in both hemispheres. Evaluating the state of research to date, we judged that, during the 1970s and earlier, an international religiopolitical interface was largely feared; this was evidenced by an uncritical reliance on the hypothesis of linear secularization, modernization, and progress (Lewy, 1974; Smith, 1974) that had characterized functionalist paradigms then dominant in postwar Western social science. Simultaneously, in a similar vein, research on Eastern Europe, made up of the once so-called "socialist" societies, also advanced the concept of linear progress. That East European societies might hatch conservative and fundamentalist politics was virtually excluded as a possibility (Misztal, 1978).

We found several compelling reasons to advance our proposition that modernity is not a linear paradigm of progress but rather a dialectical, contrasting, and indeed challenging combination of social processes and cultural tendencies; that improvement in the organizational order of industrial production, societal consumption, and distribution of cultural values by the media does not yield adequate mapping of the world by masses of people living in the West and the East; and that the continuous processes that prompt organizational improvement also produce a hermeneutical vacuum and debilitate the cognitive abilities of both common society members and producers of ideas alike.

First, only a person lost in a coma for the brief period of the past few years is unaware that Europe—Eastern and Western—is being transfigured in ways that will radically affect its component nations' sovereignties, economies, internal politics, and, likely, religions, not only during the remainder of this century but also well into the next millennium.

Second, the recent breakup of the Soviet Union and its loss of hegemony as the Second World superpower has been accompanied by a drastic removal or reduction in regime repression of religiosity and freedom of religious expression. Indeed, with the collapse of often officially sanctioned Communist atheism, there is an ideological, not to mention a spiritual, vacuum for much of an entire generation of East Europeans.

Third, not just in Eastern Europe but in the West as well, the need exists for a consideration and reexamination of the roles religiously based social movements are and can be playing in determining the direction of social evolution. Some movements are fairly new and others are formally repressed but recently reinvigorated, while still others have existed for a good decade or longer but can only now, after the passage of sufficient time, begin to be adequately assessed.

In this volume we seek to address these epistemological and methodological shortcomings. We have brought together scholarly theoretical and empirical treatments that focus on fundamentalist Christian social movements, or Christian movements with relevance to fundamentalism, and conceptual essays that delve into the relevancy of such movements. We also believe that a strong case can be made for a phenomenon of global fundamentalism. In line with earlier studies (Hadden and Shupe, 1989; Misztal, 1992), we find that for the individual mind caught between two types of hegemonic yet contradictory secular and religious explanations of modernity, with the claims to control the public sphere being made by several equally powerful actors, there exists a generically fundamentalist religious response to the modern world situation that is the monopoly of no single faith. However, for the sake of clarity of discourse and for obvious length considerations, we did not include in this volume discussion of Buddhist, Islamic, Jewish, or other varieties of fundamentalism, although we would maintain that the definition of fundamentalism we present in the first chapter would lend itself to analyses of those religions as well. Our focus will be on Christian Fundamentalism.

We explicitly divide this volume's contents into comparative, limited sections. In Part I we consider the concept of a global fundamentalist resurgence that, as we say, has the potential to be used interreligiously. We also present an analysis of American Christian Fundamentalism in its relation to modernity and the production of symbolic capital, as well as of how energetic, even radical religious movements, such as fundamentalist ones, gradually mellow or accommodate to the various social institutions they set out to purify or reform.

In Part II we examine fundamentalist religious revival in previously Eastern bloc countries. Poland, in a sense, gained visibility as one of the first nations to challenge the Communist Party's hegemony, but it was hardly the last. And nobody could have anticipated the fall of dominoes it precipitated.

In Part III we examine religious revival in North and Latin America—from the New Christian Right and its auxiliary anti-evolution Creation Science controversy to Protestant Fundamentalism and Pacifist resistance in Latin America.

Finally, in Part IV we attempt predictions as well as social theorizing to outline what we can expect of regularities in social movements' relations to regimes and cultures: how they create, sustain, and "normalize" social change in today's societies and in future ones.

Research on religiously based social movements in the western hemisphere has been ongoing for several decades and has already provided dividends to the subdisciplines of social movements and political sociology. The region of Eastern Europe, by contrast, is only now beginning to be explored and the progress of its movements charted and monitored. It is a valuable living laboratory for those interested in studying the mobilization of religious movements and their potential to influence mass movements and to restructure political institutions. Our goal as editors has been to encourage the wedding of insights derived from research in both blocs or hemispheres and thereby stimulate a better appreciation of the religiopolitical change that is sweeping over our planet.

Part I ————————————————

THE GLOBAL FUNDAMENTALISM PHENOMENON

1

MAKING SENSE OF THE GLOBAL REVIVAL OF FUNDAMENTALISM

Bronislaw Misztal and Anson Shupe

The present combination of a twenty-first century culture with society still adrift in the nineteenth cannot be maintained much longer. Either this contradiction will lead to a complete disintegration of society, marked by sudden rushes of violence and irrationality, or it will be overcome.

Alain Touraine, *Return of the Actor*

Sociological hermeneutic endeavor has been overall an optimistic one. Society, as Touraine pointed out (1988: xxi), was seen as a movement from tradition to modernity, from beliefs to reason, from reproduction to production, from Gemeinschaft to Gesellschaft, from the sacred to the profane. Because society was clearly identified with modernity, its actors were identified either as agents of progress or as obstacles to modernization. We call this the linear concept of history. It is based on simplifying or reductionist, ontological, and epistemological premises. The first premise is economistic: it sees society as a market in which free actors enter licitation, bidding at the submission of captivating ideas of development and progress. The second premise is psychologistic: it sees individuals as soliciting the simplest possible, most adaptive, and least expensive—in terms of cognitive dissonance—explanations of the environment. Several prophets in the unilinear historical concept have predicted that humanity will be captivated by the grand ideas of progress to the extent that the demise, or radical overhauling, of traditional religion will eventually become imminent (Cox, 1965: 1–4; Wallace, 1966: 264–65).

In the meantime the unpredicted happened. On the one hand, the grand ideas of progress began to crumble (Harrington, 1989) and conservative projects emerged (Bloom, 1987) to reveal, by the early 1990s, that modernity has brought about freedom but not democracy, greater equality but not justice, abundance but not affluence, education but not enlightenment. The intellectual, political, and economic edifice of the socialist world system has gone bankrupt. It therefore orphaned intellectuals of both leftist and rightist persuasions—the former were rendered helpless in their attempt to see a progressive alternative to capitalism, while the latter were devoid of a meaningful foe. On the other hand, many a prophetic scholar's expectations that the progressive social (possibly labor) movements would one day change the surface of planet Earth (Touraine, 1988) were a bit imprecise, since at times progressive social movements, such as Solidarity in Poland, have yielded otherwise rather libertarian politics, or—to much surprise—social change came about without progressive movement, or any movement for that matter, as in the Soviet Union. Moreover, theoretically grounded beliefs that a universal civil society would bring together both realistic and idealistic approaches to democracy (Alexander, 1991: 170) derived from the egalitarian status of citizenship, which approximates only the initial phase of transformations that we witness nowadays.

As the twentieth century comes to an end, we find many powerful movements that invoke some type of religious tradition to refute the progressive differentiation between the sacred and the secular in institutions. Militant Sikhs in India, Hindus, antiabortion Roman Catholics, ultraorthodox groups of the kind of the Haredim and Gush Emunin in Israel, Fundamentalist Muslims in Algeria and Egypt, Buddhists, Tamils, Shi'ite Muslims, New Christian Rightists, charismatic Protestants in North and Central America, Japanese neo-Shinto nationalists, Creation Science advocates—all represent a resurgence of conservatism that may broadly be termed *fundamentalism*.

Fundamentalism constitutes an attempt to reclaim sacred authority and to use it in the service of reorienting (within their own regions and cultures) the seemingly relentless process of historicity or the capacity of a society to construct its practices from cultural models and through conflicts and social movements (Touraine, 1988: xxiv). It wages an attack on public space, on culture, and on the intellectual ability to explain and think of the world (Lemert, 1991: ix), and it appropriates the mobilization potential of the masses against the ideas of universal progress, captivating social consciousness with religious, ideological, and otherwise nonempirical or nontheoretical imperatives. Says Jeffrey Alexander:

Any sober look at real societies reveals that [the social requisites of democracy] are never fully achieved. . . . When rapid social change wrenches the social fabric, the societal community becomes polarized into different camps, left and right, modern and traditional, secular and sacred. As particularistic ideologies become stronger and power blocs threaten the autonomy of different institutional domains, crises emerge that threaten to tear society apart. (Alexander, 1991: 171)

Religious fundamentalism is an instant heuristic remedy to the situation of rapid change, frequently the change that is imposed from without or from above. People initiate social change when dissatisfaction with current conditions reaches critical mass and when they anticipate that it would remedy some immediate problems of their life-world. But the processes of social change often continue spontaneously, and the avalanche cannot be stopped. Soon the magnitude of changes overwhelms those who not so long ago were for the change, as it can best be seen in the former Soviet Union where posters of Stalin reappear in the hands of recent supporters of the *perestroika*. It is precisely at this point where polarization of the community occurs, which requires the dichotomized parties to come up with arguments to support their causes. With a paucity of arguments, fundamental values replace reasoning. Fundamentalism can therefore be viewed as a cognitive perspective concomitant to that of modernism, not an alternative to it. It is prompted not by social change, but by the pace of the transformative process and by its magnitude that goes beyond culturally and intellectually determined possibilities to comprehend the world.

Despite claims that "there is no weapon in the theoretical arsenal of the social scientific study of religion or of political science that can attack the problem of worldwide religious resurgence" (Swatos, 1989a: 1), we are more heuristically optimistic. In this chapter we attempt to identify the various phenomena that have come to be known collectively as *globalization* and we argue that this overall process has simultaneously set in motion spontaneous revivals of conservative religion that might initially seem antithetical to the former. Resurgent religious fundamentalism, we posit, is not some atavistic or anomalistic creature experiencing its "last gasp" at the end of the twentieth century, but, rather, it represents a widespread worldview that is frequently held in the wane of other, more adequate means of comprehending the magnitude and the pace of the processes of social change.

THE EMERGING ERA OF GLOBALIZATION

Since the 1960s scholars have argued that a world-system with economic, cultural, and political dimensions is evolving to the effect that it can be interpreted as a totality, wherein discrete selves, nation-states, and traditions of civilizations are interconnected by complex relationships of competition and compromise, discordance and détente. Each element is couched within the frame of the whole so that action must be referenced against the coordinates of the world and not simply against limited geopolitical segments (Garrett and Robertson, 1991: ix).

Likewise, globalization is seen as a process in which action by or within one unit is increasingly constrained by the necessity to take into account in some manner actions or implications for action of other units on a worldwide basis (Simpson, 1991: 31). The result is an interpenetration and interdependency of economic currencies, ownership, and markets accompanied by the growing power of multinational corporate conglomerates; the decreasing functional importance of national sovereignties; dissemination of the technology necessary to create a media "global village" capable of instantaneous information and image reception; and a parallel progressive erosion of the authority of religious symbol systems that claim monopolies on ontological world views. Such developments are obviously unprecedented in human history.

Historical documentation and theorizing (albeit with a deterministic bent) regarding the processes of globalization has been assembled by Immanuel Wallerstein (e.g., 1989, 1980, 1979, 1974). This process has been taking shape since the Age of Exploration, the Protestant Reformation, and the dawning of the industrial revolution. While one could argue as to the extent that the institutions of any particular nation-state are being subsumed under a global umbrella, it is indisputable that such overall process has affected countries and cultures on virtually every continent. In this macro scheme of social, political, economic, and cultural earth shifts, religion is given variable emphasis. Wallerstein's analysis of the world system entails the view that secularization is a unilinear, nonrecursive fact. Thus it takes for granted the eventual demise of organized religion as a significant social force. Accordingly, this perspective sees religious resurgence as a deviant occurrence in the broad sweep of history (Swatos, 1989a: 2).

Alternately, Roland Robertson, who more than any other sociologist has suggested that the religious factor can play a critical role in globalization, believes the unilinear secularization hypothesis both premature and false. The expansion of nation-states' spheres of operation under the guise of enhancing the quality of life inevitably leads the polity to cross over institutional lines into religious or sacred realms (Robertson, 1985b: 348).

There are built-in limitations to the secularization process that eventually set in motion the dynamics to enable religion to assert itself as an important social fact. Accordingly, the globalization process itself raises religious and quasi-religious questions because it is increasingly concerned with matters traditionally associated with the religious domain (Robertson and Chirico, 1985: 239, 225). We agree with this latter suggestion, but there is still more to the story of the resurgence of fundamentalism.

THE EMERGING ERA OF FUNDAMENTALISM

In the West the term "fundamentalism" is associated most commonly with a type of conservative Christianity that developed out of a liberal-conservative schism in American Protestant evangelicalism during the early years of the twentieth century (Hadden and Shupe, 1988: 107–8; Marsden, 1980). The Fundamentalist movement obtained its name from a series of ten paperback volumes entitled *The Fundamentals* published between 1910 and 1915 and privately financed by two businessmen brothers. The volumes consisted of edited chapters authored by leading conservative theologians who defended biblical inerrancy and attacked the evils of what they perceived to be secular, atheistic modernism. Scholars have since regarded the necessary existence of these volumes as a patently transparent rearguard attempt by conservative Christians to reassert truths and doctrines that they believed to be seriously endangered. In this narrow sense, fundamentalism is a phenomenon barely a century old and associated with distinctly evangelical Protestant Christianity.

By the term fundamentalism, however, we intend a more inclusive and globally relevant meaning. In our view fundamentalism is not simply characterized by rigid doctrinaire movements that reject the modern world. *Global fundamentalism* can be defined as a series of related responses to the globalization process per se (Shupe and Hadden, 1987). *Secularization* is a self-limiting process that folds back on itself at some point and allows—however inadvertently—spiritual-sacred explanations and world views to fill a void left by purely secular processes and ideologies. Common to the infrastructures of fundamentalist movements is a resistance to the institutional differentiation process (secularization), which progressively renders religious institutions and belief systems irrelevant and marginal to culture. Resistance to global economic interdependence is a secondary reaction, grounded in the perceived threat to their religious beliefs, and is not necessarily a nascent nationalism—although it may exhibit attributes of nationalism (Shupe and Hadden, 1989: 111).

Global fundamentalist religious movements can be characterized in several ways. First, fundamentalist prophets commonly issue a call to return to a pristine tradition now largely abandoned, a loss that has caused current levels of immorality, a lack of self-determination, and other innumerable woes. Second, these prophets posit a society gone astray, providing a litany of symbols, conspiracies, and villains. Third, the modern revival is conscientiously aligned with both the mythic tradition and the modern world to build credibility in its potential for realizing significant change. Fundamentalism is therefore a vigorous attempt to use aspects of a religious tradition for both coping with and

8   Bronislaw Misztal and Anson Shupe

reshaping the changing world. The dynamics of globalization have promoted the dynamics of fundamentalism in a dialectical fashion (Shupe
and Hadden, 1989: 112–13).

In short, secularization (among other forces) serves as the "thesis" that
eventually sets in motion the "antithesis" of fundamentalism, promoting
attempts through social movements to "resacralize" the social order. We
concur that much of the fundamentalist phenomenon within any religious tradition, whether conservative Pentecostal Christians in Central
America (Poloma, 1986), *Soka Gakkai* or xenophobic *minzokuha* groups
in Japan (Shupe, 1991), or Dakwah supporters of an Islamic state in
Malaysia (Mess and Pearce, 1986), reasserts the importance of the desired
role that a revived religious dimension should play in secular society.
The contrast between such a desired role for religion and the appearance
of religion's compartmentalization within secular society is, after all, why
the fundamentalist issue is notable to social scientists in the first place.

But the other tensions created by the globalization of markets, cultures,
and politics should not be relegated to a secondary status in stimulating
resurgent fundamentalism. Citizens of national communities react au-
thentically to the perceived weakening of the latters' sovereignties (and
therefore to the loss of their self-determination, if not hegemony). These
concerns dovetail with the resacralization motif, although they are not
totally subsumed by it. Nor is resistance to economic codependency an
ancillary reaction, as American protests in the 1990s over alleged Japanese "predatory capitalism" and unfair trade practices demonstrated.
In a sense, expressions of nationalism and economic grievances are political manifestations of revitalization movements (Wallace, 1956), while
fundamentalism is the religious analog. Both types represent responses
to globalization.

The fortunes of fundamentalist movements depend on the events and
trends within their larger societal contexts to create "symbolic capital"
(Bourdieu, 1991) to be used in their growth, as much as they depend
on the particular grievances of the persons attracted to them. However,
the reaction against globalization—not just as blanket rejection but as
creative reorientation—is undeniable. Globalization breaks down barriers of polity and culture, but it also prompts movements to reassert
identities and self-determination, at least at this point in history. At the
minimum we can conclude empirically that the globalization process
produces yawning gaps between the ideological (even metaphysical)
needs of peoples to maintain a meaningful Weltanschauung and the
capabilities of culture-producing political regimes to provide them.

It should not be surprising that religion emerges as the crucible within
which ideational responses to globalization form and interact. Despite
the anticipation of many contemporary social scientists that religion's
influence over individuals would be largely privatized and thus become

sociopolitically inconsequential, religion still retains a symbolic capital. This capital may even be growing (Hadden, 1989). Driving group resistance to the differentiating effects of globalization is a dialectic between Gemeinschaft and Gesellschaft class dimensions (Robertson, 1987a, 1987b). The restoration or maintenance of self-identity (be it religious, nationalistic, or ethnic) becomes a key element.

The widespread institutionalization of mass media, with satellite transmission, cable capabilities, and the rest, has not transformed the world into a cultural "global village," despite early optimistic predictions (McLuhan and Fiore, 1967). In fact, instantaneous, image-rich video news coverage may actually have exacerbated tensions among peoples of different nationality, ethnicity, and faith backgrounds rather than brought us all together (Shupe and Hadden, 1989: 116–19). Religious conflict is a staple of modern news reporting; hence, there is no reason to think such reporting will not feed into existing tensions.

CONCLUSION

Fundamentalism on a global scale is no mysterious "reappearance" of a once-believed declining cultural form. Indeed, if current world-system theorists are correct, from the trends building from the sixteenth century to the present, religion's resurgence might even be said to have been anticipated (if only less obvious). At the same time, the current proliferation of fundamentalism does not ensure a reversal of secularization: "It is all too easy to fall into the temptation of arguing that the greatly increased visibility of religion across the contemporary world signals or manifests a definite reversal of the process of secularization" (Robertson, 1987a: 31). The phenomenon is simply too recent for us to know.

2

FUNDAMENTALISM IN AMERICA REVISITED: THE FADING OF MODERNITY AS A SOURCE OF SYMBOLIC CAPITAL

John H. Simpson

Classic interpretations of Christian Fundamentalism in America view the movement as a reaction against the culture of modernity (Mencken, 1925).[1] Thus, for its adherents, Fundamentalism's biblical literalism provides grounds for denying the validity of unfriendly scientific evidence found in geological data and the claims of the theory of evolution. The Fundamentalist reading of the Bible supports patriarchal and traditional norms of sexual behavior and marriage patterns vis-à-vis modern social and legal permissiveness. Fundamentalism's vesting of ultimate, absolute, and triumphal authority in written scripture and its strictures underwrites firm boundaries between the "saved" and the "unsaved" and, thereby, weakens sociocultural flexibility and the type of empathy in human affairs that is deemed to be afunctional in modern, complex, diverse, industrialized societies (Simpson and Hagan, 1981; Winter, 1991).

Although the interpretation of Fundamentalism as a reactionary movement has its uses, it is by no means clear that Fundamentalism's present visibility and persistence can be understood entirely in those terms. Thus, I shall argue that Fundamentalism's strength in the contemporary situation is not due to an increase in the popularity of its oppositional values or the number of individuals endorsing its doctrines but, rather, to trends and events in surrounding contexts and environments that provide the movement with new exogenous opportunities. Those opportunities can be understood as a *pool of symbolic capital* that Fundamentalism can now draw on to affirm its boundaries and promote its cause.

Symbolic capital is created, destroyed, or modified when some interpretive social process confers a generalized value on the identities, goals, interests, and ideologies of some social unit (cf. Garfinkel, 1956). The ebb and flow of events and trends and the extent to which they can be interpreted as enhancing or undermining the identities, goals, and so forth of a social unit is the major factor that determines the amount of symbolic capital available to a social unit at any given time. A unit's symbolic capital increases when some public interpretive process assigns a positive general value because some event or trend is viewed as favoring such identities and goals. Alternately, symbolic capital decreases when the logic of public interpretation devalues these identities and goals.

Symbolic capital (Bourdieu, 1991) should not be confused with cultural or social capital (Coleman, 1990). *Social or cultural capital* constitute means that can be used to achieve outcomes or goals in specific contexts or circumstances. Social relations and networks, information, education, individual and collective orientations, capacities, and skills are the elements of social and cultural capita. They are factors that affect the instrumental dimension of action. *Symbolic capital*, on the other hand, encompasses the evaluative dimension of action. It consists of images, reputations, and publicly held notions of worth and value that are socially pervasive.

Although symbolic and social or cultural capital are analytically distinct, there is, nevertheless, a relationship between them. Thus, the differential assignment of value to social units through public interpretive processes may affect the extent to which instrumental means can be effectively employed by units to achieve desired outcomes. Conversely, instrumental outcomes may change the attribution of value and worth to social units. Finally, when public interpretive processes are the object of instrumental action, as in advertising, public relations, or news work, the images and reputations themselves become instrumentalities and commodities in a market.

In establishing the claim that a set of events affects the amount of symbolic capital available to social units, the central question is: What makes it possible for the units, themselves, and others, as well, to interpret events as going their way—that is, as enhancing an identity or a set of interests? That is a complex question since it is possible for the same set of events to create symbolic capital for different social units with interests that are opposed or even unrelated. The creation and use of symbolic capital, in other words, is not a zero-sum game. Different interpretive sets can produce symbolic capital from the same events. Furthermore, a set of events in one locale may create symbolic capital for units in another locale that is far removed geographically, socially, and intentionally from where the events occur. In a rapidly globalizing world, in fact, it is difficult to identify all of the units, locales, and networks where symbolic capital can be created or destroyed by a particular set of events or trends.

Although it is not inconsistent with other approaches to understanding fundamentalism, the symbolic capital perspective avoids some of their pitfalls. For instance, the characterization of fundamentalism as reactionary may describe certain important substantive features of the movement, but it offers little in the way of explaining why some individuals are attracted to those features in the first place. Explanations that answer the attraction question in terms of personality or motivational factors often are misspecified or lack scope. For example, the presumption of an affinity between the authoritarian personality type and Fundamentalist ideology (Johnson and Tamney, 1986) overlooks the affection of some authoritarians for rigid left-wing ideologies. Explanations anchoring motivations in threats to status or lifestyle (Lipset and Rabb, 1981) fail to consider the constant nature of such threats to many groups and communities in modern societies including Fundamentalists. While threats are constant, a group's visibility, efficacy, and power may ebb and flow over time. Perceived threat and group vigor do not vary concomitantly. Hence, resource mobilization approaches (Liebman, 1983; McCarthy and Zald, 1977) describe how movements and their associated organizations become forces to be reckoned with by capturing and "metabolizing" resources in their environments. Resource mobilization approaches, however, tend to neglect variation in the capacity of societies to create and supply resources and to determine what can serve as a resource for a movement in a particular circumstance. Because they fail to consider variation in the resource-generating capacities of societies, mobilization explanations so far have added little to the comparative study of movements such as Fundamentalism.

In revisiting Fundamentalism[2] to better understand its presence and vitality in the contemporary situation, I will describe some salient features of the environment of Fundamentalism in modern North (and increasingly South) America. That environment stretches far beyond the bounds of American society itself and requires an analysis of events and trends that have global significance (Robertson and Chirico, 1985; Simpson, 1991). In that regard the analysis focuses on the decline of modernity and completes the circle, so to speak, encompassing the dynamics of Fundamentalism. Thus, Fundamentalism's origins can be ascribed to a reaction against the ascendance of modernity while its vigor in the present situation must be attributed, at least in part, to the presence of symbolic resources created by the passage from modernity to postmodernity.

THE FADING OF MODERNITY

As the twentieth century winds down, intellectuals and academics face two questions: What is or was modernity, and how do we know that it is disappearing, if indeed it is? These questions admit no simple answers. Debates rage around the notion of postmodernity, its critical substance, sources, permanence, and political meaning. Those debates thematize such notions as the end of the Cold War as the end of history, the epistemological status of texts (Derrida, 1990), and "political correctness" (D'Souza, 1991).

By way of entry into a sociological answer to questions about the nature and status of modernity and postmodernity, I will focus briefly on a pattern of elements that appears to signal the emergence of what could be called the *postmodern factor*. The postmodern factor is defined by a sociopolitical dimension, a cultural/interpretive dimension, and a human rights dimension.

The term *factor* is deliberately used here in its formal methodological sense to draw attention to the systemic and polarized nature of the contemporary situation. Thus, for some actors and social units, history (in the Hegelian sense) may have ended; for others, the struggles of history are unabated. For some, there may be no firm ontological or epistemological grounds on which evidence or truth rests; for others, the notion of objectified, discoverable truth is central. Finally, not all human beings everywhere are socially constructed individuals with rights *as individuals*. Many humans still live out their lives as "unindividualized" parts of collective units.

The postmodern factor emerges from the epistemic correlations between those dimensions. The correlations imply tension or conflict between units at different locations on a dimension, while the existence of the factor implies the conditional affinity between a specific location on one dimension and a specific location on another dimension. Thus, if history has "ended" for a unit, then it is unlikely that the unit is embedded in a context where a notion of objectified truth finds support and a weak version of individualization exists.

The Sociopolitical Dimension

Whether or not history, in fact, "ended" when the Berlin Wall was breached, the disintegration of communism's geopolitical base in Eastern Europe and the former Soviet Union unquestionably marks the end of an era. The question is: What era? Does the decline of communism signal a move beyond modernity or simply a new stage of "the modern project," especially with reference to religion?

One hallmark of modernity is the notion that state, economy, and society or the civil, private sector constitute a system of autonomous, differentiated, institutional elements that have empirical integrity and a natural systemic construction in terms of the nation-state myth. Viewed in that way, religion was a problem for modernity and modernity was a problem for religion. Religion was a problem for modernity because the autonomy of the institutional sectors implied the replacement of tenacious universal religious logics of action by rationalized and specialized secular logics. Especially important in that regard was the development of civil society or the public domain where all interests, including religious interests, were regarded in principle as equally privileged (Habermas, 1989). Modernity was a problem for religion because it required religion to invent itself—that is, to construct its own rationalized logic for action as an autonomous institutional sector.

Modernity constrained and differentiated institutional sectors including, paradoxically, religion itself, to discover how to proceed as if God did not exist. At the same time, the progressive crystallization of the modern nation-state—the basic site for implementing "the modern project"—required not only a culturally powerful story line justifying national unity but also the construction and display of an appropriate identity in the international arena. Both needs raised the question and problem of civil religion (Bellah, 1967). At the level of the nation-state, then, a classic predicament of the modern project was the need, on the one hand, to "clip the wings" of religion in order to underwrite rationalized autonomous institutional action and, on the other hand, to project a collective national identity incorporating powerful symbols that conferred a sense of national unity and transcendent purpose. In many circumstances such symbols were constrained by history in religious or quasi-religious directions.

Various solutions to the predicament were implemented, as the thematizations of church and state and civil religion attest. What is of interest here is the peculiar ambiguity of the Communist solution to the problem of religion in the modern circumstance. While national regimes varied somewhat, all Communist regimes modernized the relationship between religion and the state by radically separating the organization of religion from the state. The state, however, was not neutral toward or tolerant of religion as an autonomous institution, as was the case generally speaking in the West. Rather, Communist regimes competed with religion by deliberately promoting and institutionalizing a "transcendent" utopian secular ideology complete with appropriate rituals and ceremonies. The ideology suffused all institutional sectors and constituted an official "text" requiring, of course, a "catechism." In that sense Communist nation-states were much more "religious" than the industrialized Western nations, which had solved the religion predicament in ways that undid religious monopolies and encouraged potentially debilitating competition between voluntary religious persuasions.

The breaching of the Berlin Wall signaled the demise of the Communist "caesaro-papist," "religious" monopoly and can, therefore, be interpreted as a secularizing event. The state-sponsored official "sanctity" of Marxist-Leninist ideology was undone. The collapse of the Communist monopoly in Eastern Europe and the Soviet Union, then, was a move in the direction of completing the modern project. Institutional sectors were freed to implement rationalized logics of action that are germane and effective as far as specialized purposes are concerned. At this point, however, it is by no means clear what the eventual outcomes will be. Especially crucial in that regard is the extent to which civil society—that is, the institutional arena that is able to form and act independently of the state—becomes an effective reality in the various national jurisdictions formerly monopolized by communism. The development or retardation of civil society will, in turn, affect the direction that religion takes. It is possible that in some jurisdictions religion will simply replace communism and enter into a relationship with the state that is functionally the same as the relationship between the state and the Communist Party under the old regimes. Poland may be a case in point. Some have argued that under communism the Roman Catholic Church was, in effect, the location of civil society in Poland (Michel, 1990). But is the church still the location of civil society now that it is no longer in opposition, so to speak? Civil society requires not only independence from the state but also an infrastructure that supports pluralism and competition within the civil or public arena. Is the Roman Catholic Church in Poland content to be one actor in an arena of formally equal actors, or does it seek to be more?

Contemporary events and directions in Eastern Europe and the former Soviet Union are, of course, conditioned by a host of extremely complex conditions and circumstances. Variation within and between national jurisdictions can render precarious any sweeping generalizations. Nevertheless, the collapse of communism does seem to indicate a move in the direction of completing the modern project throughout the entire European world. At the same time, however, the winding down of the Cold War has a distinctly postmodern twist, for, viewed in the context of twentieth-century history, it points to a slackening of the grand politics of will within the West.

For anyone born in the twentieth century, it is likely that major life-focusing events are linked in one way or another to war—World War I and World War II; regional conflicts; the admixture of limited wars, police actions, and popular uprisings; and the threat of nuclear destruction that accompanied the Cold War. The politics of memory of most populations is embedded in the dramas of violence that have been enacted in the twentieth century.

While there have been other centuries of violence within the West, what set violence in the twentieth century apart from earlier episodes was its link to totalitarian forms of imperial or national domination grounded in secular ideologies. Bureaucracy plus modern communication and transportation technology made it easy to control large populations through a combination of indoctrination and force. The number of actions and structures that could be directly controlled from a distance was greatly enhanced in modern times.

Modern technological and bureaucratic control were accompanied by the secularization of Western thought. Secularization began in the Age of Enlightenment as an elite cultural expression and eventually evolved into forms of mass political ideology and action that, on the one hand, assumed that God was dead and, on the other hand, legitimized action in terms of some ultimate secular horizon or the wisdom resident in some abstract, nontranscendent category: blood and soil, the people, the proletariat, workers and students, and so forth. It is within that general notional framework that the grand politics of will was defined and played out in the twentieth century. Its "prophet," whose metaphors encapsulate the century, was Friedrich Nietzsche (1968): he (correctly) proclaimed that God had died, and he replaced God with the superman who created and willed his own values.

Joining modern technology to models of absolute domination that were justified in terms of mundane values, Joseph Stalin and Adolf Hitler embodied Nietzsche's superman metaphor. Their values were ultimately arbitrary and in the service of power for power's sake. Those values underwrote the grand politics of secularized will that has been the hallmark of politicized violence in the modern West during the twentieth century. More modest and less virulent forms of political and scientific "vocation" were proposed by Max Weber (1956) but they, too, rested ultimately on Nietzsche's superman and the secularized will, albeit on a mitigated and latent version of that master metaphor.

The outcome of World War II and the destruction of the Berlin Wall mark the end of the grand politics of will within the West. Abstract categories used to justify action—blood and soil, the people, the proletariat—have been replaced by more organic, empirical dimensions, many of them ethnolinguistic. Democratic forms of representation have cut the nerve of single-party domination based on bureaucratic technologized absolutism. Violence in the service of values at the nation-state level can now be challenged by models of conflict resolution that assume a set of interests, especially economic interests, that are not well served by interstate violence. While the capacity for violence, especially violence based on ethnolinguistic differences, remains, history has "ended" *within* the West, at least for the moment, as far as the grand politics of will at the interstate level is concerned. I stress the qualification "within the West" because, as the conflict in the Persian Gulf made clear, the grand politics of will remains alive and well at the global level in the form of essentially intercivilizational conflict.

The Cultural Interpretive Dimension

The notion of cultural modernity is at once both variegated and expansive and limited and specialized. Thus, it can be argued that modernity encompasses the totality defined by the rise of science and technology, democracy/totalitarianism, and capitalism/socialism and their admixtures in local jurisdictions and systems throughout the West—a mélange thematized and labeled as "progress" in the latter half of the nineteenth century. On the other hand, modernity can refer to the advent of a new form or critical technique within a specialized area of cultural production, especially in the arts or literature but also, more generally, in the interpretive and humanistic disciplines. In some cases the invention of a discipline is an indicator and expression of modernity, sociology itself being a case in point.

Perhaps the most characteristic general feature of modernity is its way of reinventing itself so that what is modern is what is "newly new" in the present. The understandings, actions, and productions of the past and near-past become old-fashioned and "unmodern." It is forgotten that they too were once modern.

The sense of achieved distance and difference from the past that is at the core of modern sensibility rests on a peculiar compounding of realism and nominalism. That amalgam provides both the grounds for a notion of objectivity and structure and the concomitant sense that the objective is merely a named construction, a consensually validated act of imagination or imaging with no real or objective referent.

The spirit of objectivism that informs the modern temper has deep roots in the development of science and the notion of an external world in conformity with categories of the mind that give rise to laws and predictions about the state and direction of the physical world. The spirit of objectivism reached its apogee in the doctrine of positivism where the real was identified with those things that are empirically measurable. Within the social sciences, objectivism has been expressed in a variety of structuralisms—some materialist, others idealist—positing externalities that determine the course of human action. Thus, for example, Marxist theory has assumed that the locus of control of the means of production was the ultimate constraining externality in human systems of action, while Parsonian structural-functionalism has assumed that a set of collectively held values was the constraining externality that could be invoked to explain action.

Nominalism has roots in science, too. In particular, the claim that scientific knowledge is produced by a methodology that is nonrhetorical and self-correcting on the basis of empirical evidence effectively brackets and, for practical purposes, suspends questions about the ultimate nature of the objects of scientific work. Whether, in fact, scientific methodology is brought to bear on either an external objective order or a purely imaginary order constructed by the mind makes no difference in applying its methodology or in validating the findings it produces. The ontological "agnosticism" of scientific methodology tends to underwrite the nominalist bent in modernism by depriving any posited necessary external order. Nominalist tendencies also find support in the principled impermanence of scientific knowledge where things are not only not what they appear to be from the perspective of ordinary naive perception, but also what they are found to be is subject to revision, inversion, or even radical transformation (Kuhn, 1970).

High modernism, then, incorporates a paradox. Both an objectivist, realist mode and a prominent nominalist tendency are found in the modern sensibility, and the tension between them is never finally resolved. Among other things, the paradox of modernity has been fruitfully exploited in the development of certain theoretical perspectives in sociology that proceed on the assumption of a dialectical relation between an objectified social order, system, or structure and the aggregation of subjective actions that produce that order, system, or structure (Berger and Luckmann, 1967; Giddens, 1985). In those perspectives social structure is constructed from the subjectivities of action and is then deemed to exist as an externality that "causes" real effects, but, itself, is subject to revision and rests on two broad premises: (1) every text or—within the social science frame of reference—set of facts or data is infinitely meaningful; there are no privileged interpretations and (2) somewhere in every text there is a *rhetorical* device or premise—usually implicitly assumed or hidden—that belies any claim in the final analysis that the text contains a consistent logical argument, rests on a purely logical foundation, or exhibits logical completeness and closure. In other words, all texts, facts, data and sets, and their interpretations, contain the rhetorical grounds of their own undoing. Because interpretations are themselves texts, deconstruction theories claim that, in principle, there is an infinite regress of meanings resident within any text. Neither can the text itself stand as an isolated externality, or the object of privileged interpretation, nor are there any grounds for critique and interpretation that ultimately lie outside the text itself.

Deconstruction can be viewed as a radical solution to the unresolved ambiguities in the paradox of high modernity. Where the locus of meaning vacillates between the presumption of objectivity and methodologies that reduce and transform objects, meaning has no fixed ground. Deconstruction fixes the ground of meaning by (paradoxically) asserting that there is no ground because there is, in principle, an infinity of grounds. Nothing is privileged, therefore everything is privileged, in postmodern sensibility. In that circumstance the correlatives of meaning, structure, and substance give way to style and domination based on aesthetic criteria. Method is a way of viewing and reading transformation in action (see, e.g., Durkheim, 1965/1915).

Of all the sociocognitive problems that modernity is thought to pose for individuals and collectivities, perhaps none is more prominent than the problem of meaning. Is there meaning in a world of rapid, constant change, and, if there is, where is it found and how is it constructed? The unresolved tension in the paradox of modernity, the tension between objectivities, and the deconstructive and reconstructive capacity of modernism's nominalisms—all lie at the root of the modern problem of meaning. Where meaning is thought to lie in an external objective order and its interpretation, the critical reduction of that order to other terms is assumed within the modern paradigm. "Meaning" is not intrinsic and sustainable. On the other hand, where it is claimed that method and critique themselves provide a basis for meaning, ontological "agnosticism" invariably hides assumptions of objective externalities or absolutes which Western thought cannot really seem to escape. Caught between the objective but reducible and the externalities on which reductions rest—usually unacknowledged but reducible, themselves, when found—the ground for establishing meaning in the modern circumstance is never firm.

There are clear signs, however, that the fortress of high modernity and the ambiguous solution to the problem of meaning that it guards is now under serious siege.[3] Most visible in that regard is the self-consciously postmodern critical mode that has come to be known as *deconstruction* (A. Morris, 1984). A social base for the deconstructive urge and the triumph of the aesthetic can be found in postindustrial populations. Upscale elites and their imitators "worship" in the temples of the arts, especially the visual arts, while the masses find their senses pleased and understood in the icons of the consumer society and, especially, in the art of the television commercial and the video (Jameson, 1991). Popular religion becomes a form of play and lucid entertainment, a "pretend as if" activity that underwrites and celebrates lifestyles. It no longer serves as a coat of meaning that legitimizes societies and rationalizes the lives of individuals according to the function assigned it in the classic modern sociological formulations (Yinger, 1957). In short, the problem and pathos of meaning found in the heart of modernity by intellectuals and analysts from Søren Kierkegaard to Max Weber has lost its salience. Postmodern persons do not ask, "What does this mean?" They ask, "How does it look and how do I feel?" Logos has been submerged in eros.

The Human Rights Dimension

In sketching some of the general features of change in the contemporary world, I have, so far, dealt with attributes of the distribution of global power and the sociocultural and epistemological trends that define what counts as knowledge. The sea of changes in Eastern Europe and the former Soviet Union—the end of the fundamental political reality of the past forty-five years—and the rise of poststructuralist critical thought—deconstruction in particular—signal new directions in politics and culture that are moving the world beyond modernity. What will the terms of participation in that world be for collectivities and individuals? In other words, are there any general diffuse authoritative rules or understandings that orient and constrain the actions of social units in the emergent situation?

It is at least arguable that the notion of human rights now constitutes a set of prescriptive ideas that is institutionalized at the global level, where it operates as a standard for judging the actions of states and nations. While codifications of human rights emerged in the West in the eighteenth century, their effective scope as a resource and standard for action was limited to the intrastate level until after World War II. Of the four major Allied powers in World War II (Great Britain, free France, the United States, and the Soviet Union), three had institutions and mechanisms that effectively subjected their political, legal, and judicial systems to the norms of the human rights tradition that focused on the individual as the unit endowed with rights. The emphasis was on the freedom of the individual. The fourth, the Soviet Union, subscribed to a notion of human rights that was consistent with the ideology of Marxist-Leninism. It located rights at aggregate or collective levels and stressed the equality side of the freedom/equality dialectic. In all cases, human rights were "in the hands," so to speak, of the nation-state.

The adoption of the Universal Declaration of Human Rights by the General Assembly of the United Nations in 1948 marked a departure from the development of human rights as a set of standards for evaluating and judging action. The development was essentially procedural rather than substantive. While the Universal Declaration codified the understandings of the Western human rights tradition—understandings which, themselves, were not new ideas—the breakthrough occurred in terms of the collective agreement among a substantial number of nations that human rights constituted standards that should be applied in principle to evaluations and judgments of their own acts and behaviors as nation-states in an international arena. In other words, human rights passed into the jurisdiction of the system of nation-states and no longer existed as only rules and norms to be enacted at the level of the nation-state. Nation-states became in principle the objects of human rights as collectively enacted normative standards, and not only subjects or independent actors that could either honor or disregard the notion of human rights in keeping with a particular national history, civilizational attachment, or the requirements of political expedience.

There is, of course, no way at present to enforce the observance of human rights at the global level. Nation-states can and do violate human rights, but they increasingly do so at their own peril. Human rights exist as a clear and definitive focus of global discourse, and they are used on a daily basis in the media to judge and prescribe national actions. Nation-states impose economic sanctions on other nation-states for perceived violations of human rights. On a bilateral or multilateral basis, nation-states agree to observe human rights in exchange for desiderata. Violations of human rights by nation-states become rhetorical resources in the public relations arsenals of oppositional and liberation movements. Watchdog organizations make a global business out of detecting and publicizing the plight of individual victims of human rights violations. In short, human rights are a major element—perhaps *the* major element—that serves as an evaluative standard for action in the emergent global culture (Livermore, 1989).

The institutionalization of human rights as a global standard means, among other things, that the participation of individuals in collectivities and the relations between collectivities including nation-states are increasingly likely to be judged and contested in terms of human rights on a worldwide basis. Thus, movements in the West, and especially in North America, to "degender," "derace," and "desex" stratification systems—movements that tend to be intensely expressed in local jurisdictions and organizations—ultimately find their justification in human rights claims. At the other end of the scale, with the demise of communism as a world-ordering possibility, it is now likely that the drive for justice in the world system of nation-states will increasingly be articulated within the framework of human rights as a set of standards to be applied in reforming regional, national, and local venues.

Finally, it can be asked: What is postmodern about the institutionalization of human rights on a global scale? The answer lies not in the pervasiveness of the notion, but in the capacity of the idea of human rights to organize interventions and movements that change understandings governing participation and action in collectivities from the household to the nation-state. In particular, notions of human rights relativize and loosen the hold of collectivities on their members by raising the question of what constitutes a fair exchange of duty and conformity for rights and due process. The global institutionalization of human rights, with its exclusive focus on the rights side of the equation, rationalizes and routinizes the basis for questioning any social contract—totalitarian or democratic—and can in that regard be viewed as the mainspring of the multitude of local and national movements for change that have swept the globe in recent years. In many respects those movements render the individual-society relationship problematic by tying an attribute or property of an individual (such as race, sexual orientation, gender, or ethnicity) to a set of actions and processes that routinely change "the way things are done." The person/structure dialectic on which so much classical sociology turned no longer exists when properties or attributes (rather than persons, centered egos, or citizens) have rights that are expressed as absolute demands in a rapid flow of events (social movements) that submerge and efface the collective sites that rights *and* duties once defined and structured. The media image of attributes-as-individuals-pursuing-rights has become an autonomous end in itself.

FUNDAMENTALISM IN A POSTMODERN WORLD

Given the end of the Cold War, the rise of poststructural criticism, and the institutionalization of the notion of human rights as a global standard, what can be said about Fundamentalism in North America and its future? As noted in the introduction, I am developing the view in this chapter that the larger sociopolitical and cultural environment within which Fundamentalism finds itself produces events and trends that can be used as resources, resources that solidify and enhance Fundamentalism's self-interpretation and internal organizational requirements and entrench its position in the larger system of which it is a part. Thus, my analysis is intended to complement and advance the sociological interpretations and explanations that came into the literature in the 1980s to account for the persistence of Fundamentalism in America and its then newly visible efficacy as a cultural and political force. This chapter, then, could have been subtitled "Beyond Revitalization," for the problem that analysts face today is not how to account for the appearance in a secularized environment of an oppositional movement based on traditional values but, rather, how to describe and understand the social "metabolism" of a movement that uses events and trends in a larger world to maintain its strength and achieve its goals.

In the remaining portion of the chapter, I will argue that the larger environment—not entirely wittingly, of course—has produced events and trends that establish new sources of symbolic capital for Fundamentalism. Those new sources of strength are drawn from the events and trends described above as the sociopolitical, cultural/interpretive, and human rights dimensions of the contemporary situation.

The faltering of communism in Eastern Europe and the former Soviet Union is an event that significantly increases the pool of symbolic capital at the disposal of Fundamentalism in North America. The epithet of the Christian Right—"Godless communism" (e.g., Bell, 1964)—sums up both the former threat and the nature of the interpretive victory that is now available to those in the Fundamentalist camp. The decline of communism is, of course, a general resource for many North Americans, but in a very specific sense it can be claimed by the Christian Right as the climax of long-standing ideological and organizational opposition to the forces of "Godless communism." The sympathies that lay behind the ideology of such organizations as the Christian Anti-Communist Crusade now seem vindicated, while the "un-American" techniques—from a liberal point of view—that they employed have been forgotten. Fundamentalists can see themselves in their own terms as on the winning side and as, indeed, having contributed to the outcome of the central global, political struggle of our time. That is also true, of course, for many Roman Catholics as well, including, especially, Pope John Paul II.[4]

While the demise of communism in Eastern Europe and the Soviet Union has provided palpable symbolic capital to Fundamentalism in the United States, the interpretive field of endeavor marked by the rise of poststructural/postmodern critical modes offers more diffuse resources. At one level those critical modes of discourse are far removed from the life-world of Fundamentalism and, indeed, from the general quotidian concerns of most persons, with the exception of a few academics and intellectuals here and there (e.g., D'Amico, 1990). Notwithstanding the considerable gap between the languages of ordinary discourse and "intellectual" postmodern discourse, however, there is a sense in which the latter reflects the former.

The continuous discontinuities, the fragilities of the moment, and the parade of novelty that is encountered and experienced on a daily basis either directly or vicariously through the media lend credence to the sense that everything is revisable and nothing has permanent standing. The notion that the present moment is produced by something—a structure of action—that exists prior to the moment and will endure beyond the moment to produce another moment is called into question by the nature of experience itself. Structures are not superseded, overcome, replaced, or changed because they are not there to begin with as experienced objectivities with legitimate rules of their own. Life is one frame after another and what exists, exists in the moment. There are no privileged frames with special meaning, although some moments may be more entertaining or more "fun" than others. "Specialness" and "quality time" are thematized as possibilities because there is no "specialness" or "quality time" in the ordinary course of things.

Assuming, then, that postmodern sensibility is not foreign to populations in advanced/postindustrial societies, including the United States and, therefore, that postmodern criticism is in correspondence with some of the diffuse popular sentiments of those populations, in what way is that a resource for Fundamentalism? Postmodernity is a resource for Fundamentalism because it makes new neighbors out of old enemies from the culture wars of high modernity. Old enemies become new neighbors because postmodern criticism poses a threat to all the camps on the battlefield of high modernism. That is especially true of the great objectivisms that struggled with one another, such as Marxism versus action theory and science versus religion. In each case an objective, knowable, external order was assumed to exist by the opposing parties in the struggle. Thus, the devotees of the culture of science assumed an effective correspondence between testable logical propositions referring to the empirical world and the empirical world itself. In the case of religion, liberals accepted the assumptions of the culture of science and then had to struggle with the problem of finding an objectivity that was their own and which they could use to do "business," so to speak. Among the nonorthodox modern theologians, none solved the problem more elegantly than Paul Tillich (1967) who invoked the classic Western philosophical notion of being as a knowable order, knowable in a way that, according to Tillich, is not inconsistent with the assumptions of the culture of science.

Religious orthodoxy in the modern period, on the other hand, rejected the notion that the only real knowable order was to be found in the empirical world with the method of science. A perch of objectivity was established by inputting absolute authority to something empirical, from whence a particular tradition could be defended as reasonable and internally consistent. In the case of Roman Catholicism, the doctrine of papal infallibility invented in the nineteenth century provided a perch of objectivity: words spoken *ex cathedra* by the Pope. Fundamentalism also created its perch of objectivity in the nineteenth century by assigning absolute authority to a text: the verbally inspired, inerrant Bible.

From a historical perspective, conflicts between the culture of science, Protestantism, and Roman Catholicism defined a field of symbolic, cultural, and political struggle that set Western civilization on the road to modernity (Wuthnow, 1989). Those conflicts were still alive in modern times. Despite such conflicts, however, postmodernism defines them all as neighbors because they all depend on the assumption of some type of objective external order. Postmodern criticism undoes that assumption and renders it doubtful by locating the rhetorical grounds in any objectivistic claim. While the substance of objectivistic claims differs greatly between, say, science and Fundamentalism, postmodern criticism suggests that the form of the claim is the same in each case and, therefore, that both the texts of science and the texts of Fundamentalism ultimately rest on rhetorical and not logical assumptions. Critique does not deny the great practical or pragmatic differences between, say, a scientific text and a Fundamentalist text, but it does make them neighbors in the sense that they both can be found to contain rhetorical claims.

New neighbors are not necessarily new friends, and it is not to be expected that Fundamentalism will now join ranks with, say, evolutionism and launch an assault on the common postmodernist enemy who can point to the rhetorical biases in both camps. The mutual hostility generated by conflicting ontological and epistemological assumptions remains. Yet where the implications of postmodern criticism are realized, Fundamentalism ironically stands to gain. In the milieu of high modernity, Fundamentalism was seen as purveyor of rhetoric and science was seen as a source of universal objective truth. That no longer completely remains. Thus, postmodernism with its "nose" for rhetoric renders the creationist/evolutionist conflict somewhat moot.

Finally, the institutionalization of human rights as a global standard for judging the actions of nation-states and other corporate units can provide a resource for Fundamentalism in the form of new oppositional possibilities. Particularly strong opportunities to define and reinforce firm cultural and organizational boundaries exist for Fundamentalism, where the notion of human rights is brought to bear on the extension of full political, economic, and social rights to women and homosexuals.

Fundamentalism's endorsement of a patriarchal-heterosexual model as normative is derived from its view of the Bible as an inerrant authoritative text to be read literally. That hermeneutical-ethical complex runs counter to the notion that women and homosexuals ought to be full and equal participants in all of the institutional sectors of a society. Thus, where strong pressures exist to ensure full and equal participation in collective life, Fundamentalism has an action opportunity. Using the social logic of contrast, distinction, and difference, it can set itself apart and reinforce the boundaries separating it from those who advocate equality for all, irrespective of gender and sexual orientation. Constructed differences become a basis for oppositional action.

Body-oriented issues—such as who should control the body or what are the limits to bodily expression—are inextricably implicated in the full extension of human rights to all categories in any population. Given the global institutionalization of human rights, Fundamentalism now has a vital antithetical resource that it can use to create strength through opposition for some time to come.

CONCLUSION

Fundamentalism in America arose in response to conditions of rapid social change in the latter part of the nineteenth century. Under the influence of secularizing trends, the purposes of institutions and leading organizations were increasingly justified by myths of progress and the advance of knowledge divorced from religious milieux and, especially, the influence of Protestant Evangelicalism that had been a paramount factor in American public life since the Civil War. In that circumstance, Fundamentalism evolved as a differentiated response to the secularizing trends of modernity and, thereby, participated in modernity on the basis of a claim to legitimacy and authenticity founded on its own specialized autonomous cultural perspective. Fundamentalism bought into the modern project as a pluralistic field of culture combat where it was willing to defend its own claims (Lechner, 1985, 1988).

Today, Fundamentalism exists as an institutionalized movement that survived and grew within the larger field of modernity. With firm boundaries and a well-established organizing capacity, Fundamentalism is now positioned to use the trends and events of the postmodern world to its advantage. Ironically, the very trends and events that are creating the postmodern world appear to run in Fundamentalism's favor. Perhaps that trend, more than anything else in contemporary North America, signals the decline of modern times.

NOTES

1. "Fundamentalism" herein is used in its original—not generic—sense. Thus, *Fundamentalism* is a set of Christian beliefs and experiences that include (1) subscription to the verbal, plenary inspiration of the Bible and its inerrancy; (2) individual salvation through an acceptance of Christ as personal Saviour (being born-again) on account of Christ's efficacious substitionary atonement for sin in his death and resurrection; (3) the expectation of Christ's premillennial return to earth from heaven; (4) the endorsement of such Protestant orthodox Christian doctrines as the Virgin birth and the trinity. Fundamentalism can be measured and analyzed as a property of individuals or collectivities. (For problems of measurement, see Hunter [1981] and Smith [1990]). Ammerman (1987) is an excellent study of Fundamentalism as the defining feature of a local American congregation and its members. Marsden (1980) provides a history of Fundamentalism in North America.

The popular view of Fundamentalism in North America (which I would argue is also the "classic" view held by the majority of American intellectuals and knowledge workers) was inspired by H.L. Mencken's (1925) account of the so-called "Scopes monkey trial" and his successful rhetorical degradation of Fundamentalism's chief protagonist at the time, William Jennings Bryan (see also, Manchester [1986: 160–86] and the film *Inherit the Wind* [1960]). Hadden and Shupe (1988) document the powerful effects that Mencken's image of Fundamentalism continues to have in the American public arena today.

2. This chapter is a "revisit" in the sense that the burden of work among sociologists studying and interpreting Fundamentalism in America ten years ago was to account for its resurgence in the American public arena after a "siesta" of over fifty years (see, for example, the essays in Liebman and Wuthnow [1983]). Other problems now confront analysts, including the problem of understanding Fundamentalism as a modest but persistent element in the American public arena. This "revisit" can be contrasted with my previous "visits" (Simpson, 1983, 1985, 1988, 1989) in that the latter (perhaps, naively) did not bear the marks of suspicion that something called "modernity" was ebbing away.

3. On postmodernism see Featherstone (1988), Hutcheon (1989), and Jameson (1991).

4. "The Fatima message—pray for the demise of Communism which will end in the lifetime of Lucia, the sole surviving visionary—perfectly suited John Paul II's life-long mission against the oppressor of Eastern Europe. The recent implosion of Communism has further inflamed devout Marianists who see in the Soviet collapse the logical triumph of their prayerful efforts" (Kapica, 1991).

3

THE ACCOMMODATION AND DERADICALIZATION OF INNOVATIVE RELIGIOUS MOVEMENTS

Anson Shupe

During the past several decades, virtually all scholarly studies of religious movements of the cult-sect type have emphasized the latter's formative problems and struggles. These include studies of *why* such innovative groups arise (e.g., Aberle, 1962; Bainbridge, 1985; Barber, 1941; Linton, 1943; Wallace, 1956; Wuthnow, 1982), studies of *where* such groups arise and proliferate (e.g., Belshaw, 1972; Stark, 1985), studies of *how* such groups operate internally and successfully with their environments (Bainbridge and Stark, 1980a; Bromley and Shupe, 1979; Gordon, 1987; Richardson, 1988; Shinn, 1987; Stark, 1987; Wallis, 1972; Wilson, 1987a), and studies of the subsequent societal *reactions* such groups provoke (e.g., Beckford, 1985, 1983; Shupe, Hardin, and Bromley, 1983; Shupe and Bromley, 1980). There have been exceptions, with scholars looking to the future of such groups as Sun Myung Moon's Unification Church and the Hare Krishnas (see, in particular, Bromley and Hammond, 1987), but they are conspicuous against the overall trend toward analyses on issues of formation and growth.

Likewise, analyses of the conflict between new religious movements and mainstream social institutions have emphasized and catalogued how they deviate from ordinary societal expectations. But, despite the familiarity of Weber's (1956: 20–32, 46–59) concept of the "routinization of charisma" to virtually all sociologists, relatively little has been posited by recent researchers as to (1) how these groups might accommodate culturally and behaviorally (whether deliberately or otherwise) and (2) specifically how some of their more controversial traits evolve into less flamboyant or offensive patterns. A growing literature on one American-born religious movement that has been elevated to preeminent status as *the* most analyzed group now clusters around the Church of Jesus Christ of Latter-day Saints (the L.D.S. Church). Both Mormon and non-Mormon scholars have written of specifics in the Utah-based Mormon Church's accommodation on the most important points of its subculture, such as polygyny, that once brought it into violent conflict with the larger American society, but most of this work is historical and, sociologically speaking, fairly atheoretical (e.g., Alexander, 1986; Arrington and Bitton, 1979; Shepherd and Shepherd, 1984; Shipps, 1985).

In this chapter I suggest a conceptual approach for analyzing the accommodation/deradicalization process that religious movements undergo as they lose much of their novelty and moderate their conflict with host societies. I explicitly assume that unless a group is radically isolationist and economically independent of its larger society it will experience strong pressures to accommodate, or, using an organic analogy, to "mature." The real question for virtually all religious movements, therefore, is not "if" but rather "in what ways." My examples come from the experiences of movements that originated primarily in twentieth-century Asia and moved into North America and Europe after World War II. In following the logic sketched below, I believe we can better understand the relationship between resource mobilization concepts and that which I term the *deamplification* of religious conflict.

THE DEAMPLIFICATION AND INSTITUTIONALIZATION OF CONFLICT OVER RELIGIOUS MOVEMENTS

British sociologist Bryan Wilson (1982: 233–34) has observed, "The impact of a new movement on the world may be, at times, considerable: but the impact on any new movement, of the need to survive in the world must, in the long run, be somewhat greater." Few religious movements ever exert more than a purely local influence on the larger society that usually rejects and/or ultimately engulfs them. The fate of the vast majority of cults and sects is extinction within a few generations or a coming to terms with society. This second process can variously be thought of as routinization, accommodation, compromise, or deradicalization. It literally represents a sort of truce—a willingness by the deviant, rebellious group to drop certain parts of its innovative profile in exchange for peace, or détente, with the larger social system.

Sociologically, this moderating process is the reverse of what is called *deviance amplification*. Wallis (1977), for example, utilized the concept of deviance amplification in his analysis of how conflict between the Church of Scientology and various government officials both in the United States and elsewhere escalated within a spiraling, dialectical relationship that bred mutual suspicion, recriminations, and reprisals. Deviance amplifi-

cation proceeds thus: (1) initial deviations from valued norms lead to
(2) punitive reactions, which then lead to (3) further alienation of the
deviants, which leads to (4) further deviations, which lead to (5) increased
punitive reactions, which, in turn, lead to even more of (3) in an am-
plifying spiral.

In *deviance deamplification*, an opposite process occurs. The dialectical
interaction reverses the escalation of norm violation and societal reaction.
Deviance deamplification proceeds thus: (1) moderation of some radical
characteristic or practice leads to (2) the appearance of reduced threat
to a mainstream cherished value, which then leads to (3) reduction in
hostility and fears about a person or group regarding that characteristic
practice, which, in turn, results in (4) further encouragement to moderate other radical characteristics (through decreased hostility), which
can feed back into more of (2) in a deescalating spiral.

This stepwise process of deamplifying the tension between religious
deviance and society's hostile responses to it is not inevitable, and when
it occurs it often results in a reduction of only part of the overall tension.
In the United States, for example, the Mormon church has, since its
founding in 1830, experienced the most virulent persecution in the
nation's history. Communitarian economic experiments, theocracy, political adventurism by its founder-prophet Joseph Smith, and plural marriage were among the issues that won it opposition. In this century,
however, the L.D.S. Church has seen its members become well integrated
into virtually all areas of the nation's occupational structure and its public
reputation as a wholesome family-oriented religion soar. Nevertheless,
a reserve of hostility toward it still remains among many conservative
Christian groups that routinely denounce Mormonism as a "cult."

What pressures incline a struggling religious movement toward an
accommodationist posture? At the social psychological level, the most
frequently provided answer is that a religious group's followers eventually become weary of frantic, intense lifestyles and become in danger
of "burning out." Or the charismatic leaders die, and no one follows
who can rally believers to continue their activities at a fever pace. Man-
agerially, the leaders are constantly under a mandate to maximize the
group's survival chances, as well as to press for whatever advantages can
be gained for dialogue and exchange with liberal parties within the larger
society.

But such answers do not point to what aspects of a given religious
movement are especially prone to revision. They imply that an across-
the-board reduction in radicalism will ensue until the group is more or
less absorbed into the larger religious establishment and culture.

A more organizational-structural answer, based on the various works
of German sociologist Max Weber and his pupil Ernst Troeltsch (1960),
and elaborated by Thomas O'Dea (1966), is that certain standard *internal*

pressures for doctrinal orthodoxy and conformity, ongoing efforts to legitimize and aggrandize authority, an expanding division of labor, and similar factors lead a surviving, growing religion to turn into the very worldly, sprawling ecclesia that as a charismatic movement it once rejected.

However, I suggest that resource mobilization theory, currently in vogue among many social movement researchers, is a more fruitful organizational perspective that takes into account the new religion's *interaction* with its sociocultural environment. *Resource mobilization theory* assumes that social movements are best understood as systems with ongoing needs that lead their operatives to mobilize, or accrue, "raw materials" in order to satisfy them (e. g., McCarthy and Zald, 1977; Zald and Ash, 1973; Zald and Berger, 1978). These organizational resources can be obvious tangible "inputs," such as recruits or converts, money and property, and motivating ideologies as well as more abstract ones, such as public reputation and publicity, legitimacy, particular leadership styles, and so forth.

What a resource mobilization approach would generally predict with regard to this process of accommodation, I hypothesize, is that:

1. Those institutional arenas in which a religious movement's resource aggrandizement activities more often threaten or violate traditional values will evoke the greatest reaction of hostility from larger society.

2. Accordingly, a reduction in the radicalness of a group's innovative resource mobilization strategies will call forth less public opprobrium.

3. And, therefore, analysts ought to anticipate signs of accommodation in precisely those institutional arenas where resource mobilization has most threatened or violated key values.

In other words, new religions ought to be under the greatest pressures (or temptations, from insider purists' standpoints) to compromise their strategies of gathering resources where these strategies are the most unconventional *and* where such innovations have run up against critical, or key, values of larger society. Therein lies the guide to the most likely directions of accommodation. Pressures for accommodation, as perceived by a group's members, will not be randomly or equally distributed. Rather, such pressures will center on specific forms of resource mobilization. If the conflict is to deamplify, accommodation should occur there first rather than somewhere else. In the following pages I wish to illustrate this approach by focusing on two exemplary key values that have most often been threatened and/or violated in the West, particularly North America, by innovative religious movements.

ACCOMMODATION AND CHANGES IN
RESOURCE MOBILIZATION

The two core North American values I have selected to illustrate (but obviously not to test in any rigorous sense) this resource mobilization approach are *capitalist individualism* and *nuclear family lifestyles*. These economic and familial values might seem narrowly cast characteristics of the modern North American middle class, but they overlap with values in other industrialized societies. Thus, they are broad enough to have cross-cultural relevance but also institutionally specific enough to provide recognizable, reliable examples.

Capitalist Individualism: A Violated Economic Value

Capitalist individualism is an important value in Canada and the United States, Japan, and many parts of Europe. While new religious movements have also violated many of the economic understandings of citizens' obligations to the state in democratic socialist societies (see, e.g., Shupe, Hardin, and Bromley, 1983), the greatest popular reactions against current new religions have been in predominantly capitalist systems.

A considerable literature in social science concludes that the plethora of new religious movements in post–World War II America engaged in a broad pattern of economic experimentation and diversity of fund-raising mobilization strategies. The stereotypes of "cults" (largely based on mass media coverage of Unification Church and Hare Krishna fund-raisers) portrays their followers as largely depending on street solicitations, often incorporating deceit and ploys involving less than full disclosure of group affiliations and ultimate purposes for the money (Bromley and Shupe, 1980.) However, the reality is that various groups tried different strategies of mobilizing funds at different times; many strategies were eventually rejected as inefficient; and in any case no group relied exclusively on any single strategy. During the 1970s, for example, the Hare Krishnas (in addition to soliciting donations in exchange for flowers, lapel pins, or record albums) operated lucrative businesses that sold incense, cosmetics, perfume, and publications other than those offered in exchange for donations. Members of the Guru Maharaj Ji's Divine Light Mission often operated communally based businesses such as bakeries or health food stores. The Church of Scientology never sought charitable contributions on the streets but, rather, secured its financial base by selling courses in its brand of philosophy/psychology as well as publications authored by its late founder, L. Ron Hubbard. In addition, various Jesus Movement groups sought donations for their literature, raised their own food on their farms, and bartered crops and craft goods for needed supplies (Richardson, 1982).

Even these ventures, however, were criticized as unfair competition with similar secular businesses, primarily because religious members worked for far below standard wages, volunteered parts of their labor, or turned much or all of their incomes over to some central controlling religious ownership. Like the more visible street solicitation strategies, such cooperative enterprises violated the basic values of individual advancement, entrepreneurship, and self-interest intrinsic to capitalism. But they never aroused as much ire as did charitable solicitation practices.

Toward the end of the 1970s, however, mass media coverage of the short-run lucrative returns from street/airport solicitations by the Moonies, Krishnas, and others had made the public wary of donating and gave such groups good reason to seek alternative sources of income (e.g., Bromley and Shupe, 1979). As a result, more and more time and effort had to be expended to gather the same *per capita* fund-raiser amounts, and these became viewed internally as counterproductive. Thus, the Hare Krishnas in most locations eventually abandoned selling their books and seeking contributions in airport waiting areas. They increased their publishing efforts and engaged in a variety of other entrepreneurial activities. Their West Virginia temple complex, New Vrindaban, for example, became a major regional tourist attraction, particularly on weekends, during the 1980s until internecine warfare erupted among factions of the movement. During the early 1980s in Dallas, Texas (among other places as well), the Krishnas opened a popular vegetarian-style Indian restaurant (complete with gift shop and complimentary tour of its adjoining temple) that belonged to that city's Chamber of Commerce. A decade ago it received a maximum four-star rating by a Dallas newspaper and continues to cater to a Yuppie clientele in their late thirties and forties. (Tipping of the Krishna waiters and waitresses is encouraged.)

Similarly, the Unification Church for a time operated a chain of "Go N' Joy" delicatessens/convenience stores run by Moonies on a sort of "mom-and-pop" cooperative basis, then added sales of designer jewelry and various craft items (such as mounted butterflies in glass cases). One of the Church's initially most controversial projects began in the late 1970s when Rev. Moon announced a prophecy that his movement "must turn to the sea." The Unificationists began buying up fleets of fishing boats, boat-building facilities, and cannery plants in Louisiana, Alabama, New England, and California. The fishing industry, a family and tradition-oriented trade economically precarious in the best of times, reacted vehemently. Visions of "Moonie" fishermen reducing existing fish stocks and undercutting other fishermen's prices because of their communal and voluntary labor fueled hostilities. Yet the Unification

Church's lack of expert fishermen and limited membership that could be spared to work at these ventures ensured that nonmembers would be hired and brought into the business.

In fact, the Unificationist fishing enterprise has opted for capitalism. A report on the Unification Church's activities in the Alabama community of Bayou La Batre, that state's most important fishing locale on the Gulf Coast and a leading manufacturer of work boats and seafood trawlers, found that an accommodation between the initially hostile, suspicious community and the entrepreneurial Unification Church agents developed and conflict eventually subsided. (Reid and Starr, n.d.: 379) It notes that "most employees of the boat building firm bought by the Moonies were retained, often at improved wages, and found their new managers to be fair and efficient. The 'Moonies' also proved to be good customers for local suppliers" (Reid and Starr, n.d.: 379). By the 1990s the Unification Church was shifting its resources back to Asia and investing in classic entrepreneurial fashion heavily in the People's Republic of China while courting the politically shifting powers in the Soviet Union (Shupe, 1990) for further investment.

Meanwhile, Scientologists during the 1980s began to sell high-quality leather goods on a "direct-sales" commission basis in the mode of companies such as Amway or Herbalife. Even the now-defunct California-based Synanon, which began as a controversial drug-rehabilitation program later to turn into a full-blown authoritarian cult community, became involved in a number of relatively conventional economic ventures, such as acting as a middle agent between factory overstock items and "distressed merchandise" and tax-exempt organizations that provided corporate donors' receipts to be used for tax deductions (Ofshe, 1980).

To be sure, not all such efforts are profitable for these groups. Cases in point were the Hare Krishnas' *Back to Godhead* magazine, Scientology's *Freedom* magazine, and the Unification Church's daily newspapers in New York City and Washington, D.C. (The Unificationist newspapers, in fact, have proven to be an enormous drain on the movement's resources, absorbing over 20 million dollars in operating losses [Bromley, 1985].) Likewise, the Unification Church's commercial film-making venture, specifically the critically disclaimed motion picture *Inchon*, lost over 50 million dollars and closed at American movie theaters almost as soon as it opened.

But the point is that these innovations, successful or otherwise, were usually inspired as responses to negative publicity over what were usually more controversial violations of a prime Amer-European value: capitalist individualism. The changes described above have been attempts to return financial resource mobilization to a pattern more in keeping with the values of individual profit-making and capitalistic enterprise. Many individuals in such groups now have personal and financial incentives to make money for its own rewarding sake rather than for purely larger, altruistic, communal purposes. The upshot is that various movements have moved in the direction of providing goods and services that non-members are willing to purchase for their direct economic values rather than out of sheer philanthropy. If nothing else, the financial activities appear more normal (i. e., understandable) in terms of capitalistic activity to nonmembers, and in many cases hostility has been muted as a result.

Nuclear Family Lifestyle: A Violated Family Value

Undoubtedly the institution most directly and significantly affected by many new religious movements has been the family, whether in the United States, Europe, Japan, or elsewhere. Some groups, such as the Unification Church and the Hare Krishnas, have required a full-time commitment of members, necessitating a communal lifestyle and whole-sale abandonment of former careers, obligations, and associations, some-times including the biological family. Frequent physical separation of mobile or geographically distant members from biological families and kin has been a notorious complaint. In addition, the consuming demands of some movements on members' energies and revised priority of life goals accepted after conversion leave little time for frequent or even regular communication with their families.

Added to these factors is the inability of many families to understand their members' new faiths and commitments, as well as the latters' seem-ing willingness to cede to leaders, such as Sun Myung Moon, "Moses" David Berg, or the late Bhagwan Shree Rajneesh, authority which these young adults would assuredly deny their own parents. Such new, intense loyalties have only exacerbated families' sense of alienation (Shupe and Bromley, 1980).

In addition, related to the violation of the previous capitalist individ-ualism values has been a sense of breached reciprocity that the "aban-doned" families feel at seeing young adult offspring rejecting their parents' lifestyles and the often expensive investments the parents have made in formal education for their offsprings' career preparation. At the very least, many parents undoubtedly look forward to some vicarious satisfaction in their children's presumed career and educational accom-plishments as they mature. The social embarrassment of having an off-spring in a strange "cult," the confusion and hurt feelings at being suddenly the object of his or her rejection and even outright scorn, and the sense that this promising young adult is "wasting" his or her best years and opportunities have proved powerful motives for families to oppose many new religious movements.

During the past decade, however, a loosening of the authoritarian demands of notable groups has been occurring, and even the groups of

Oriental origin, such as the Hare Krishnas and the Unification Church, have begun altering their courtship and mating practices, as well as other more mundane lifestyle customs, in the direction of mainstream culture. Some changes have been pedestrian, indeed. Male Moonies, for example, wear their hair more stylishly long and women can now be seen—at least at formal occasions with non-Moonies—wearing make-up. Another example: In the late 1970s one could not entice a Moonie to enter a bar even if the Moonie did not imbibe alcohol. Within a few years he or she would accompany a person into a bar but would only drink mineral water with a twist of lime. By the early-to-mid 1980s at banquets held during Unificationist conferences chablis wine was served, and Moonies sipped rather naturally alongside guests.

More significant changes can be observed in Unification Church wedding arrangements. Engagements more along the conventional lines of American society (complete with rings and designations of future partners as "fiancées") are now held (though physical intimacy is still discouraged during this period), and partners can indicate several preferences before being "matched" by Rev. Moon (who still, in the Korean patriarchal manner, oversees the pairings). Though it is not officially condoned or publically discussed, private conversations with members also reveal that contraceptives and other means of birth control are becoming more prevalent, despite official church encouragement to embrace large numbers of children, as has the founder himself.

Likewise, there seems to be an increasing number of, and acceptance of, married Hare Krishna members, greater provision for the group's own education of its growing ranks of children, and an enlarged flexibility and tolerance toward couples who decide to divorce (Knott, 1986: 51). Older adult members now encounter many typical middle-class American situations, such as teenage children who wish to date other young Krishnas and even non-Krishnas, who want a driver's license, and so forth.

The Krishnas also have their own mundane accommodationist lifestyle changes. Many members with professional responsibilities and who deal regularly with the non-Krishna community now use their pre-Krishna names on business cards and in correspondence. Shaved heads are declining in frequency, and, when Krishnas are on errands away from their temples and communities, the traditional orange robes are largely dispensed with in favor of loose-fitting cotton street clothes.

In addition, the Hare Krishnas and the Moonies both have begun serious encouragement of "associate" or non-full-time members. At one time, for example, the Unification Church claimed tens of thousands of such sympathetic part-time members, but the numbers were largely illusory. The millennial, communal nature of the 1970s and early 1980s Unification Church simply had no role for "part-timers" to play. The same was once true of the Krishnas. But times have changed. The Krishnas, in particular, have been successful in serving as a cultural beacon for persons of Hindu sympathies and ethnicity in larger cities and who attend temple services for worship, contributing to temple expenses. More so than the Moonies, the Krishnas have sought prestigious "affiliate" converts to advertise in movement publications (such as a former Miss Denmark, who is also a professional fashion model, and an heir to the Henry Ford automobile fortune). Scientology has followed suit, becoming adept in recruiting movie actor John Travolta, actress Karen Black, and jazz musician Chick Correa, among others. Japan's American branch of Nichiren Shoshu Buddhism publicizes its own celebrities, such as singer-actress Tina Turner and jazz musician Herbie Hancock.

Finally, not all groups are attempting to downplay every exotic aspect of their religion. For example, the Hare Krishnas have staged their traditional and colorful Festival of the Chariots in San Francisco, Los Angeles, New York, and other American cities to give the public a first-hand view of their members and subculture. In 1982, in fact, the Dallas, Texas, Hare Krishna temple entered a float in the annual Cotton Bowl parade and won honorable mention from the judges.

In sum, the initial attraction of various religious movements for many new members in the 1960s and 1970s may have been alternative lifestyles and countercultural customs, the relative "strangeness" of which mystified and even frightened outsiders (particularly families), and even separation from mainstream society. Currently, however, within various groups there is a normative drift, occurring over a surprisingly short period of less than a decade, back toward those very middle-class customs that members once rejected with such gusto. Moonies, for example, seem to take the same pride and enthusiasm in talking about their fiancées as do most other young Americans, and it seems likely that using such terminology provides both them and their concerned families with a more familiar reference point to understand events in their lives (Bromley, Shupe, and Oliver, 1982). In using this terminology, such groups repair much of the perceived damage to middle-class family values and restore the appearance of "normality" to their new kinship arrangements.

ACCOMMODATION AND RESOURCE MOBILIZATION: THE PERENNIAL SHIFT

In this chapter I have dealt with only a few of the many religious movements now operating within North America, Europe, and Asia. Many more instances of accommodation along the lines of resource mobilization strategies could be provided. The Nichiren Shoshu movement in Japan and the United States, for example, has moderated many of its belligerent, abrasive attitudes toward other Buddhist and Shinto groups (e. g., the discouragement of *shakubuku*, or "breaking and subduing"-style forceful conversions in favor of *shoju*, or tolerant conversion through gradual means) and has instituted a major political party (the "Clean Government Party," or *komeito*) that is now the third largest in Japan (Shupe, 1991, 1986). Likewise, Glazier (1986) reports that various religions of blacks in the Caribbean islands have shifted their radicalism toward cooperation with different political parties and candidates in recent years.

In the same way, the anticult movement (or ACM) in the United States has undergone its own accommodationist transformation during the past two decades. Originally this opposition movement consisted of outraged parents and families of "cult" members operating in ad hoc (and sometimes unlawful) vigilante ways (Shupe and Bromley, 1980). Best known of their tactics was *deprogramming*—the abduction and forceful retention of members from cults, browbeating and haranguing them until they recanted. However, the most significant ACM change has been a steady *professionalization* of this countermovement's leadership and strategies. While many of the founders and early activists of the ACM in the early 1970s were professional persons (physicians, lawyers, clergymen, and educators), the actual permanent coopting of the countermovement by full-time medical, psychiatric, and psychological professionals who were not personally affected relatives did not occur until the mid-to-late 1980s.

Such professionals allied with the mental health professions have coopted the ACM and transformed it into a "growth industry" for therapists (Clark, Langone, Schecter, and Daly, 1981; Shupe, 1985; Singer, 1985). The redefinition of religious innovation and deviance as psychological pathology in a religiously pluralistic society continuously generating such religions makes such professional imperialism almost a certainty (e. g., Robbins and Anthony, 1982). The same tendency toward the professionalization of originally voluntary, nonprofessionally driven social movements (at least in the United States) has also occurred before, as in the anti–family violence/anti–woman battering movement (Shupe, Stacey, and Hazlewood, 1987).

In sum, what social science currently knows of how so-called new religious movements mature is that they stave off persecution and negative public reaction by shifting their strategies of resource mobilization away from controversial, toward more conventional, methods. Their accommodation need not be total or equally spread over component activities. In fact, it is usually focused and mostly occurs at the most critical points where the group attempts to amass necessary resources.

But shifts in resource mobilization, insofar as we have sufficiently *recent* data, only inform us about short-term strategies. The long-run goal is only beginning to be researched. Some older groups, such as the Mormons, have received the necessary historical scrutiny to make their survival sociologically meaningful. For most existing groups we do not know, for instance, what minimum time factor is necessary to produce tolerance and the public definition of legitimacy.

We are at a fortunate point in the history of social science of being able to observe more sociological processes than just origination and formation. To the extent that we regard these religions as problem-solving, resource-gathering organizations, we may be able to extend social science's understanding of them beyond what has been done before.

Part II ———————————————

RELIGIOUS REVIVAL IN THE EASTERN BLOC

4

THE VANISHING POINT: THE RELIGIOUS COMPONENTS OF PEASANT POLITICS OF PROTEST IN POLAND, 1970–1980

Krzysztof Gorlach

THE RELIGIOUS COMPONENTS OF PEASANT CULTURE

Religious components in peasant movement ideology in Poland during the 1970–1990 period are not exceptional phenomena. On the contrary, one can argue that the pattern is similar to that of the workers and intelligentsia protest movements. Such a statement is evidenced by Polish history and cultural tradition and is characterized by the victory of the Counter-Reformation movement in the sixteenth and seventeenth centuries. The strong position of the Roman Catholic Church during the partition period in the nineteenth century and in independent Poland before the last war further enhanced the role of religious components in politics of protest. Researchers point to other contributing factors: the lack of significant ethnic and religious minorities in Polish society, along with the functioning of the Roman Catholic Church as the only institution not effectively controlled by the Communist state (Ramet 1987: 55–79).

However, a more detailed analysis of this problem (i.e., the presence of strong religious elements in social movements challenging the Communist system in Poland) requires a more precise framework. The religious component may be seen in three elements of social movements. First, it may be present in the religious values and beliefs that undergird a movement's ideology or agenda: some of the movement's values or demands may be inspired by religious values. For example, some goals presented by the intelligentsia, workers, or peasant movements in Poland have been inspired by the Roman Catholic Church social doctrine and/

or have directly contained elements of such a doctrine. Such issues as social justice, human dignity, personal human creativity, human rights, freedom of speech, and freedom of religion were on the agenda of the Solidarity movement. Whether this inspiration was based on religion or simply on the liberal tradition or the humanistic component characterizing European culture remains to be proven. In 1970–1990 Poland, the justification for these values, goals, and demands were primarily found in the social and moral doctrine of the Roman Catholic Church.

Second, the religious meaning may characterize the symbols that incorporate the movement's social identity since some religious elements can be found within the repertory of "material" symbols (banners, badges, and so on). Religious elements can also be found within rituals or behavioral patterns produced by a movement. In Communist Poland one saw these elements in both dimensions. The portrait of Pope John Paul II on the main gate of the Gdańsk shipyard, the portraits of the Black Madonna on workers and peasant banners, and public masses and prayers that begin workers' and peasants' organization meetings are good examples. Strong Catholic symbols, however, especially among the workers' and peasants' protest movements, were understandable in a situation in which the Communist authorities presented themselves as heirs of the radical and popular worker and peasant tradition in Poland.

Third, the religious component may be visible in the close organizational connections between protest movements and the Roman Catholic Church. Meetings in local parish buildings, or simply in churches, and the presentation of protest movements in the Catholic press were a common practice in past decades. In the 1980s the church became the main institutional channel of communication between ordinary people and protest movements, including those which, due to their ideology, were not of a Catholic character. This was quite clear in many cases of movements and organizations among the intelligentsia.

This chapter attempts to analyze the problems of religious components of peasant movements. Three main issues will be addressed here. First, in what way and to what extent is a religious component present in contemporary peasant culture in Poland? Second, in what way did religious elements become components of the peasant movement's agenda in Communist Poland? Third, in what way were these components present in the Peasant Solidarity movement, which was an important element of the struggle against the Communist system in Poland?

The starting point is made by considering the main characteristics of peasant culture, where two theoretical traditions exist: American anthropology that deals with peasant studies of Latin America or Asia, and the East European sociological tradition that deals with peasantry as one of the major social forces in the history of its society. Two concepts of peasant culture with special focus on religious elements form the intel-

lectual tool of my analysis. These concepts have been formulated by Eric
Wolf (1966) and Kazimierz Dobrowolski (1971), respectively.

Wolf's theory focuses on the gap between the peasant culture and the
culture of the rest of society. This is premised on the thesis that peasant
culture, as well as peasant communities, form a minor element of society
and, according to their nature, consist of subversive parts of social order
controlled by other groups and their cultures. This idea was formulated
by Robert Redfield (1953, 1955) as the concepts of the so-called *great*
and *little* traditions in human civilization. Peasant communities and peasant cultures are essential elements of the little tradition. This involves
the problem of peasant religion "since it cannot be explained solely in
its own terms." If it functions to support and balance the peasant ecosystem and social organization, it also constitutes a component in a larger
ideological order. Responsive to stimuli that derive both from the peasant
sector of society and from the wider social order, religion forges one
more link binding the peasantry to that order (Wolf, 1966: 100). Religion
is seen as being strongly connected with peasant culture and peasant
communities and fulfilling needs and requirements substantially different from those of other social collectivities, groups, or classes:

Although peasant religion and specialist religion [that is, religion characterizing
the dominant group in society] intersect, they respond to different needs and
processes. The peasant remains absorbed in the requisites of his narrow-gauge
social system. It is not that the peasant is ideologically uncreative; he is limited
in his creativity by his concentration upon the first order of business, which is
to come to terms with his ecosystem and his fellow-men. (Wolf, 1966: 102–3)

I therefore propose that when the process of modernization starts in
a peasant community it will break the barriers between the peasantry
and the rest of society and cause the step-by-step disappearance of social
and cultural gaps between the two worlds—that is, the peasant world
and the world of "others" (other strata or social classes), respectively. It
prompts basic elements of peasant culture, including religious values
and norms, to enter the state of transition.

This argument is further corroborated by Dobrowolski's (1971) theory
of traditional peasant culture. This culture had emerged in feudal society
where strong social divisions prevailed, becoming its subversive element.
Peasant culture was founded on such characteristic elements of society
as primitive agrarian technology and stability of peasant communities.
Hence, peasant conservatism and the importance of oral transmission
of cultural content and values have formed the backbone of peasant
culture. Anonymity of cultural products and strong connections between
the culture and the power structure of peasant communities, as well as
the importance of magic and religious values, are also evidenced. "One

of the salient features of traditional culture was the unusually great role allotted to magical beliefs and practices compared with activities based on empirical and rational foundations" (Dobrowolski, 1971: 288). Religious beliefs systematically present in peasant traditional culture have played an important role in preserving values and norms in its content. Underlying those beliefs was a deep-rooted belief in a divine omnipotence that created and controlled everything, and in the will of God equally regulating the social order and the destiny of individuals, as well as controlling the laws of nature. Against this there developed a system of transcendental sanctions, including religious commands and prohibitions. Those who broke them would meet with God's punishments; those who accepted them and acted in accordance with the "will of God" could reckon on his support, since the ultimate mastery of things and people lay with him (Dobrowolski, 1971: 290).

In Dobrowolski's theory, the peasant traditional culture is a *sui generis* reality with its own dynamics. There are, however, factors that cause disintegration of peasant culture: the growing infiltration into the villages of products demanding higher technical skill and knowledge about how to use them; a more intensive exchange of goods between town and country, and the breaking up of the spacial isolation of the countryside; the development of rural education; and the wider connection of village populations with social, political, and cultural movements on a national scale (Dobrowolski, 1971: 297). Consequently, traditional peasant culture has become a peasant culture in industrial society because the tide of displacement of elements of traditional culture was not an even one; slow at the end of the feudal epoch, it speeded up at the turn of the nineteenth and early twentieth century, and became rapid in the new Poland.

THE PEASANTRY AND CITIZENSHIP PROCESSES

The processes of social reconstruction in Communist Poland have removed the barriers between the traditional "own" peasant world and the "foreign" outside world. Subsequently, the traditional rural community, whose confines were constituted at the same time the boundaries of the peasant world were, have disappeared. This has been reflected in peasant consciousness in a variety of ways. Disintegration of the former multifunctional but monocultural integrated structure, which was the traditional peasant community, involved as well the destruction of "the system regulating the relation man-nature, operating on a level outside consciousness, and created strong demand for doctrines justifying man's role" (Pawluczuk, 1968: 261). Possibly for this reason the doctrines of peasant political movements appeared in a period when the isolation of the peasantry was diminishing. In the same period there occurred deep transformations of religious consciousness, along with the birth of national consciousness.

The religious transformations of Polish peasantry have been erroneously interpreted by the mainstream Communist scholars, who concluded that these changes should be interpreted in terms of the processes of secularization, and not in terms of the modification of the model of Catholicism in Poland. These changes bear witness to a gradual loosening of ties with the church and the parish rather than a conscious decision in favor of the model of "open" Catholicism (Pawelczynska, 1971: 72). The alleged secularization consisted in the assumed departure from a distinct religious model of Catholicism existing in traditional rural communities, where the Roman Catholic faith, embodied in the parish, was the basic system of reference regarding the formation of world view and moral and ethical attitudes. Sociologists of religion saw religiosity as the condition of social degradation of the peasantry that was not a consciously chosen culture, but one that had been introduced from outside (Ciupak, 1961: 17). Strong religiosity of the traditional and local rural community was seen as resulting from close contact with nature, dependence on factors outside human control, technological obscurantism, and the isolation of the traditional, local rural community. Sociologists concluded, therefore, with a simple thesis that, as a result of the change in those factors, in the outcome of advancement of industrialization and urbanization of the countryside, and in the cultural and technological advancement of the peasantry, the rural model of Catholicism would atrophy, the role of the parish would be limited to the narrow sphere of religious life, and the authority of a priest would be reduced to religious matters.

The justification for this thesis had been sought in anticlerical tendencies among the peasantry, conspicuous largely in more radical trends of peasant social and political movements in the inter-war period. The processes mentioned above created a type of parish—most commonly represented in rural areas—where in an "open" village community the church was a place of worship and the vicar and the vicarage were the administrative offices to arrange weddings, christenings, and funerals. Such an approach replicated the analyses of Western industrialized societies and secularization processes. It missed, however, certain specific Polish aspects of the church and religion in Polish society. The specific role of the church was a substitute for state organization. This role was created during the period of partitions and led to an exceptionally strong integration of religious and national values.

The imposed character of industrialization in Communist Poland had transformed work, the role of education, and occupational structure, but it failed to diffuse or radically transform the sphere of religious values. The measure adopted by the Communist state to implement the secularization program brought results other than intended. The issues of religion, freedom of religious practices, and religious instruction at schools caused serious anxiety among the peasantry. The former peasant anticlericalism no longer functioned in Communist Poland. The vicarage and religious observances appeared to the peasantry as the mainstay of peasant identity, ownership, and Polish customs (Golebiowski and Hemmerling, 1982: 25). The fact that the Communist state meant, in the eyes of the peasantry, an institution whose actions were directed against peasant interests further hampered the process of secularization (Gorlach, 1989). There were not only such drastic manifestations of official policy as, for example, the enforcement of collective farming with a whole range of concomitant actions, but also the presence in rural communities of state administrative or economic agencies, which, instead of helping and facilitating work, hindered or even harmed farm management.

Although some scholars (Golebiowski and Hemmerling, 1982) pointed to serious restraints on a parish function in the life of rural community as an argument that the process of secularization of peasantry was well advanced, they overlooked the active role of the church, which, as an institution and a body inspired by an idea, has adjusted to the processes of modernization of society in Poland.

The millennium program strengthened religion and national tradition ministering to the social wants of various groups, taking a position on important issues of public life. Consistently, the church played an important role as a mediator between Communist authorities and protest movements, especially in the 1980s. An alternative picture of the role of religion in Poland thus emerges:

The religiosity of peasants in rural communities is characterized by stability and continuity, though primarily on the national level. Because on this level religion functions as a common value inherited from forefathers which enables a vast majority of Poles to retain their national identity. This value is reaffirmed through religious practices on a mass scale where the motivation is both religious and national. When the concepts of God and the Fatherland, the Church and the Nation are closely identified, religion can easily fulfill the function of integration. (Piwowarski, 1984: 40)

The sphere of religious values is only narrowly separated from national contents in Polish society (Chrypinski 1984; Wierzbicki, 1976: 173–80). Subsequently, religion was identified with nationality, becoming a "trigger" that released the process of ethnic self-defense in the face of a cultural threat, thus consolidating national values beyond the level of a local community. The decisive step in the awakening of national awareness among peasants was made when the peasantry released itself from the restraints of traditional local community. Consequently, the peasantry had a chance to broaden its outlook beyond the locality.

The historical process of gradually increasing national identification of the peasantry lasted throughout the nineteenth century, reaching completion at the dawn of political independence in 1918, when massive participation of the peasantry in the war against Soviet Russia in 1920 in defense of the newly regained independence was historical proof of the process. National consciousness was established firmly in peasant communities in the interwar period. The peasantry organized in several political parties, then fought for a democratic state against authoritarian regime beginning in 1926. The citizenship process was therefore completed. This transition found its best manifestation in the attitude of peasants during World War II and the Nazi occupation. The main peasant political party in that period, the Polskie Stronnictwo Ludowe, organized an independent military organization, the Bataliony Chlopskie, to fight the Nazis.

The most important aspect of peasant national consciousness in Communist Poland was a deep mistrust of the peasantry toward the state as an institution. It was rooted in the Communist attitude toward the foundation of peasant existence—the family farm. Concerns were voiced in protests against state agricultural policy that had favored the collectivization of farming and in demands of guarantees for family farms and respect for the economic interests of the peasantry. Peasants saw the nation as a community of which they were full and important members. Hence, they were extremely sensitive to all manifestations of being treated as "second-rate" citizens—those who are called on to give but are given nothing in return.

"FOLK RELIGIOSITY" AND THE PEASANT MOVEMENT IN CONTEMPORARY POLAND

A particular kind of *folk religiosity* has arisen based on the peasant cultural tradition. It is characterized by eight distinctive components:

1. Denominational nationalism, consisting of a fusion of Polish and Catholic elements;
2. Religion as primarily an aspect of social life and a group characteristic while its individual aspect takes second place;
3. Religion connected with everyday life—work, family, and so on;
4. Religion of a sensualistic and practical nature, bent to fit in with the peasant tradition;
5. Religion that is doctrinally poor, which is not knowledge, but an experience;
6. Religious behavior of a traditional and ritualistic character;
7. Religion with an ethical content more important than religious dogma;
8. Religious behaviors and attitudes that include great respect for the official

representatives of religion (the clergy)—priests that are authorities on all
religious and nonreligious issues.

Folk religiosity in contemporary rural environments is not an un-
changeable quality; on the contrary, it undergoes constant changes on
several levels: global attachment to one's religion, religious knowledge,
religious and moral convictions, religious practices, and one's attitude
to the parish and to the clergy (Marianski, 1983: 241–80).

Some elements, however, are either permanent or undergo limited
changes: quite far-reaching homogeneity in global attitudes toward religion, traditional and conformist justification of one's religion, as well
as obligatory religious practices both single and repeated. The priest still
has significant authority in a village, but he is not the only person with
such authority and his powers are restricted by part of the Catholics in
the countryside only to matters pertaining to religion and the church.
Ties with the parish as a local community become weaker in certain
aspects. The social form of religiosity in the rural community is shaped
within an institutional framework that is revealed in concrete contacts
with the parish.

Changes in religious consciousness are rather slow as far as negating
or undermining the dogmas, but they are more conspicuous in their
views on moral principles. For example, progressing social liberalism in
relation to the principles of sexual and conjugal morality points to the
negative direction of changes in folk religiosity. Changes in religious and
moral consciousness are broader in the sphere of ritual and cultural
behaviors. The latter, although isolated from the whole of collective life,
are characterized by considerable stability.

Numerous spheres of cultural traditionalism in the parish undergo
drastic reduction. One sees the disappearance of folkloristic elements of
folk Catholicism, practices concerning magic and beliefs, as well as folk
rites directly associated with religion. The cult of patron saints undergoes
changes in the parish. Together with the disappearance of customs,
certain attempts to revive and reactivate old customs are made, but they
are provided with new meaning and motivation. Folk Catholicism becomes less "common" and "parochial" but more "institutionalized": "The
weakening of the folk element in favor of the institutional one and
shifting from the folk credo to the official one, which is the case with
folk Catholicism, brings danger of the rise of selective treatment of
religion and of partial identification with the Church" (Marianski, 1983:
280).

Such fundamental changes in the religious consciousness of the Polish
peasantry attested to the ideology of the Peasant Solidarity movement.
First pre-Solidarity peasant organizations emerged in 1978–1979 in central and eastern Poland and in southern provinces as local parish scale

bodies. They were strongly connected to the church in ideological as well as institutional dimensions. Leaders of these groups presented themselves as activists, defending Polish peasants and rural people of Catholic tradition in the face of Communist authorities. It should be stressed that local priests were among the leadership groups in each case mentioned here.

First, Peasant Solidarity organizations were founded in the fall of 1980 as a part of a great national movement challenging the Communist system. From the very beginning these organizations had some universal as well as similar features, the latter meaning that peasants were the only group to found a separate "Solidarity" organization. This fact confirms the feeling of specific identity among farmers as a distinct social category, testifying to the peculiarity of their class and occupational interests and demands. According to one of the leaders, Farmers Solidarity is the only trade union in Poland that fights for means of production necessary for its members to work and live. The demands of farmers included the following:

- Recognition of peasant agriculture as a permanent and equal element of the national economy, along with securing appropriate conditions for its further development, and the blocking of the mechanisms of land turnover, which tends to destroy a peasant economy;
- Securing favorable management for the peasant economy, its further development through stable supplies of the means of production, and a proper level of income for the peasants;
- Equalization of individual farmers with other socioprofessional groups with regard to social benefits;
- Creation of conditions for the functioning of local administrative and economic structures based on the principle of self-government. (Halamska, 1988: 150)

Farmer demands in the 1980–1981 period covered general social and national concerns of the recognition by the state of the role played by the church in social life, the recognition of Catholic national tradition, and freedom of religion. The Peasant Solidarity program was therefore of multidimensional character, containing social-national issues (national and religious freedom), social benefits (subsidies and pensions for farmers, equalization of living conditions among the rural and urban population), and "the spirit of entrepreneurship" (the freedom for economic activity of private farm owners) (Wierzbicki and Rambaud, 1982).

Organizational division inside the movement was different from that of workers' Solidarity. Three peasant solidarities existed in the same period—Independent Self-Governing Trade Union for Individual Farmers Solidarity, Peasant Solidarity, and Rural Solidarity—each concentrating on different farmer demands. The Independent Self-

Governing Trade Union for Individual Farmers Solidarity pointed out the entrepreneurial elements in farmers' demands and presented the idea of agriculture and farm consistent with West European standards. At the same time, Peasant Solidarity stressed social and national elements in these demands, including the political agency problem and regional or even local peculiarities of the rural question. In turn, Rural Solidarity, whose members recruited from various groups (including nonprivate farm workers), mainly concentrated on equalization of rural people's living standards with those of other social and occupational groups. In spring 1981 the three factions were united and were registered as one structure. During this period they stayed in close link with the church, and the leaders of the movement were supported by the Polish Episcopate officials and the Pope himself.

When martial law was proclaimed in Poland in December 1981, the farmers' Solidarity organization, as well as the whole Solidarity movement, and other independent organizations were banned and forced to act illegally. As a matter of fact, they endured the 1980s because of the Roman Catholic Church's strong support—especially through the local church structures (such as village parishes), which in many cases provided facilities for the existence and activities of various semi-legal peasant groups and organizations.

The peasant movement has experienced changes and transformations too. The effect of these changes became quite visible in the late 1980s. The success of round table talks, the foundation of the new Solidarity government in 1989, and the initiation of economic reform processes have created a totally new situation. Generally speaking, the peasant movement has reacted to this situation in a class manner, concentrating, first of all, on economic problems and farmers' demands connected with the functioning of Polish agriculture. Interestingly, while the peasant movement had demanded introduction of market mechanisms when Communists were still in power, it became the most radical critic of the new economic policy when the postsolidarity government was formed. Polish peasants' organizations (including post-Communist organizations) organized a few unique protests against governmental policy, including the blockade of main highways in July 1990 and March 1991, protest marches in spring and fall 1990 and spring 1991, and a sit-in strike at the Ministry of Agriculture building in July 1990. The three basic social and economic demands of farmers were state guarantees for minimal prices of agricultural products, preferential governmental credits for farm owners, and restricted food imports especially from European Economic Community (EEC) countries. In fact, national and religious connotations almost disappeared from the movement demands. The rhetoric inspired by national and Catholic tradition is hardly apparent in documents and comments presented by the leaders of the movement.

On the contrary, it is now quite similar to the rhetoric of farmers' movements in Western countries.

CONCLUSION

In conclusion, I argue that religious components were present in the peasant politics of protest as a result of folk religiosity that developed as a component of traditional peasant culture and survived industrialization and urbanization processes. They included close links between religious and national values, the group nature of religious experience, and the primary role of the symbol and the religious ceremony, as opposed to doctrine and the dominance of ethical and emotional aspects over intellectual and cognitive ones in religious thinking. Present protest politics were fused with the emotional and moral load included in the political programs that were presented, particularly during the period of great social and political tensions of confrontation with the Communist system. Religious symbols were used as elements of identity for both the peasant population and the organizations fighting for peasant interests. The church as an institution was used as a basis for its institutional network. Tendencies that were present in an embryonic form in the traditional model of religion were strengthened (in spite of the processes of industrialization and urbanization) by the political situation that arose in the Communist system. The lack of democracy, and the lack of free expression of group interests and points of view on public issues encouraged the tendency to substitute ways of social and political expression. To a great extent this was simply the result of circumstances. The consequences for the political life in a democratic and free market system, however, remain to be seen.

5

RELIGIOUS REVIVAL OR POLITICAL SUBSTITUTION: POLISH ROMAN CATHOLIC MOVEMENTS AFTER WORLD WAR II

Janusz L. Mucha and Maciej K. Zaba

In this chapter we deal with certain Roman Catholic religious revival movements in Poland during the three decades preceding the breakdown of communism. We argue that peculiar national, social, and political situations and the influence of Vatican II on the Roman Catholic Church have been conducive to enhancing those movements' popularity. In essence, new religious movements occurred in Poland, both as a result of a decline of community life and due to forced secularization of the public source. In turn, this secularization was largely a result of the Communist Party's efforts to purge religion from public life. The movements ultimately were not organized for political reasons, though, for a brief time, some of them were politically involved.

Social movements of religious revival or renewal occur in various regimes. The movements to be discussed in this chapter have mostly an urban character. Interestingly, some of them "operated" to some extent in the countryside and in villages but never became significant there. We analyze specific movements within the Roman Catholic Church. Rural religious movements (such as Jehovah's Witnesses and Pentecostals), at least in Poland, frequently are departures from the Catholic Church. In this sense, the rural religious renewal movements are more culturally radical. If one follows sociological theories of social movements, one finds more cases showing that the urban situation has made some grievances within the Roman Catholic Church more possible and acceptable and has given some resources to those movements within the church. Thus, we do not compare the rural and urban situations here but rather focus on operating within major urban areas, most of which were also important academic centers.

FACTORS RESPONSIBLE FOR THE EMERGENCE OF THE RELIGIOUS REVIVAL MOVEMENTS

The second part of the 1950s brought increasing cultural and political freedom, opportunities for cultural development, and increasing participation in public life and the decision-making process. However, this process lasted only ten years. The mid-1960s witnessed a new process called *small stabilization*. Political and cultural freedom became restricted as more and more people were discouraged and withdrew from participation in public life. Most people were narrowly preoccupied with attempts to improve their standard of living. Community life declined, and individualistic, egocentric attitudes prevailed. Primary ideals and primary group values were on a decline (Cooley, 1962). The Gesellschaft type of societal organization dominated, overpowering the old Gemeinschaft community values (Tönnies, 1957). The "profane," ordinary sphere of everyday pragmatic life gained importance over the "sacred" sphere (Durkheim, 1965/1915).

Such processes continued, despite brief periods of economic prosperity stimulated by international loans that had little effect on Poland culturally or spiritually (Nowak, 1982). Economic crises of the late 1970s and of the 1980s compounded the worsening situation. The youth were first affected by such a "spiritual deprivation." Schools were subjected to total bureaucratization. The educational system ceased to be a channel of upward social mobility. Access to good schools, even on the secondary level, was determined by the parental socioeconomic position. The old ethos of hard work was no longer held as an important social value. Family life became disorganized. Informal peer groups were very weak because of the intentional influence of organizations and activities supported by the state. In short, the social fiber of urban Poland was disintegrating.

Vatican II, on the other hand, emphasized the need for debureaucratization in the Roman Catholic Church, for involving laypersons in church affairs, and for strengthening community life within the church structure. It also strengthened the church's role as a countervailing force to prevalent trends.

A crisis in community values is often an important source of new spiritual movements (e.g., Robbins and Anthony, 1979: 76). Such was the case in Poland. Emerging religious movements were in some respects similar to the so-called New Social Movements, studied by West European and North American sociologists. Such movements' antimodernist persuasion rejected the notion of a society that would be grounded solely in the value of its economic growth (Polish economic growth was undeniably slower than in the Western democracies). Instead, movements' programs focused on issues involving the superstructure, proposing small-scale, decentralized organizations; they were antihierarchical in their own practice, and their emphasis was on self-help, self-organization, self-actualization, and participation. Those movements drew membership from all parts of the class structure. Polish spiritual movements had the characteristics of bridging movements, since they bridged the gap between various segments of social class structure (Johnston and Figa, 1988; Klandermans, 1986). Their aim was not only the equality of rights but also the right to be different (e.g., Melucci, 1984: 830). Consisting mostly of young, relatively well-educated people, these Polish religious movements have also included members of other social groups. The aim was not to remake society, but instead to change themselves and their immediate social environment.

The ensuing religious revival in Poland was a reaction to forced policies of secularization. Secularization was partly the result of actions taken by the political authorities and partly a spontaneous reaction to the elimination of the sacred sphere from the public and often from personal life. In this sense Poland was not unique. An interesting discussion of the American case is presented by Mark Chaves (1989). Likewise, Rodney Stark and William Bainbridge make a strong argument that because religion satisfies universal human needs, secularization ultimately results in religious renewal, revival, and religious innovation (1985: 1–2, 429–56). Nor was the Polish situation unique in that the supporters of post-materialistic values came into conflict with a political and social system that had been chiefly materialistic (Klandermans, 1986: 22). Thus, one could refer to all the social movements that operated in Poland as the "social movement sector" (see McCarthy and Zald, 1977).

In the 1960s, most social movements in Poland were religious movements. In the rural areas they were non–Roman Catholic, while in urban areas they were Roman Catholic. The situation changed in the second half of the 1970s. Social movements emerged within the Roman Catholic Church and various non-Catholic (Protestant/sect) groups sought converts. A variety of Catholic, non-Christian, astrological, occultist, Oriental, and parareligious spiritual movements (e.g., Doktor and Kosela, 1984) existed at large.

Finally, political and democratic opposition movements emerged as a third type of social movement. Yet there were hardly any relations between Catholic and non-Catholic religious movements or between religious and nonreligious movements until the late 1970s and into even the very early 1980s when Catholic movements developed ties to nonreligious political and democratic opposition movements.

In the remainder of this chapter, we focus only on the Roman Catholic movements of religious revival in Poland and only on the most important organizations within this movement. We do not discuss regular Catholic organizations such as those of Catholic lay, youth clubs, "family ministry," clubs of Catholic intelligentsia, religious education of schoolchildren, or parish councils (see for more information on these, Slominska, 1987).[1]

The thesis of this chapter is similar to that of Bert Klandermans (1986). Although they were spiritual and apolitical, the religious revival movements came into conflict with the political and social system of Communist Poland. Because of this conflict they became politicized. We view these movements primarily as religious movements that have had a secondary political function and not as political opposition movements that developed under the protection of the Roman Catholic Church.

We shall now look at somewhat different opinions on somewhat similar issues. In her article on "civil religion" in Poland, Ewa Morawska describes "Polish romantic faith as a civil religion, constituted and reconstituted through sustained conflict between the . . . civil society and imposed alien rule" (1984: 29). For her, "civil religion" is "a set of religiopolitical symbols and rituals regarding a nation's history and destiny"; she states that the major function of this civil religion has been to delegitimize alien rule "by rallying Polish society around a counterview of a past and future free, independent Poland" (1984: 29). In this chapter, we present some examples to show that this was really true, not only in the nineteenth century but also in the period following World War II. We agree that "home, church, and informal social gatherings were the main institutional 'carriers' of popular 'civil religion' in partitioned Poland [the nineteenth-century situation] and had remained with them until the end of the 1980s" and that "the relations between Polish 'civil religion' and the Catholic Church has been complex and ambivalent" (Morawska, 1984: 30). Unlike Morawska, we are not interested in "civil religion" but in movements of religious revival that function within the Roman Catholic Church.

The link between the Roman Catholic Church and political opposition in Poland has been frequently stressed. The church had material resources, cadres, buildings, equipment, and access to mass media. These resources played an important role in the opposition process. They could be used because of their protected status, particularly as the Communist regime's need for legitimation increased (Borowski, 1986; Johnston and Figa, 1988).

Subsequently, a "religio-oppositional subculture" (civil religion) emerged in Poland. This subculture is thought to have been a product of repression and of restricted political discourse. Prohibited national and religious traditions and holidays commonly took on political significance. This subculture was passed and refined through family and youth activities taking place under church auspices, away from the scrutiny of the regime (Johnston, 1989: 496–97).

Interestingly, the "religio-oppositional subculture" may also emerge (and actually had emerged) when purely religious and not necessarily political discourse is being restricted, when public character of religion is being denied by political authorities, and even when charitable activities must be supervised by the state authorities.

DESCRIPTION OF FOUR MOVEMENTS OF SPIRITUAL REVIVAL

In what follows, four social movement organizations are analyzed. We contend that these are the only large-scale, Roman Catholic, religious revival movements in Poland—hence the focus on the spiritual and political functions of their activities.

Oases of God's Children

Oases of God's Children is the oldest and the original Polish spiritual movement. It was initiated by Rev. Franciszek Blachnicki in 1954 and has been known under various names (Life-Light Movement, Oases, and Oases of the Live Church: Light-Life). The movement had an ostensibly spiritual character, but during the Stalinist period, when it was founded, it had obvious political ramifications. Its objective was the strengthening of the religious experience in the antireligious political climate of Communist Poland. The instigator and leader of the movement started it as field trips organized for his altar boys. He followed some boy scout traditions, but the purpose of the trips and camps was to change the whole individual life of the participants: their life was to become enlightened and highlighted by the word of God. However, Reverend Blachnicki strongly believed that religion was a public phenomenon, and this belief had important consequences for the movement.

Vatican II and its ramifications transformed the Roman Catholic Church. The role of laypersons in the Church became more important, and they were exhorted to first become spiritually transformed themselves. Father Blachnicki helped organize many Oases of the Live Church in the "desert of materialistic world." Eventually, these groups were established in many urban parishes. The movement came to embrace not only youngsters but also their adult relatives. Yet, the youth branch remained the largest. In the mid–1980s the whole movement numbered about 70,000 people.

The movement was organized by priests and subsequently has been supervised by parish pastors. It has consisted of small groups of parishioners who have been meeting every week for prayer and Bible study. The members of the Oases were to transform themselves into "new people"; true members of the Church understood it as a community of the faithful and the clergy.

The main objective of the Oases movement, as perceived by the modern clergy, has been the transformation of parishes into "communities of communities," that is, into groups of people who are responsible for strengthening the Catholic faith and for its propagation. Propagation was seen as a social activity and a confrontation with people for whom other values are much more important. Propagation was interpreted as "to go and to preach," to help other people transform themselves. Another objective has been "to give witness," to live according to one's own principles and to show that this was not only desirable but also possible, even in a hostile milieu. Additional fields of activity have been charitable work and helping pastors with their tasks (Bolczyk and Wieczorek, 1987: 26). The most important "external" activity, however, has been of an apostolic, evangelizing character. It opened a field of social conflict between the evangelists and the potentially evangelized, and also between the movement and the political authorities. Some members of the Oases chose to withdraw, to retreat within the group of the already convinced. Still, at the end of the 1970s, the Oases constituted the only large movement of young people, completely independent of state authorities.

There were at least two "political" interpretations of the Oases spiritual movement until the late 1970s. According to Communist authorities, activists, and ideologists, the movement was first of all disseminating anti-socialist values and therefore was mostly of a political—moreover, illegal—character (e.g., Brodzki and Wojna, 1988). According to many Catholic intellectuals and some socially oriented activists, however, the movement concentrated itself too much on the spiritual renewal of its individual members and small religious communities, and it did not pay enough attention to the outside world. This second group of critics pointed to evidence proving that when the members of the movement were temporarily leaving their Oases and went out to the "desert," or the "profane," everyday life world, they were helpless, completely unprepared to deal with the social, political, and cultural reality in which most Poles lived.

Why, then, the Communist "accusations"? The problem originated at the end of the 1950s when priests organized field trips and camps without asking for permission to do so from the local administrative authorities. Not only did these priests pull youths out of pro-regime organizations, associations, and values, but also they constantly and without hesitation broke the administrative regulations that demanded registration of every trip, camp, or other overnight activity. What was defined by priests and participants as a religious spiritual gathering was defined by the authorities as an illegal camp. The priests refused to apply for administrative permission. The local authorities, encouraged by their supervisors, punished every unauthorized action. Heavy fines were often imposed on the priests who organized these activities, on the laypersons who helped them, and on the farmers who had given permission for their land to be used for these retreats. Priests and farmers appealed to the bishops, and the conflict escalated politically. Throughout the 1950s, 1960s, and 1970s, the movement became politicized by the very fact that it was labeled political and because it became a target of authorities (for this phase of the Oases movement, see e.g., Bolczyk and Wieczorek, 1987; Cviic, 1983).

At the end of the 1970s, the political context within which the Oases movement found itself had changed. On the one hand, within the Roman Catholic Church, various previously informal structures became more formalized. This change also affected the Oases. In big cities, their presence became rather a rule than an exception within the parishes. Earlier, Church authorities were surprised but delighted if an Oasis was organized within a parish; now they expected this kind of activity. By the mid–1970s a network of local groups had been established throughout the country. Its activity was coordinated by a chaplain appointed by the Primate. On the other hand, since 1976 an organized, democratic opposition operated in Poland. Although this opposition was illegal and heavily persecuted, it broadened the public sphere and gave a new meaning to public and political activities. The public and the political ceased to mean the acceptance of the Communist regime.

In March 1980, a few months before the Gdańsk and Szczecin strikes that resulted in the emergence of Solidarity, the Fifth National Congregation of Directors of the Light-Life Movement was held. It published (via underground press) a *Declaration of Intentions* that defined the overall situation in Poland as a deep cultural crisis, characterized by humiliation, lack of individual freedom, and total dependence of individual human beings on state authorities. Passivity and escapism were not only potential dangers but also the reality within the Life-Light Movement. What was to be done, asked the congregation? Its answers: cooperate with the democratic opposition, "give the witness," and publicly present one's own moral convictions. The *Declaration* also addressed the problem of participation of Catholics (not only the movement's members) in the public sphere still controlled by the Communist authorities. Such problematic participation included their membership in the Communist Party and their voting in the local and national elections organized by the party. The *Declaration*'s tone was decidedly activist, not retreatist. Individual conscience was to be, however, the supreme judge of everyone's social activities. As a result, between March 1980 and December 1981 the Oases movement participated very actively and more and more overtly in Polish political life.

During martial law (1982–1983) and later during the so-called period of normalization (1983–1988), the situation changed again. Rev. Blachnicki, the instigator and leader of the movement, emigrated to West Germany and became an extremely radical, militant anti-Communist activist.

In Poland the Communist activities started a very strong ideological and political campaign against the Oases. Oases' leaders realized that continuation of any public activity would jeopardize not only the position of the movement, but also that of the Roman Catholic Church. The movement retired to the enforced isolation from the public sphere and to the concentration on religious and spiritual issues (Nosowski, 1989).

The Barrel

A different, local, social movement organization represents the kind of organization that is very active in cities and academic centers. This group has operated in Cracow, a medieval city with the second oldest university in Central Europe. It is called the "Barrel" (Beczka). It was organized at the Dominican Father's parish in Cracow's downtown in the 1960s, in large part as a result of Vatican II influence, and originally was a college students' ministry. The laypersons were to be mobilized to take new responsibilities within the church. The Barrel Club, at the beginning of its activity, was a real spiritual oasis in Cracow's secularized cultural life of young people. Its objectives were to facilitate a spontaneous expression of religious faith, to find new forms that would make the authentic religious experience possible for adolescents, and to find a new, attractive form of religious gathering for young people. The movement attracted not only college students but also many high school seniors and young college graduates. Rock and roll masses in the Dominican Church became very famous and controversial; field trips and camps became very popular—yet the basic activity was purely spiritual and religious. Bible studies, theological discussions, group religious experience, group prayer, and singing religious hymns were among the frequent activities. Until 1976, there had been no political interests demonstrated by the movement's members. The only exception was charitable activities and, even here, the motivation seems to have been nearly purely religious.

In 1976, when a movement of democratic opposition emerged, the Roman Catholic Church had begun stressing the existence and significance of inalienable human rights. Taking advantage of the intellectual resources of Cracow, the leaders of the Barrel established an educational center, called the "free university." It functioned in 1977 and 1978, using the church material and organizational resources as well as some resources of Jagiellonian University of Cracow. For example, some of the university's professors became teachers in the "free university." After a short break in 1978, the teaching activities reappeared. According to the estimates of organizers and participants, about 500 students were coming to every lecture. The subjects were varied: ethics, Russian literature, Eastern Orthodox culture, culture and religions of the Far East, Marxism

and contemporary philosophy, history of the Roman Catholic Church
in Poland, modern history of Poland, and social stratification in contemporary Poland. There was a distinct shift of subjects away from the purely
religious to the cultural, social, and political spheres.

Student ministry lost its spiritual character and became involved in
social and political activities. The Barrel attracted more and more young
people who were less interested in religion and more in criticizing the
Communist economic, social, and political system in Poland. They were
using the resources of the Roman Catholic Church to carry on their
political activities. The new situation opened discussions within the Barrel concerning its own structure and activities. Internal conflicts
emerged. Many students and old members were still interested much
more in purely religious activities and did not like the transformation
of their movement into anything else. Other old members were simply
afraid of the danger of ideologization and politicization of Catholicism.

The situation changed again in December 1981 after the declaration
of martial law. It became impossible to continue any kind of political or
even pseudopolitical activities of other than a pro-government character.
The movement developed now in two directions. One was the strengthening of the charitable activities. Not only physically and mentally hand-
icapped people needed help, but also the internees of the martial law
and their families. The Barrel organized a group of members who engaged strongly in this kind of work. The charity gained something of a
political reputation, though this was still more strongly emphasized by
observers than by those who were engaged in it. The second direction
was of a totally religious character. The Charismatics, or members of
the Movement of the Renewal in the Holy Spirit, became the largest
component of the Barrel—a few hundred members. The Charismatics
had been active within the Barrel before, but their communities had
been very small. Under martial law their relative importance thus increased, which again resulted in some conflicts within the student ministry. Thus, the parties of the internal conflict were, on the one hand,
the Charismatics and, on the other hand, the more socially and intellectually oriented students as well as the Dominican Fathers who preferred to support more intellectual than emotional religious activities
(Ruszar, 1983).

It is important to remember that the influence of the clergy on the
Barrel movement, as well as on every other religious movement within
the Roman Catholic Church, has been very strong. Using the church's
financial, material, organizational, and symbolic resources, the movement has had to accept the supervision on the part of the church hierarchy. On the other hand, members of the movement have considered
themselves first of all Roman Catholics, and the discipline has been an
important element of this self-definition. They have been extremely

sensitive to the accusation of schism, of building a new sect, and they reiterate that they had not separated from the body of the Roman Catholic Church. Yet the accusations mentioned above have been heard not only in informal discussions but also during the meeting of some of the Vatican committees dealing with new religious movements (e.g., Wilkanowicz and Turnau, 1987). We shall return to this problem at the end of this chapter.

Charismatic Renewal

A third religious movement organization is the Charismatic Renewal. According to its theoreticians and leaders, this movement is actually not a new phenomenon. Indeed, they interpret the essence of the Roman Catholic Church as charismatic. Charisma is a gift given by the Holy Spirit to all Christians during the baptism rite, and it is the foundation on which the Church community had been built. Some would argue that the charismatic character of the church is much more important than its official, formal structure. While formal charisma of the church offices must be recognized, it cannot reduce the significance of the individual charisma of all Christians. The brotherhood of all Christians is, again, more important than patriarchalism and paternalism (Greinacher, 1987).

The origin of the Christian charismatic movement cannot be discussed here. It is worth mentioning only because the strongest wave of this religious current, Protestant Pentecostalism, originated at the very beginning of the twentieth century. Neo-Pentecostalism, or its Roman Catholic variety, became possible only in the post–Vatican II ecumenical atmosphere. The new movement began at the dormitories of two Roman Catholic universities in the United States, in Pittsburgh and Notre Dame, in 1967. It was an offspring of ecumenical prayers of Catholics along with representatives of Pentcostalist communities.

The Pentecostal Movement in the Catholic Church was growing very fast, and in 1971 its first international congress was held at Notre Dame. During the 1980s the center of the movement shifted to Rome. According to the estimates of *L'Observatore Romano* of June 1987, membership of the movement exceeded 20 million people.

The Catholic Charismatic Renewal came to Poland in 1976, brought by two Polish priests, who participated in gatherings and prayers of the movement in Italy and the United States. The official name of the movement (from the beginning strictly controlled by the Roman Catholic Church hierarchy) has been Catholic Movement of the Renewal in the Holy Spirit. It has been active mostly in large cities: Cracow, Gdańsk, Warsaw, Bialystok, Wroclaw, Lublin (a site of the Catholic University), and Lodz. The First National Congress of the Renewal in the Holy Spirit was held in Czestochowa (a site of the Black Madonna shrine) in 1983. There were around 7,000 participants. The last known convention was held in 1986. More than 25,000 people from all Polish dioceses attended, and the estimates are that twice as many people belong to the movement. Most of them are young people with at least a high school education.

There are virtually no differences between the Roman Catholic Charismatic Renewal in Poland and this same movement in other countries. What is important here is that the movement embraced a lot of people and that it became an important phenomenon on the local level of parish life, although it never had an explicitly political character or functions. Proceedings and the recollections of participants of the above-mentioned congress and observations at the local level all make it clear that the renewal of spiritual life, the renewal of the sense of belonging to a community, of the sense that one's own life was inspired mostly by religion and that religion radiated from it, were of particular importance for the movement's members. What is also significant is that the Church hierarchy did not lose control over this highly emotional movement. It has been highly centralized and only the lowest, at the parish and community level, seems to be relatively informal.

Obviously, there have been many conflicts. Some lay leaders of both larger communities and small groups within the communities developed the idea that God spoke through them—that they were the true prophets who should have led their groups, regardless of the opinion of pastors. As a consequence, there have been some schisms. While their number has not been large, the danger of schism has been real; however, it has been one of the sources of tension between the groups and the pastors (Dembowski and Turnau, 1987; Pasek, 1989).

The charismatic movement has been organized on four levels: the national level with the national chaplain and national conferences; parishes as "communities of communities"; communities belonging to parishes; and eventually small groups within the communities. The movement has developed strong informal bonds between members of communities, and particularly between members of small groups. They have not only prayed together and studied the Bible, they have also discussed their spiritual problems and shared their life experiences (Pasek, 1989: 42).

Neo-Catechumenism

The fourth movement of spiritual revival within the Roman Catholic Church in Poland is the so-called neo-catechumenism. This movement, too, was imported to Poland. It was started in Madrid, Spain, in 1964. Its instigator was Mr. Kiko Arguello. Like many other "prophets," he was interested in renewal of spiritual life of Roman Catholics. He succeeded in building strong religious communities within poor parishes in Madrid, in other big cities of Spain, and, since 1969, abroad. In 1969 the movement reached Italy and in 1972 many other countries. In 1979 there were 3,050 communities of neo-catechumens in 1,584 parishes, in 390 dioceses, and 51 countries (Weron, 1984).

According to Arguello and his followers, we witness in the modern world a crisis and erosion of some supreme values. It is necessary to rebuild them. We can do this through the "second conversion" of Christians, who have become overwhelmed by the profane, ordinary aspects of life. This "conversion," or "evangelical renewal," takes place within small groups (thirty–forty persons) of adults, coming from various social milieus. This conversion after baptism is necessary if we want to find our place in the Church community and if we want to live a truly Christian life within the Church. Arguello's ideas were based on the tradition of the first centuries of our era, when candidates for baptism had to participate in specially organized rites and sacraments for the sake of their spiritual growth. Everything was done under the strict control of the Church community. The same process, Arguello reasoned, should be repeated now on a higher level in a completely changed social situation. Neo-catechumanism did not want to diminish the role of baptism of children but, rather, to revive the practice of gradual and intensive evangelization of adults. In order to find their own place in the community, believers had to destroy their own ego, give up their own sympathies and antipathies, devote themselves totally to the church community, and become parts of a whole.

The movement appeared in Poland in the second half of the 1970s when the deteriorating public situation in Poland was already under way. However, it has not tried to engage in any public activities. It has operated only on the level of parishes, with a growing number of communities that have not exceeded sixty persons each. Their main objective has been the religious self-education under the supervision of the parish priests, but to some extent performed by members themselves. Charitable activities have been the only kind of visible public behavior (Dembowski and Turnau, 1987; Szatynska, Szatynska, and Polak, 1987).

Some members of the movement have been "wandering preachers." They have been going from parish to parish, preaching to the faithful. Again, it is worth mentioning that they want, first of all, to avoid the accusation of schism. Therefore, they stop first at the rectory, speak to the pastor, and only then, having his permission, preach. The pastors have served as "guardians of orthodoxy" (Szatynska, Szatynska, and Polak, 1987: 40–41). The preaching has been obviously a social phenomenon, but it has taken place only within the parishes, on the church premises, and under Roman Catholic Church auspices.

CONCLUSION

In sum, four different social movement organizations have been presented: Oases, the college student ministry called the Barrel, Charismatic Renewal, and neo-catechumenism. There are no other important movements of religious revival within the Roman Catholic Church in Poland. Membership in the first two organizations has consisted mostly of young people (high school seniors, college students, and young college graduates). The organizations originated as purely religious, spiritual movements, with an obvious public aspect, not because of their objectives and intended activities, but because of resistance on the part of the dominant political system. In the second half of the 1970s, they became highly politicized. Many Poles who, in most respects, would not be considered very religious, identified with the Catholic Church and with Catholic-sponsored religious movements as a way of opposing the Communist regime. The martial law declared at the end of 1981 again reduced the activities of the movements to spiritual (and charitable) ones.

These organizations met some resistance within the Roman Catholic Church itself. Some priests were more, some were less, enthusiastic about the changes introduced by Vatican II. Some were more, some were less, tolerant of the spontaneous activities of the faithful. Most important was that members of the movements strongly emphasized their subordination to the body of the Church and that religious activities were much more important to them than political activities.

Two other religious movements have not had nearly as much political aspect. When they became relatively popular, the democratic political opposition was already strongly organized, and they did not have to serve as its, even partial, substitute.

NOTE

1. One important reservation has to be made here. Our analyses are based on the interpretation of the secondary data—mostly published articles, interviews with activists, and reports. The picture would be improved if it were supplemented with the findings of empirical research, especially if there were any studies of the rank-and-file movement members. Several unauthorized recollections by individual movement members whom the authors know in person do not stand the rigor of scientific inquiry and hence cannot be used here in lieu of empirical survey, the need for which we are aware.

RELIGIOUS NATIONALISM: SIX PROPOSITIONS FROM EASTERN EUROPE AND THE FORMER SOVIET UNION

Hank Johnston

The end of the Cold War holds the potential for a new international stability. At the same time, however, seeds of nationalism that have rested dormant for seventy-five years are now establishing roots and sending out shoots. As the Cold War ends, and in the sunlight of new freedoms, old ethnic enmities have found fertile soil in Eastern Europe and the former Soviet Union, insidiously covering political landscapes created by the weakening of old regimes.

In the midst of nationalist demands, one finds yet another trace of the past: frequently nationhood is legitimated in terms of a community of the faithful. The church and nation are merged. At nationalist protests one often finds priests; national anthems are sung on the steps of cathedrals. For many, religious icons symbolize the suffering of a nation. Nationalist demands give rise to calls for religious freedom.

The embodiment of a nation as a community of faithful has many historical representations in the West. In the United States, despite fundamental accord on individual liberty and religious freedom, and a constitutional separation of church and state, there has been a traditional association of God and nation (O'Brien, 1987). Today, as pluralism and secularization have spread, this seems to be less the case. Elsewhere in the West, hegemonic ties between church and state have also decreased. In many cases where the church remains instituted, in Sweden and Norway for example, the community of faithful is well below 50 percent of the population.

In certain minority regions in the West the association of religion and nationhood has lingered. This is especially true in Quebec, and also in Catalonia, the Basque region of Spain, Flanders, Brittany, Wales, Scotland, and the cauldron of Ulster in Ireland. In general, however, these linkages have attenuated in recent years. Despite pockets of religious resurgence, the aggregate trend seems to be that, under conditions of democratic pluralism, secular materialism turns attention away from traditional forms of religiosity. Institutionalized political competition gives at least partial vent to nationalist aspirations, channeling communal conflict away from potentially virulent combinations of God and nation. Most recently this is apparent in Spain. As late as 1974, both Basque and Catalan nationalisms had very strong religious components (Johnston, 1991; Pérez-Agote, 1986; Zulaika, 1988) when they stood in opposition to the Franco regime. By 1991, the linkage has almost disappeared under democracy and prosperity.

In the East, however, both economic growth and political freedoms have been severely restricted, and in many minority national regions the association of religion and nation is still strong. Despite Marxist-inspired efforts at expunging both God and nation from public discourse, current events suggest that, at best, the police state only drove them underground. In the privacy of family and friends they were nurtured and passed to new generations, awaiting a time when social control was eased and they could be voiced in public again.

The focus of this chapter is the persistence of the linkage between religion and nation under conditions of repression. My goal is to suggest several propositions about this relationship as it relates to nationalist mobilization. It is a topic with pressing relevance for several regions in both the former Soviet Union and Eastern Europe. In order to first establish an empirical base, I will begin with descriptions of three movements where the fusion of religion and nationalism have been particularly strong: Poland, Lithuania, and western Ukraine.

THE PANORAMA OF RELIGIOUS NATIONALISM

At the outset it is important to emphasize that nationalist movements are usually motivated by political, not religious, interests, and, while the degree of the religion-nation merger will vary, eventually political forces dominate. The politicization and secularization of nationalism occurs not as a conscious decision by the clergy to retreat to spiritual matters (although this occurs frequently) but, rather, as a function of the changing context of mobilization and the opening of political opportunities. It appears that religious aspects of nationalism consistently play a role in the early stages of nationalist mobilization and before that, in what might be called the abeyance phase of a movement (Taylor, 1989). This is when, under unfavorable structural conditions, deeply held sentiments are maintained by dedicated activists.

In considering premobilization patterns, it is important to distinguish between religious beliefs and the social organization that in part sustains those beliefs. Social theory and church theology both recognize that one cannot exist long without the other, but in the former Eastern bloc state policies often have driven a wedge between the two. The effect was frequently to force aspects of religious organization into more informal social structures such as friendship networks, "home churches," and families. Shlapentokh (1984, 1989) has noted how state repression privatizes social discourse in the sense that people tend to rely more on trusted inner circles of family, friends, and acquaintances. While much of his argument derives from the Russian case, it makes sense that when repressive policies are applied in a minority national context against religious practice, historical links between nation and religion are reinforced and embedded in the content of privatized interaction. As will be apparent, the public-private axis is a key variable in understanding patterns of religious nationalism.

Privatized Religious Nationalism: Ukrainian Uniates

The most poignant example of privatization is the maintenance of the Ukrainian Uniate Church despite what can only be described as the most ruthless campaign of religious persecution in a state not reputed for its tolerance. It is known that religious beliefs and customs can be secretly maintained in fear of severe sanctions for centuries, such as the "Crypto-Jews" in New Mexico (Teltsch, 1990: 30) and underground Catholics in Sagara, Japan. In 1946 Stalin's dissolution of the Uniate Church forced a similar "catacomb strategy" on Ukrainian Catholics.

The Uniate Church possessed strong nationalist connotations because of its distinctive merger of Ukrainian Eastern Orthodoxy and Catholicism. Also, it has been noted that its allegiance to Rome and generally Western historical traditions threatened the Communist regime's hegemony in the region (Hvat, 1984). When western Ukraine was annexed by the former Soviet Union after the war, the Uniate faithful numbered over 4 million and had a well-organized, Westernized, and nationalistic clergy of almost 3,500 (Markus, 1975: 104). To consolidate control, the Communist Party staged an ecclesiastic council called a *Sobor* in L'vov, western Ukraine, where under duress several priests conspired with ersatz bishops to dissolve the Union of Brest (which had joined the Uniates to Rome centuries earlier). Henceforth, Uniate churches were closed or transferred to the Russian Orthodox Church. The legitimate hierarchy was arrested, and many recalcitrant clergy were exiled (Bociurkiw, 1977; Markus, 1975).

In response to these events, the Ukrainian Uniates went underground, forming a clandestine church that endured persecution and repression for almost forty-five years (Bociurkiw, 1975; Hvat, 1984). In some Western *oblasti*, it is reported that Uniate faithful attended the few Latin rite Catholic churches that were open, especially the Catholic cathedral in L'vov, thereby eschewing any compromise with Orthodoxy. On holidays, the closed churches were often surreptitiously opened for worship. Other times, covert priests traveled and administered sacraments at services in private homes. Some priests outwardly acquiesced to the Orthodox patriarchate in Moscow but duplicitously kept Uniate liturgy and sacraments for the faithful. Authorities often knew of these activities and arrested or fined those involved (Markus, 1975: 107–9). More dissident Uniates, those who demanded official registration of the church according to the Soviet constitution, were imprisoned and exiled (SMOT, 1980).

Under these conditions, the Uniate Church was able to exist without a formal structure but, rather, through trusted networks of believers. How it was accomplished has now been studied in depth. One observer characterized Ukrainian Uniate Catholicism as "a psychological attitude and national-cultural identification, with a certain set of customs and practices zealously kept. Major religious feasts are observed within the family or among close friends (Easter, Christmas Eve, religious namedays, etc.). Baptism, religious nuptial rites, and funerals are frequently performed by a Christian priest, often secretly, and sometimes even by a Uniate priest" (Markus, 1975: 108). Acted out in the most intimate reaches of social life, all this proved to be exceedingly difficult to repress.

The Uniate Church represents the most privatized and clandestine enclave of religious nationalism. Because it was a church without official structure, its organization was almost entirely private or, even more remarkable, duplicitous. Its primary locus was the shared meaning given by adherents to membership and rituals, supplemented and reinforced occasionally by surreptitious meetings. However, deprivation of organizational resources imparted to the Uniate Church a symbolic strength and moral high ground unparalleled in the U.S.S.R. Church organization took a secondary role to church symbolism in the nationalist cause. Since the mid–1960s the secular Ukrainian dissident movement drew on the church as a symbol and supported the Uniate cause as a central nationalist grievance. In 1989, under pressure from the Ukrainian Nationalist Front (RUKH) the Uniate Church was granted full religious freedom.

Nationalism and Church Organization: Poland

It is widely recognized that the Roman Catholic Church played an important role in the original emergence of Solidarity. As Laba (1991) observes, the symbolism was especially strong: pictures of Pope John Paul II and of the Virgin of Czestochowa carried in protests, the cross in the background at the signing at the Gdańsk accords, pilgrimages to the Jasna Gora monastery as assertions of resistance, and Cardinal Stefan Wyszynski himself as a symbol of resistance.

The role of the Polish church went far beyond the purely symbolic. Because its organization was public, and its resources considerable, it played a substantial role in the initial mobilization of the opposition. Unlike any other country in Eastern Europe, the Catholic Church in Poland had schools and universities. It had freedom to teach the younger generation. By its unique relationship with the Communists, its organization was freed from the demands of mere survival, allowing application of resources to more expansive goals. It is true that the state took countermeasures, and that many Poles were nationalistic and anti-Communist without being religious. It is also true that the church walked a thin line between accommodation and resistance, and was frequently criticized for its caution. Still, for a large majority of Poles, Roman Catholicism and its symbols represented an assertion of opposition to the regime.

It is important not to misrepresent the church's primary mission in Poland as anything other than spiritual. Nevertheless, its considerable resources were also put to use, directly and indirectly, in propagating the illegitimacy of the regime (Johnston, 1989). Solidarity eventually became politicized and secularized, and, with changing contexts of political opportunities, it left its roots in the church behind. Indeed, we witness today a distancing of Polish political culture from the church on several issues (Engleberg, 1991: 5). Nevertheless in the early stages of mobilization, the opposition drew on the church, and the resources the church was able to provide were important in several ways.

First, the church stood for national autonomy and the continued illegitimacy of the Communist regime. This symbolic merger had roots in the various partitions of the Polish nation during the nineteenth century. When public use of the Polish language was prohibited, and when national culture was expunged from public discourse, the church provided the few occasions where national consciousness could be expressed (Borowski, 1986: 29; Morawska, 1984: 30–31).

Second, the church was one of the few places to publicly voice dissent, as veiled and muted as it may be. Its teachings sharply contrasted with official atheism of the regime and represented a challenge to the world view of Marxism-Leninism. Catholic journals were important sources of information for the opposition. The weekly *Tygodnik Powszechny* (Popular Weekly) and the monthly journals *Wiez* (Bond) and *Znak* (Sign) appeared under the auspices of the church and provided forums for not only Catholic writers but also other branches of the opposition. Another important underground publication was *Spotkania* (Encounters), published by Catholic students and intellectuals.

Third, the church had access to considerable resources that were free from direct control by the regime. Churches had been used for hunger strikes, the most famous being the one at Saint Martin Church in Warsaw organized in support of the Committee of Workers Defense (KOR). KOR was probably the most important pre-Solidarity dissident organization, and while it was for the most part secular, several activists had strong ties with the episcopate. In the pre-Solidarity period, there were also linkages with other human rights groups such as the Movement for the Defense of Human Rights (ROPCIO), and with progressive Catholic and intellectual groups. Church-owned buildings were sometimes used for lectures and debates, providing for a level of freedom that was impossible at government-sponsored events. Several members of early opposition groups came from the church-based "academic ministries" that were affiliated academic institutions. In the earliest stages of Solidarity, churches were often used as meeting places. Several chapters of Rural Solidarity grew out of militant sectors of the Catholic Oases movement. Groups like these and others helped overcome the gap between different social strata in Poland: intellectuals, workers, peasants, and students (Borowski, 1986). The effect was to broaden the base of the opposition and, in part, to lay the groundwork for more mobilization of Solidarity.

An Intermediate Case: The Catholic Church in Lithuania

As in Poland, the Lithuanian nation was in many ways synonymous with the Catholic Church. Also, like Poland, Lithuania was a highly homogeneous region and did not present the kinds of regional or religious diversions that the state could play on, as it did in Ukraine. These factors combined to moderate repression when compared with Ukraine and opened opportunities for maintaining a merger of nation and church.

Because the Soviet constitution ostensibly guarantees "freedom of belief" for all citizens, restrictions on Lithuanian Catholicism occurred behind a facade of religious freedom. Churches were burdened with exorbitant rents and utilities charges. There were severe restrictions on religious instruction: priests were commonly fined for proselytizing, and religious youth were labeled and sanctioned in schools and secondary associations. Also, there was a constant barrage in the media and the workplace of atheistic campaigns. Nevertheless, in contrast to the Ukrainian Uniates, it seems that the resource base available to the church was sufficient to permit a surplus that freed some priests and laity from purely spiritual ministrations.

In the early stages of *Sajudis* (the Lithuanian nationalist movement) the Catholic Church was an active presence—priests took part in demonstrations; churches served as gathering places for protests. For its part, early demands of the *Sajudis* front included full freedom for the Catholic Church, for imprisoned Catholic activists, and the return of confiscated churches. Like Poland, many Lithuanian dissidents came from Catholic sectors. During the 1970s, *samizdat* publications emanated almost wholly from Catholic activists. More than any minority republic in the Soviet Union, national consciousness in Lithuania is tied to religious symbols and practice. The Hill of Crosses at Siauliai continues to play a role in nationalist symbolism that parallels the Jasna Gora monastery in Poland.

However, compared with Poland, the campaign against Catholicism in Lithuania was intense. This has been extensively documented, and I will not review it here (see Bourdeaux, 1979; Vardys 1965, 1978 for full accounts). Less well documented are the individual strategies of religious practice through which Catholicism survived and was blended with Lithuanian nationalism in the private corners of social life, primarily among family and trusted friends. Since World War II, Lithuanians have borne the brunt of anti-religious and atheistic campaigns waged by the Communist Party. Recognizing the role of the family in religious maintenance, the state instituted boarding schools called internats, along with "Summer Youth Days," to break the continuity of socialization. Nevertheless, it has been estimated that 70 percent of Lithuanian youth are religious communicants (Vardys, 1978: 217). According to one observer, in a period prior to glasnost, "preschool education, generally accomplished in the home, is done in such a way as to nurture and develop a national consciousness: to teach the language, the customs, and the national character" (Finklestein, 1977: 64). To this must be added Lithuanian Catholicism.

These strategies of national-religious survival parallel Uniate Catholicism. They are embedded in processes of primary socialization in the family that for the most part lie beyond penetration by the state. The central role of primary relations was crucial in all three cases I have discussed, but in varying degrees because they were supplemented by varying levels of public religiosity in the form of organizational participation of the church. These ranged from the relative freedom of a quasi-institutionalized church in Poland, to suppression in Ukraine, and to marginality in Lithuania. What then can be generalized from these three accounts?

PROPOSITIONS ABOUT RELIGIOUS NATIONALISM

One can postulate six propositions about religious nationalism. The first is:

1. Under conditions of repression, nationalist sentiments are kept alive and passed through primary socialization in a religious-nationalist value system.

The basis of this proposition is the relative impenetrability of these primary social relations. Except under the most extreme conditions of state terror, such as under Stalin or Pol Pot, when children have turned in parents, the effect of repression, while not completely absent, is significantly attenuated here. Trusted relations become the building blocks of a private social structure that stands in opposition to public society. As long as the trust holds, state surveillance is next to impossible. It also complicates a social science of these societies.

By definition, nationalist mobilization requires moving from these privatized relations to public actions. Although there is a certain risk (not to mention a psychological cost) involved in maintaining a belief system on an everyday basis that stands in opposition to the official reality of the regime, it takes a great deal more risk to voice it publicly. In all three of the cases cited above, there appears to be high visibility of activists from religious-nationalist backgrounds, especially in early stages of mobilization. While on the individual level dedication to one's beliefs and even a sense of martyrdom (see SMOT, 1980: 273) no doubt motivate some activists, in the aggregate several structural and organizational variables can be identified. These are expressed in the following propositions.

2. Under conditions of repression, there is a linear relationship between the level of that repression and the role of church resources in nationalist mobilization.

Personal courage aside, the support of a church organization is often crucial in moving individuals from a private attitude of religious nationalism to public assertion. This proposition refers to the early stages of mobilization rather than to the broader and widely recognized relationship between mass mobilization and countervailing force. Its importance lies in the efforts of clergy and laity to channel, either officially or informally, resources into religious-nationalist activities that are ancillary to the spiritual calling of the church.

Where state repression was the greatest, the Ukrainian Uniates directed their attention almost wholly to survival and the spiritual needs of the faithful. The religious-nationalist link seems to have been almost wholly privatized, or emphasized by more secular quarters of the opposition. Repression was so extreme that clergy and laity often drew on the resources of the Roman Catholic and Russian Orthodox churches to meet these spiritual goals. Little was available for nationalist-oppositional aspects until repression eased significantly.

At the other end of the continuum was Polish Catholicism, where the application of organizational resources to national-religious, but ostensibly not oppositional, activities was protected by concordance with the

Vatican. The intermediate case is Lithuanian Catholicism. While local churches survived, they were heavily taxed, and often fined for illegal proselytizing. This depleted the resources of the clergy available to more nationalist/oppositional activities. Nevertheless, some clandestine activities of a religious-nationalist sort, and some *samizdat* publications were produced.

3. There is a curvilinear relationship between repression and the importance of religious symbolism in nationalist mobilization. Freedom to employ religious icons and public rituals increases the importance of these symbols, but as repression closes off public expression, their role decreases, but at a decreasing rate. Eventually the decline bottoms out, whereby the importance of religious symbols begins to increase in lieu of any other public expression.

Although both the Polish and Uniate examples represent strong symbolic mergers of religion and nation, they are polar opposites in terms of level of state repression. While this proposition is tentative, and concrete measures of the importance of religious symbolism are difficult to come by, my reading of events suggests that increased repression can augment reliance on the symbols and rituals of religion and nation, in effect substituting them when public action is not possible. Figure 6.1 is a graphic two-dimensional portrayal of the relationship. A more accurate graphic representation would be three-dimensional to include a third variable of public versus private expression. As repression increases, the locus of religious symbolism shifts from public discourse to private relations outside of state control. Religious symbolism was widely in evidence in the mobilization of Solidarity, but, more importantly, it was taken into the public realm with a vengeance (Laba, 1991: 132). As repression increases, religious symbolism is forced into increasingly privatized social spaces. In the absence of public expression, it makes sense that religious symbols will play an increased role at a psychological level also. The importance of Marian cults in Spanish Catalonia (Johnston, 1989), the Basque region (Zulaika, 1988), and Poland during periods of intense repression points to this relationship.

Again, these patterns seem to hold at earlier stages of mobilization. Because nationalist movements are complex in their composition, the use of religious symbolism is a double-edged sword. On the one hand, there is much to be gained from the emotional appeal that religious symbolism has for large sectors of the public. Moreover, they are often vivid images from an aesthetic perspective, and they carry great mobilizing potential. On the other hand, these symbols come at a price: a diversion from the nationalist political agenda that could alienate secular supporters. The key factor here is the strength and pervasiveness of the religion-nation linkage in the region, and to that I turn with the next proposition.

Figure 6.1
The Importance of Religious Symbolism in Nationalist Mobilization
According to Level of State Repression

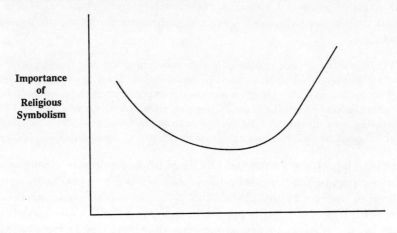

Importance
of
Religious
Symbolism

Level of State Repression

4. The historical depth of the church-nation linkage is fundamental to the te-
nacity of religious symbolism in the national movement.

   In all three of the examples mentioned above, the linkage of religion
and nation have deep historical roots, reaching back to the late middle
ages, and becoming ingrained in the modern nationalist mold during
the nineteenth century. This contrasts with other minority regions where
religion has played a much more diminished role in nationalist mobili-
zations, in Estonia and Latvia, for example. Here national identification
with the Lutheran Church is but a shadow of that found in Lithuania.
During the 1970s, there was no *samizdat* equivalent in Estonia or Latvia
of the *Chronicle of the Catholic Church in Lithuania*. The presence of Lutheran clerics and symbolism is relatively sparse, compared with that of
Catholicism in neighboring Lithuania.
   It is clear that Protestantism is symbolically austere when compared
with saints and holy places of the Roman Catholic Church, and the
centralized authority of Catholicism is an important factor which I will
discuss shortly. Nevertheless, comparison with the other Baltic republics
emphasizes the role of historical continuity, particularly during the age
of nationalism in the nineteenth century.
   Lutheranism in both Latvia and Estonia was imposed by the Germans.
During the nineteenth century, church administration was dominated
by German clerics and German pastors were common at the parish level.
Any identification of Lutheranism with the nation had to overcome these

earlier associations. When Estonian and Latvian independence was won in the early twentieth century, administration of the church was indigenized. Nevertheless, the association of Lutheranism with Germany seems to have attenuated the association of religion and nation and left both to their respective spheres. In contrast, Lithuanian priests were all local, and had been for two centuries. The imperial policies of Russification during the nineteenth century constituted both attacks on the nation and on the church, and further reinforced the association. In a pattern paralleling Poland during partitions, the threats by neighboring empires melded nationalist and religious identities.

5. Internationalization of church hierarchy increases the likelihood of Maximalist demands about national autonomy and even independence.

It is no accident that the three cases outlined earlier all involve Roman Catholicism. The relationship seems to work on two levels. First, at the level of collective definitions, ties to a Western church in part define what it means to be Lithuanian, Ukrainian, and Polish. For these nationalisms, and for others, Catholicism shapes a Westward-facing definition of the nation that carries with it a rejection of links with the Communist and Orthodox East. Similar processes can be observed in Croatia and Slovenia in their relations with Serbia.

Second, the global organization of Catholicism provided concrete channels for Westernized definitions of the nation. This can occur through organizations that have international scope, such as Catholic Action and Pax Christi. This is especially true where Catholic youth groups are the only alternatives to state- and party-controlled youth organizations. In Poland international contacts in Catholic youth organizations and church-affiliated Boy Scout troops were particularly worrisome to the regime. In both Spanish Catalonia and the Basque region during Francoism, groups such as Catholic Worker Youth, Catholic Student Youth, and Catholic Agricultural Youth were sources of new ideas. These came through counsel-priests and through occasional international contacts available to select members. It is not surprising that in the Soviet Union these types of international linkages were severely repressed.

6. The centralization of authority in the Roman Catholic Church strengthens the merger of religion and nationalism, especially under conditions of repression.

Again, this proposition works on the level of collective definitions and church organization. First, the structure of Catholicism, centering on a priesthood and a hierarchical organization of spiritual authority, bestows structural and moral clarity for the body of faithful. On an individual psychological level, and in terms of collective resistance to the state, the firm structuring of belief and practice is no doubt fortifying.

Second, steadfastness in nationalist demands can also be strengthened by organizational discipline within the church. This effect, however, is complicated by the organizational scope of national churches and depends on several factors. The most fundamental is whether or not the national hierarchy has been compromised in its relations with the regime. It has been widely noted that the Polish hierarchy sought to moderate the actions of Solidarity (see, for example, Johnston and Figa, 1988; Laba, 1991), especially through several calls for cooperation made by Cardinal Glemp during the heat of mobilization. In Spain, the Catholic hierarchy sided with Franco and supported his uprising as a religious crusade against the atheist left. This created a dilemma for both priests and laity in Catalonia and the Basque region, who, for nationalist predispositions, sided with the Second Republic, guarantor of autonomy for the two regions.

Another factor complicating church discipline is the organizational disjuncture between national hierarchy and local parish. It may be that the church hierarchy moderates its statements to placate the regime while at the same time turning a blind eye to parish radicalism. Otherwise, a moderating or conservative hierarchy might not be aware of local radicalism because only partial reports of activities are made. For Catholics, a division of labor by different orders, and by the numerous ancillary organizations the church supports, opens opportunities for nationalist priests at the local level.

Despite these caveats, it makes sense that the global scope of Catholicism and its authoritarian structure would mitigate cooptation. The Communist Party has had greater success in controlling Orthodox churches because of their national organization. The complicity of the Russian Orthodox Church is well known (although its resurgence today may vindicate its policies). In Georgia and Armenia, charges of complicity and cooptation have often been voiced. Indeed it has been observed that the Autocephalous Georgian Orthodox Church has been subverted by the state, and even infiltrated by KGB agents (Reddaway, 1975). Scandals and corruption have greatly weakened its moral authority and robbed nationalists of its traditional role in defining the Georgian nation.

CONCLUSIONS

The above propositions are necessarily tentative. Further comparative analysis needs the kind of detailed empirical base for nationalisms in the former Soviet Union and the Eastern bloc that we have for Western movements such as those in Quebec, the Basque region, Catalonia, and the Celtic regions. I have in mind ethnographic studies of communities and the movement cultures themselves. Surveys can provide information about attitudes on religion, nationalist demands, competing ethnic groups, economic and political grievances, and primary networks of relations. Hopefully these data will be forthcoming soon.

Two of the above propositions suggest a special affinity between nationalist mobilization and Roman Catholicism. This affinity derives from Catholicism's strict spiritual authority, its international scope, and its organizational centralization. Unfortunately, while these relationships between Catholicism and nationalism are provocative, they are also the most tentative. Comparative analyses of nationalism merged with Catholicism versus those of other religious traditions is a particularly promising approach. On all three parameters, comparisons with national regions where Orthodoxy prevails, such as Serbia, Georgia, Moldavia, and (while not Orthodox) Armenia, would put these two "Catholic propositions" to the test and provide a base for refinement of the others. An especially important empirical question is what kind of local and even privatized nationalism may have been encouraged by Orthodox priests while the ecclesiastical hierarchy compromised with the Communists.

Part III ⎯⎯⎯⎯⎯⎯⎯⎯⎯⎯⎯⎯⎯⎯⎯⎯⎯⎯⎯

RELIGIOUS REVIVAL IN THE WESTERN HEMISPHERE

REASONS FOR THE GROWING POPULARITY OF CHRISTIAN RECONSTRUCTIONISM: THE DETERMINATION TO ATTAIN DOMINION

Bruce Barron and Anson Shupe

As the Christian Right took shape during the late 1970s, previously little-known names like Falwell, Robinson, Jarmin, McAteer, and LaHaye became widely recognized in North America. The name of Rousas John Rushdoony, however, remained virtually unknown. Thus, it may seem strange that Robert Billings, a leader in the Rev. Jerry Falwell's (now-defunct) Moral Majority organization during its heyday and later a member of the Department of Education under President Ronald Reagan, should have remarked during a backstage moment at the 1980 National Affairs Briefing in Dallas, Texas: "If it weren't for [Rushdoony's] books, none of us would be here" (quoted in North, 1982: 12).

Just what had Rushdoony done that was so formative? Since the late 1950s he had been churning out imposing, sophisticated material on the relevance of the Bible—particularly biblical law as found in the first five books of the Old Testament—to every facet of human society (see, e.g., Rushdoony, 1986, 1973). Though Billings may have overstated Rushdoony's significance as catalyst in the birth of the Christian Right, there is no question that Rushdoony had been stimulating those conservative Christians who read him to think politically for over two decades.

If Rushdoony did indeed help the Christian Right get off the ground, that phenomenon's more highly visible political activists have since effectively, albeit unintentionally, returned the favor. Their reawakening of evangelical interest in impacting politics and culture has considerably broadened the market for books like Rushdoony's, and several of his colleagues and disciples (more given to popular styles of writing than Rushdoony himself) have seized the opportunity. Now, after thirty years of prolific writing, Rushdoony is no longer an obscure author existing on the fringes of contemporary Christian literature. He is the recognized founder of a distinct social movement known as Christian Reconstructionism.

Reconstruction has affinities with the Christian Right, but its scope and goals are broader. In the words of Gary North, probably the movement's most prolific author and popularizer (and son-in-law of Rushdoony), "the Bible presents mankind with a God-mandated set of social, economic and educational, political, and legal principles that God expects His people to use as permanent blue-prints for the total reconstruction of every society on earth" (North, 1990: 6). Whereas the Moral Majority, for example, affirmed political pluralism and denied that it sought to establish a theocracy, Reconstruction just as openly rejects pluralism and proclaims "the moral obligation of Christians to recapture every institution for Jesus Christ" (North, 1984: 267). Rushdoony and his supporters are not the least bit bashful about declaring that their goal is total world transformation.

THE DOMINION MANDATE

Seen in the broader context of American evangelical efforts to penetrate and transform public life, Christian Reconstruction is the most developed variation of a more general Christian Right world view often identified as *dominion theology*. The distinguishing mark of dominion theology is a commitment to carrying out an approach to building (or rebuilding) society that is *self-consciously defined as Christian* rather than based on a broader consensus. While the contemporary evangelical discussion is far too complex to be reduced to a rigid dichotomy, one can generally separate those who, on the one hand, emphasize the need to work cooperatively with persons "of all faiths and none" (for example, representatives of those ecumenical groups signing the Williamsburg Charter reaffirming church-state separation and pluralistic tolerance— see *Williamsburg Charter*) to improve society and culture from those who, on the other hand, believe that meaningful improvement of society can come only on Christian (or at least predominantly Christian) terms. It is this distinction that sets apart those who want to see society conform as much as possible to a biblical world view (and all socially active evangelicals, even if far apart on specific political prescriptions, agree on this general point) from those who believe that to achieve this goal evangelicals should be working together to infiltrate, radically transform, and even take over social institutions. Put more bluntly, this is the division that distinguishes those who want to change the world from those who want to run it.

Adherents to dominion theology (we will call them dominionists) are a diverse lot. While some outside observers have erred in painting them all with the same broad brush as Christian Reconstructionists (see, e.g., House and Ice, 1988; Hunt, 1988), the distinctions among them are nonetheless important. For example, Earl Paulk, a Pentecostal who built the Chapel Hill Harvester Church in suburban Atlanta into a mega-church with over 8,000 weekly worshippers, has created his own movement based on a dominionist theology called Kingdom Now. Its basic thrust is that Christians should strive to demonstrate the kingdom of God on earth now rather than wait for Christ's second coming. While differing from Reconstruction in many ways, Kingdom Now shares a commitment to seeing Christians fulfill their mandate, dating back to Genesis, to subdue the earth and take dominion over every area of life. Reconstruction and Kingdom Now both declare that this dominion mandate dates back to the first chapter of Genesis:

Then God said, "Let us make man in our image, after our likeness; and let them have dominion over the fish of the sea, and over the birds of the air, and over the cattle, and over all the earth, and over every creeping thing that creeps upon the earth." So God created man in his own image.... And God blessed them, and God said to them, "Be fruitful and multiply, and fill the earth and subdue it; and have dominion over the fish of the sea and over the birds of the air and over every living thing that moves upon the earth." (Genesis 1:26–28, Revised Standard Version)

Reconstructionists are separated by geography, and sometimes by their stances on certain issues, into various formal organizations. Among their key centers are Rushdoony's Chalcedon Foundation in Vallecito, California; North's Institute for Christian Economics in Tyler, Texas; and Gary DeMar's American Vision organization in Atlanta, Georgia. These and other Reconstructionist organizations comprise a recognizable social movement, though not a monolithic one. It may be more useful to think of these enterprises as engaged in an alliance rather than as any tightly knit or monolithic movement.

Reconstructionists have many more sympathizers who fall somewhere within the dominionist framework but who are not card-carrying members. For instance, at a 1990 Wichita, Kansas, conference sponsored by American Vision, which describes itself on the masthead of its newsletters as a "Christian educational and communications organization providing materials to help Christians develop a Biblical World View and build Christian civilization," syndicated evangelical columnist Cal Thomas was the keynote speaker. This Reconstructionist organization also invited Dr. Herbert Titus, Dean of Law and Government at Regents University in Virginia Beach (founded by Pat Robertson) to speak at its annual 1990 fund-raising event (*AV Report*, 1990: 1, 3). In the past, Titus has bristled when he and Joseph

Kickasola, a faculty member in the Regents University School of Public Policy, were erroneously identified by one of us as Reconstructionist writers (Titus, 1989). But activities such as Titus' conspicuous participation in a Reconstructionist event, or the special supplementary section for the second volume of Rushdoony's *Institutes of Biblical Law* (Rushdooney, 1986), show at least his affinity with Reconstructionists and dominionists. Meanwhile, Pat Robertson's own politically activist version of dominionist thinking, while not strictly Reconstructionist, could also mislead one to think he leans in that direction (see, e.g., Hadden and Shupe, 1988; Marken, 1988). Robertson certainly shares the dominionist goal of seeing Christians take over at the helm and guide society; in early 1991 he laid out a projected scenario according to which "a coalition of Evangelicals and pro-family Roman Catholics" would take over the grass-roots rebuilding of the Republican Party after a 1996 Democratic presidential victory and would have enough political strength by the year 2000 to win the presidency and a majority in Congress (Robertson, 1991: 6–7).

THE RECONSTRUCTIONIST WORLDVIEW

In over a hundred books and many more times that many essays and articles written since the movement began to coalesce during the early 1960s, the main proponents of Christian Reconstruction have worked on developing a blueprint for a brand new society—though they might prefer to say they are reconstructing an old one based on the guidelines God gave Moses 4,000 years ago.

At the base of Reconstructionism's intellectual edifice sits the underlying claim that the dominion mandate of Genesis 1 remains in effect and that it is thereby the moral obligation of Christians to recapture every institution for Jesus Christ. On this basis Reconstructionists promulgate an intricate, coherent program that weaves together three levels of ideology: biblical law, postmillennial eschatology, and presuppositional philosophy. This ideological foundation, in turn, directs the entire Reconstructionist worldview: its theology, sociopolitical agenda, strategies, and tactics. We will briefly sketch these three foundational elements below (for more detail, see Barron, 1990).

Biblical Law

"The creation mandate was precisely the requirement that man subdue the earth and exercise dominion over it. There is not one word of Scripture to indicate or imply that this mandate was ever revoked" (Rushdoony, 1973: 14). With this thesis, Rousas J. Rushdoony, the patriarch of Christian Reconstruction, summarized the introduction to his magnus opus, the massive *Institutes of Biblical Law*. His works embody the ultimate goal of the Reconstructionist quest: to establish godly rule throughout the earth before Christ returns.

This, Reconstructionists say, is the climax toward which human history leads. Jesus Christ's atonement restored God's people to their place of "legitimate dominion" (North, 1988: 8) after Adam's fall in the Garden of Eden and God's curse was leveled on humanity and nature. Postresurrection Jesus Christ commanded that his disciples should go into all the world and "disciple the nations" (Matthew 28: 18–20).

It is proposals like these that show why this movement is seen as calling for not just reform of society but radical reconstruction.

Reconstructionists say the tool God has called Christians to use in restoring this dominion is *biblical law*, especially the first five books of the Old Testament. They insist that these laws represent God's blueprint for all societies, not just ancient Israel (see especially Bahnsen, 1984). Reconstructionists agree that applying the Old Testament to modern society is a complex task that requires considerable "exegetical and theological homework" (Bahnsen, 1985: 7), but nevertheless they staunchly maintain that Christ surpassed only the ceremonial sections of Old Testament law, leaving its moral and civil guidelines intact. They claim that God's method of administration may have changed under the New Covenant, but his moral character has not. One cannot distinguish civil from moral law within the Old Testament law codes, for they are intertwined; nor can one find any unique feature of Old Testament Israel that would invalidate the law's relevance to modern society. Therefore, all of biblical law remains applicable to all societies today, the Reconstructionists say.

The Reconstructionists' analysis of biblical law leads them to conclude that many areas of society now impacted by civil government should actually be under the jurisdiction of families, churches, or private organizations (see, e.g., DeMar, 1988; North, 1987). For example, since the book of Deuteronomy assigns to parents the responsibility of educating children, state-sponsored schools are considered a violation of biblical law. Under Reconstruction's generally libertarian guidelines, the civil government would play no part in personal retirement plans, welfare, or regulation of business, other than to maintain order and restrain fraudulent behavior. Minimum-wage laws and Social Security would be eliminated. All inheritance taxes and gift taxes would be abolished. Income taxes would rise no higher than 10 percent of gross income.

Reconstructionists would also restore the death penalty for numerous offenses, as dictated in the Old Testament. However, Reconstruction does not import every Old Testament directive straight into the modern world. For instance, David Chilton has suggested that ancient Israel's

Jubilee law, which required restoration of all land to its original owners every fifty years, fits under the ceremonial (and thereby no longer applicable) category because "it was a symbolic prefiguring of the work of Jesus Christ" (Chilton, 1985b: 156). (Skeptics suggest that Chilton finds the Jubilee law no longer applicable primarily because it would carry socialistic rather than libertarian applications.) On the other hand, Chilton interprets the Old Testament's insistence on "just weights" in financial transactions quite literally to mean a prohibition of paper money (Chilton, 1985b: 41).

Postmillennialism

The concept of a Christianized America, let alone a Christianized world, may seem inconceivable or hopelessly quixotic in this age of radical pluralism and secularization. The Reconstructionists' residual optimism derives from their postmillennial eschatology. With Reformed thinkers of earlier times (such as American theologians Jonathan Edwards and B. B. Warfield), and in contrast to nearly all of contemporary Evangelicalism, the Reconstructionists believe that progressive, near-total sanctification of human society will take place *before* the second coming of Christ. Their confidence is further buttressed by that firm adherence, in line with their Calvinist theological tradition, to the doctrine of predestination, which promises that what a sovereign God ordains will surely come to pass and can in no way be resisted by humankind.

Reconstructionists accuse premillennialists and dispensationalists of having "left the battlefield" and abandoned society to Satan and the secular humanists. In fact, they say, the "last days" apocalyptic emphasis of so many premillennialists has aided the forces of evil. So state Gary DeMar and Peter Leithart (1988: 50): "We suggest that the present preoccupation with the end of the world may be a false alarm pulled by the devil to keep the church from working at its full mission. The devil leads Christians to believe that changing the world is hopeless." Likewise, DeMar (1988: 81) has charged that "a preoccupation with an end times scenario is cultish when it leads the church to establish timetables that assure us as to the timing of the Lord's return and when it turns the church into a retreatist institution."

Although Reconstructionist writers do not anticipate the absolute reversal of creation's curse or the conversion of every individual, and although they agree that Revelation 20 envisions one last, conclusive satanic war on the godly, they do offer a scenario for worldwide regeneration. They expect that the prosperity and blessings experienced by Christians who adopt Reconstructionist principles will cause societies to place these believers in positions of prominence. In this way, whole nations will discover the blessings of living out a Christian social order, in turn provoking other nations to imitate the practice until "the kingdom of God becomes worldwide in scope" (North, 1988: 307).

The Reconstructionists expect God to win, but they do not believe he is in any hurry. Generally they anticipate that Christians are in the Reconstructionist quest for the long haul. Chilton, perhaps as a tongue-in-cheek rebuke to those Christians who expect the end at any moment, suggests that a reference to the "thousandth generation" recorded in Deuteronomy 7:9 about 3,400 years ago implies that history as we know it must have at least 36,000 (1,000 × 40 − 3,400) years left (Chilton, 1985a: 221). Alternately, DeMar (1988: 157) says Satan's temporary authority will last only "a few generations . . . unless Christians voluntarily give him more time by retreating into cultural irrelevance." Still others, like North (1988), even while expressing hope that major revival could begin in their lifetimes, fully expect to die before the end and view themselves as setting up the intellectual foundations for eventual Restoration.

The Reconstructionists' primary tools are conversion, education, and prayer. They explicitly reject coercion. North (1987: 153), for example, declares that he and his colleagues would never consider imposing God's law on an unwilling society in some holy war: "Faithful Christians are not to preach perpetual contentment with moral evil . . . [nor] instant liberation through revolution and violence." Thus, Reconstructionists currently endorse only peaceful and democratic approaches to social change. Postmillennialism affords them the luxury of time and, therefore, patience.

Presuppositionalism

The third ideological prong of Reconstructionism is presuppositionalism, a philosophical/hermeneutical standpoint which argues that the conclusions that human beings draw from all evidence is governed by their operating presuppositions concerning God, man, law, and nature (North, 1984: 275). Relying primarily on Romans 1:18–20 and Psalm 19:1–2 for biblical support, Reconstructionalists argue that the truth about God is plainly visible to all persons and does not require intellectual exposition or apologetic defense based on reason. This logical imperiousness dismisses discussion or debate. There is no possibility of neutrality within this closed system; every culture is religious, and every individual has religious presuppositions. Those who reject the presuppositions supplied by biblical revelation do so as a matter of "humanistic faith." Conversely, in Reconstructionists' eyes, biblical presuppositionalism acts out of confident, irrefutable commitment to the self-attesting

truth of the infallible Bible. The main practical implication of the Reconstructionists' presuppositionalism is their rejection of any "natural
law" based on reason. Nature has been "fallen" since Eden, without
inherent norms. Thus the believer and the unbeliever have essentially
nothing in common, no shared convictions on which to build a law-
order. Presuppositionalism uses this radical denial of common ground
to declare all humanly devised social systems invalid and enables Reconstructionists to assert dogmatically their image of the divinely revealed, binding nature of biblical law. Reconstructionist critics fault
Christian political efforts like the Moral Majority for seeking to appeal
to a "common morality" (North, 1982: 28) and for failing to challenge
the humanistic myths of pluralism, inherent human rights, neutrality,
and political compromise based on shared reason. In the caustic words
of North (1982: 28): "Let the God-despisers get back into their closets
and keep silent. They will be silent on that final day; they should begin
practicing early."

All three legs of this theoretical tripod provide essential support and
motivation for Reconstruction's extensive, systematic efforts at conceiv-
ing a new society. Biblical law supplies guidelines, principles, and even
specific legislative commands. Postmillennialism delivers the confidence
that the Reconstructionist undertaking, even if destined for short-term
frustration, will receive God's blessing and will ultimately bear fruit.
Presuppositionalism justifies the Reconstructionists' boldness in demanding radical social transformation while paying relatively little attention to the claims and counterarguments of those who do not share
their religious presuppositions.

REASONS FOR THE GROWING POPULARITY OF
CHRISTIAN RECONSTRUCTION

No one knows precisely how many followers of Christian Reconstruction exist in this country, but mailing lists and movement leaders' personal estimates suggest there are tens of thousands of persons who
subscribe to various organizational newsletters and/or buy Reconstructionist books. Many of these books are available in evangelical religious
bookstores and appear in various nationally circulated religious book
catalogues. In the remainder of this chapter we discuss six reasons that
seem to underlie the growing visibility, vitality, and presence of Christian
Reconstruction in America: (1) legitimate social concerns; (2) the growing
Christian School Movement; (3) political pragmatism and alliance building; (4) realistic partisan allegiance and skepticism; (5) a sense of entering
a new "dark ages"; and (6) the energetic intellectual labors of major
Reconstruction proponents.

Legitimate Social Concerns

The theological agenda of Christian Reconstruction, with its elaborate emphasis on Old Testament law and its unabashed preference for theocracy over religious pluralism, may at first glance seem a bit bizarre to most Americans, Christian or otherwise. But the movement's social concerns resonate well with those concerns of many other evangelicals. Together, dominionists, Reconstructionists, and evangelicals at large are the Americans whom sociologists Jeffrey K. Hadden and Anson Shupe describe (borrowing a line from the motion picture *Network*) as "mad as hell" and who are not going to take it any longer. In their eyes, claim these authors:

Like all Americans, evangelicals shared the national sense of "malaise" that President Jimmy Carter spoke of during the dark days of double-digit inflation and the Iranian hostage crisis. Unlike others, however, they thought they knew what had caused it, and that made them angry. Following World War II and the Scopes trial, the liberals had taken control of the dominant institutions of society. More incredibly, the liberal model for America, with its naive faith in science, its welfare state, and its abandonment of biblical values, had broken down. (Hadden and Shupe, 1988: 57)

Or, in evangelical writer Jeremy Rifkin's (1979: 197) words, they have sensed that "the liberal superstructure had cracked."

Reconstructionist theonomists share the same views as other evangelicals about AIDS, sexual promiscuity, drug use, teenage pregnancies, pornography, abortion, and other social problems. Hadden and Shupe (1988) interpret the constellation of such concerns as focusing on the family institution and its loosening control over the intrusion of outside secular humanist influences. The widespread popularity of books by evangelical writers James Dobson, James Robison, and Tim LaHaye (among others) on the modern family as the crucible within which secular humanism and moral rot have subtly and corrosively taken hold testify to an acute concern for important social problems that transcends eschatological disagreements. Family members are at risk in the here-and-now, regardless of when the kingdom of God is ushered in by the second coming of Christ. Reconstructionists have no monopoly on such concerns, a fact which only widens their potential audience among socially and politically sensitized evangelical readers.

The Growing Christian School Movement

Just as important for the appeal of Reconstructionist views is the Christian School Movement in North America, which has been characterized as "the fastest growing sector of private education in the United States" (Rose, 1988: 34). Such (largely) conservative Protestant schools have been established, it is estimated, at roughly two a day since 1960, enrolling about 20 percent of the total private school population. These schools now constitute the second largest segment of private education, behind only Roman Catholic schools (Rose, 1988: 34ff).

Generally speaking, one outcome of this enterprise (or growth industry) is that more Christians have been encouraged to view their government as an ungodly enemy to be opposed and ultimately replaced (because it funds only public schools, which many evangelists no longer trust to teach traditional values and often tightly regulates private schools) rather than as an ally in keeping the peace and preserving morality. This Christian School Movement also has opened many doors for Rushdoony's influence in particular; he long ago dissected what he believed were the public school's "messianic pretentions" (Rushdoony, 1963) and has become a familiar, supportive expert witness on behalf of beleaguered parochial schools.

Most significantly, the process of developing their own schools and curricula forced Christians to begin thinking in a Christian manner about many more topics besides education of children. In this sense, education is far more than just a single issue. Parents will usually not shell out extra discretionary money and turn down the public schools' superior facilities just so their children can have a few religious programs and a daily Bible class. Rather, Christian schools, especially if formed in self-conscious resistance to state-sponsored humanism, will tend to seek distinctively Christian approaches to all areas of study, from literature to history to government and science. Reconstructionists, of course, specialize in providing the intellectual tools and arguments for just such an enterprise, overlapping the issues arising out of their biblical literalism with other conservative Christian preoccupations, such as creationism (see Chapter 8 in this volume).

Political Pragmatism and Alliance-Building

Because of their mutual interests and concerns, Reconstructionists have been willing to work pragmatically with other Christians, premillennialists included, in political ways. The reawakening of political proclivities among charismatics and fundamentalists generally has been suggested, though these have not always resulted in successful concerted efforts. Mindful of their minority role even among evangelicals, Reconstructionists are willing to enter coalitions with fellow Christians who do not share all their biblical principles but who do share an antipathy for secular humanism. For example, Rushdoony, North, Chilton, and DeMar—the most visible Reconstructionist writers in the United States—

all joined the steering committee of the Coalition On Revival (COR), an organization seeking to unify and mobilize evangelicals to transform American society. COR includes as original signers-on Robert Dugan, director of the Office of Public Affairs of the National Association of Evangelicals. As master strategist North (1988: 140) has put it about such coalition-building: "We simply don't have the funds to be hyperexclusive. We also don't have the bodies."

In Texas, for example, Reconstructionists, as well as other dominionists and premillennialists, appeared to have worked hard for the 1988 presidential primary campaign of Marion G. "Pat" Robertson alongside secular establishment Republicans. Election-day statistics show Tarrant County, an area that includes Fort Worth (home of Reconstructionism's Dominion Press and within a few hour's drive of Tyler, location of North's Institute for Christian Economics) to have delivered the highest proportion of votes for Robertson in the Texas primary. Interviews with informants in that county's Republican Party indicate that dominionists were indeed visible and active. Informants (particularly long-time party activists) could not always distinguish Reconstructionists from dominionists or just plain conservative Christians, but they did recognize books written by Gary North, among others (Shupe, 1989b). Such grass-roots mobilization of activism is consistent with the exhortations of Reconstructionists to "get involved." As DeMar tells readers:

Christianity should be involved in politics even if it is dirty. Who else has the means to clean up politics (or any other area of human activities)? If Christians do not, who will? Christians have stayed out of politics, making its corruption even more pronounced. The answer is not to consign politics to even more corruption by ignoring its potential as an area for redemption and restoration. (DeMar, 1987: 127–28)

A Sense of Entering a "New Dark Ages"

Reconstruction's commitment to firmly resisting the inroads of secularism and to proposing a comprehensive alternative, rather than to negotiating a compromise of mutual accommodation, fits well with the increasing pessimism of some prominent evangelicals who see Western civilization entering a "new dark ages." For example, Carl Henry, long acclaimed as the dean of American evangelical theologians, pronounces Western culture moribund in his 1988 book *Twilight of a Great Civilization*. Henry observes that since the late 1960s "both the pagan forces and the Christian forces have accelerated their initiatives and seem increasingly locked into a life-and-death struggle" (Henry, 1988: 19). Repeatedly deploring society's departure from absolute, transcendent sanctions for law and ethics, Henry predicts the further expansion of "raw paganism." He underscores this predicted trend with ominous language: "American culture seems to me to be sinking toward sunset." In prose reminiscent of nineteenth-century premillennial revivalist Dwight L. Moody: "We may even now live in the half-generation before hell breaks loose" (Henry, 1988: 181–82).

Likewise, Charles Colson, ex-Watergate felon and now a major evangelical thinker, declares, in his book *Against the Night*, "I believe that we do face a crisis in Western culture, and that it presents the greatest threat to civilization since the barbarians invaded Rome" (Colson and Vaughn, 1989: 23). Popular evangelical fiction writer Frank Peretti has shown the allure of this interpretation of contemporary culture in his best-selling novels *This Present Darkness* and *Piercing the Darkness* (Peretti, 1988, 1989).

Is this pessimism the stuff of Christian Reconstruction and dominion theology? No, but the grimly confrontational attitude toward the surrounding society is. Reconstructionists mix this determined attitude of resistance with the confidence that the coming time of tribulation for Christians is only a temporary setback.

The Intellectual Efforts of Christian Reconstructionism's Primary Proponents

Finally, of no small import to Christian Reconstructionism's growth is the amazing intellectual output in essays, newsletters, and books by a relatively small core of tireless authors utilizing modest but adequate resources. It could be argued without much exaggeration that the two most prominent Reconstructionists, Rushdoony and North, themselves offer a sufficient explanation for why Reconstructionism is now a widely recognized option in evangelical social theory.

For example, North has contributed not just his life and intellectual labors but also a large amount of hard cash to the cause. With a Ph.D. in economic history, North has prospered by selling economic advice (his *Remnant Review* newsletter currently costs $95 a year for 22 issues) and is thus able to invest substantial capital in his ideological commitments. For example, his Institute for Christian Economics (ICE) bankrolled Chilton to write *Productive Christians in an Age of Guilt-Manipulators*, (a sarcastic attack on the left-leaning Ron Sider's *Rich Christians in an Age of Hunger*) and *The Days of Vengeance* and has subsidized wide distributions of ICE books, often at extremely low cost. As of 1990 North personally has authored or edited thirty-three books and edited various ongoing or previous journals. In an age of word processors and desktop publishing, Christian Reconstruction in the likes of Gary North offers a good example of how social movements can prosper with limited but committed resources and a major reserve of personal energy.

CONCLUSIONS

Christian Reconstruction has certainly reaped many followers from evangelical Christian dissatisfaction with social trends in contemporary America. But it would be a mistake to cast Reconstruction as simply a backlash movement or to view it trivially, in the way that many observers summarize the entire Christian Right scene—that is, as some expression of irrational "status politics" or "lifestyle defense politics." It is more than a reaction to dozens of social problems conceivably connected by the common threads of liberalism or hedonism.

In fact, what may be happening is that Reconstruction is participating in a major realignment of cultural strains in America. For example, Grant Wacker (1984) objects to a simplistic "stimulus-response" paradigm of explaining all post–World War II evangelical activism by reference to specific threats or problems, be these pornography, rock and roll music, drugs, or AIDS. He believes that the postwar evangelical movement is more than a function of or reaction to "the immediate and transitory swings of contemporary culture" (Wacker, 1984: 27–28). Rather, Wacker conceives modern activist evangelicalism to be the outcome of the collision of vast structural changes, wrought by the processes of modernization, with the historical tension in America between two visions of ideal church-state relations: the Calvinistic custodial paradigm and the religiously pluralistic paradigm.

In the past such reconciliation of structural-cultural strains was achieved by those broad cultural transformations to which some historians refer as "awakenings." Awakenings last, by definition, at least one generation and offer a conceptual period "in which the core myths of a society are redefined or reformulated to legitimate new patterns of behavior" (Wacker, 1984: 19).

Such an awakening as Wacker posits might indeed contain the aspects of modern Christian Right activity that are structurally and culturally integrative, functional, and therefore (from the standpoint of longevity of a society) positive and value-enhancing.

This chapter is not the place to critique the assumptions and logic of the Reconstructionists and their dominionist cousins, or to challenge their ambitious rhetoric. (For such polemics, see Barker and Godfrey, 1990; House and Ice, 1988.) Suffice it to say that the goal of turning America's religiously pluralistic system into a narrowly theonomic (i.e., committed to God's law) culture is a long shot indeed. However, this segment of conservative Christianity has within it the moral backbone, the simmering anger, and the dedication to attempt such a utopian quest. It has set for itself the honorable, albeit grandiose, goal of bringing spiritual healing and righteousness to every area of culture. Dominion theology, and in particular Christian Reconstruction, may be the epitome of overconfident triumphalism in modern Christianity. Yet, tempered with more humility and with a greater submissiveness to insights from other streams, these variations on a movement may indeed emerge from their evangelical subculture and generate genuine revival and revitalization within the American democratic experiment.

SCIENTIFIC CREATIONISM AND THE POLITICS OF LIFESTYLE CONCERN IN THE UNITED STATES

Raymond A. Eve and Francis B. Harrold

As other chapters in this volume make clear, religiously inspired anti-modernist movements are no rarity in the world of the 1990s. One such movement, however, is unusual for its focused and partly successful struggle against a powerful and prestigious component of modern society, the scientific establishment. This movement, creationism, rejects the scientific consensus on humanity's evolutionary origins as inimical to religious values.

Creationism can be found wherever northern European Protestantism's more conservative forms (with their strong emphasis on the authority of scripture) have taken root, as in the Netherlands, South Africa, Australia, and Canada. But only in the United States, with its heritage of evangelical Protestantism, populism, and anti-elitism, and a highly decentralized educational system, has creationism become a formidable force. Americans are split in their beliefs about the origins of the cosmos and of humankind. Many of them believe that humanity was directly created by God within the past 10,000 years. Many others view the beliefs of the first group with dismay or outright anxiety.

One might wonder how a scientific matter has become the focus of such sociopolitical controversy. After all, one encounters few arguments over whether atoms exist or whether stars are examples of nuclear fusion. Part of the answer lies in the fact that while the creation-evolution debate revolves around the understanding of scientific data and concepts, it is also strongly affected by social and psychological forces. Few previous publications on either side of the creation/evolution debate have looked at it from a social scientific perspective, or from the point of view of social movements theory, as we will do here.

WHAT IS CREATIONISM?

Creationism is the religiously based denial of evolution, especially of human evolution. Within the broad category of creationists there is considerable diversity. Many creationists (called "young-earth" or "strict" creationists) follow a highly literal reading of the creation account in the book of Genesis, believing that the earth and all life forms were divinely created from nothing in essentially their present form a few thousand years ago. Others ("old-earth" creationists) accept some aspects of the scientific consensus, such as geological evidence for an ancient earth, but deny that humans evolved from nonhuman ancestors. Those creationists who do not dismiss science out of hand, but argue that, properly interpreted, the scientific evidence actually favors their beliefs, call themselves scientific creationists. Over the past several decades, young-earth scientific creationists have come to predominate in the creationist movement.

HOW MANY CREATIONISTS ARE THERE?

Several studies give us an indication of creationism's popularity both among the general public and within particular segments of it. These include two fairly recent national probability samples of U.S. adults, each with a margin of error of around 3 percent.

The first was conducted by the Gallup Organization in 1982 (*New York Times*, August 29, 1982: 22). Respondents were given several statements about human origins and asked which one they agreed with. Fully 44 percent agreed that "God created man pretty much in his present form within the last 10,000 years," and 38 percent agreed that "Man has developed over millions of years from less advanced forms of life, but God guided this process, including man's creation." Only 9 percent thought that "Man has developed over millions of years from less advanced forms of life. God had no part in this process." Finally, 9 percent had no opinion.

Further evidence of support for creationism is to be found in a national poll conducted by Jon D. Miller (1987). The proportion of all respondents who, when asked if "Human beings as we know them today developed from earlier species of animals," said "No" was 46 percent (a close match to the 44 percent giving a creationist response in the Gallup poll). The higher the educational level of respondents, the less likely they were to reject human evolution. Nonetheless, about one-quarter of respondents holding graduate degrees are apparently creationists.

A series of studies of college students and high-school biology teachers (see Eve and Harrold, 1991: 32–35) indicates that rejection of evolution among these relatively well-educated population segments, though lower than in the general population, is still significant. A reasonable estimate would be that, nationally, 20 percent or more of each group could be described as creationists.

In sum, there is a significant level of creationist belief, sometimes approaching 50 percent, in diverse sectors of American society. Even in well-educated segments of the population, such belief is not negligible. In a scientifically advanced nation, this state of affairs would seem to call for an explanation. The key to understanding this question lies in religious belief.

WHO ARE THE CREATIONISTS?

Creationists have been characterized in the media and in many public discussions variously as fundamentalists, born-again Christians, Baptists, evangelicals, conservatives—and in pejorative terms like "Bible thumpers." Epithets aside, such terms are often used imprecisely or incorrectly.

Curiously, the classification of believers that probably comes first to mind for most of us—denominational membership—is not the most reliable way to sort out creationists from others. True, denominations generally perceived as more conservative do tend to have more creationists than more liberal ones (Bainbridge and Stark, 1980b). However, most sizable denominations tolerate a considerable range of belief among their members. In consequence, one can certainly find Baptists who have no difficulty accepting evolution as well as Episcopalians who are creationists.

Most support for creationism comes from the 40 to 50 million American Protestants of various denominations who describe themselves as "evangelicals." There is no unanimity in the definition of this term, but evangelicals tend to hold that to gain salvation one must believe in biblical inerrancy, the divinity of Christ, and acceptance of his grace (being "born again") rather than reliance on one's good works. Evangelicals, in most formulations, include the subcategory of fundamentalists or "evangelicalism's hardliners," who emphasize among other things a highly literal interpretation of scripture. Often allied with evangelicals against evolution are members of conservative "confessional" denominations, usually of German origin, like the Missouri Synod Lutherans.

SCIENTIFIC CREATIONISM

Many creationists are either indifferent to science or actively hostile to it. (As one bumper sticker puts it; "God said it, I believe it, and that's that!") For some creationists, however, it is not enough to ignore the conflict between their religious beliefs and mainstream science. Some accept the value and authority of science; some are technicians and scientists themselves. Simply rejecting science would contradict a vital aspect of their values and world view. They attempt a resolution of this conflict by means of *scientific creationism*, which claims that the conflict between science and creationism is only an illusion. For scientific creationists the correct interpretation of scientific evidence is actually consistent with Genesis; the real problem, they argue, has been with mainstream scientists and their theories, not with science in principle. They therefore set themselves the task of finding and explaining just where the mistakes in mainstream science are to be found. In recent decades scientific creationists have come to form something of an intellectual elite among creationists, supplying intellectual ammunition for the battle against evolution (Toumey, 1990).

While scientific creationism has achieved prominence fairly recently, its origins as a putatively scientific opposition to evolutionary orthodoxy go back to the 1920s (Marsden, 1983; H. Morris, 1984; Numbers, 1986). George McCready Price (1870–1963), a Seventh-Day Adventist and self-taught geologist, proposed that deposits from Noah's flood accounted for the geological and fossil records. Scientific creationism began to achieve formal organizational status in 1963 when a group of creationists with scientific and technical backgrounds met to form the Creation Research Society. The most important figure in this group has been Henry Morris. Morris, a Baptist, effectively founded modern scientific creationism when he published *The Genesis Flood* with an associate, theologian John Whitcomb (Whitcomb and Morris, 1961). In this book "flood geology" was set out in complex detail for the first time by a hydraulic engineer (Morris) who maintained not only that strict creationism was scientifically defensible but also that mainstream geology and evolution were badly flawed. Although the book was little noticed in the secular scientific world, it had a galvanizing effect among evangelicals, especially those with scientific or technical backgrounds.

In 1970, Morris organized the Institute for Creation Research (ICR), which soon became the leading scientific creationist organization. Staffed by several Ph.D.'s in fields ranging from engineering to biochemistry, the ICR produces numerous books and videotapes and sends speakers and debaters from its Santee, California, headquarters all over the country to make the case for young-earth scientific creationism. The ICR operates a small graduate school (currently in danger of losing its state authorization to award degrees) and claims to support a program of creationist research. Not only has evolution not been directly observed, claim ICR personnel, but transitional fossils documenting it are unknown. Furthermore, evolution would violate the second law of thermodynamics. These and other arguments are delivered in profusion, not to the scientific community, which does not consider them valid, but to a lay audience already predisposed to believe in a young earth.

The ICR's "research" consists, not of building or testing creationist scientific theory, but of attacking evolutionary science from an outdated viewpoint. This perspective, called Baconianism, characterized much scientific thought before the twentieth century. It regards science as the collection of facts, and distrusts theories and hypotheses as mere speculation (Cavanaugh, 1983). Clearly, the ICR's main task is promoting scientific creationism to the lay public in order to reassure the faithful and convert or neutralize others.

There are other scientific creationist organizations, such as the less sophisticated Bible Science Association, or the smooth, soft-spoken Foundation for Thought and Ethics, but the ICR is the dominant spokesman for the cause, largely setting the terms for the debate.

WHAT CREATIONISTS ARE *NOT*

It would be a mistake to assume, as many evolutionists have, that creationists must be simple-minded or uneducated. There is evidence (Eve and Harrold, 1986; Harrold and Eve, 1987) that while creationist college students tend to have slightly lower grade point averages and to read somewhat fewer books than others, these differences are actually relatively small. It is clear that there are many creationists who are of above-average intelligence and academic performance.

The creation/evolution debate involves much more than is commonly perceived. As with all social movements, members find themselves immersed in group dynamics that tend to generate a certain view of reality for adherents. Creationists and evolutionists structure their perceptions of reality in different ways based on different cognitive principles and on different assumptions about the rules for "knowing." Thus any social analysis of these movements must deal not only with natural science but with social psychology and the differing world views of various human groups.

VIEWS OF THE ETIOLOGY OF CREATIONIST BELIEF

Early explanations for the existence of creationists tended to rely on images of them as deviant, illogical, or even backwoods ignoramuses. As Garry Wills (1990) has noted, mainstream secularists are continually being surprised by the discovery that their religious traditionalist opponents are numerous and frequently influential, intelligent, and well educated.

Several accounts (e.g., Moffett, 1988) attribute creationism to author-

itarian, reactionary tendencies in the personalities or culture of creationists themselves. However, in keeping with recent trends in the study
of social movements (Cavanaugh, 1987; Fireman and Gamson, 1979;
Freeman, 1979; Klandermans, 1984; Zald and McCarthy, 1979), it seems
clear that personal pathology is not adequate to explain most conservative movements, including creationism.

The concept of the authoritarian personality was developed by T.W.
Adorno and colleagues (1950) to explain certain individuals' suscepti-
bility to fascism and antidemocratic ideas. It is hard, though, to see how
the authoritarian personality, often said to be the source of creationism,
can simultaneously account for the fact that most creationists favor populism and uphold parental or local autonomy in conflicts with state or
federal authority in educational matters. This is hardly the behavior that
one would expect in a homogeneously authoritarian personality.

Instead, we will emphasize here the importance of vertical status
groupings (rather than horizontal or class-based ones). Such vertical
groupings (Max Weber's *Stände*) cut across class lines in their promotion
of a particular world view and lifestyle. Some of these vertical status
groupings are locked in a struggle to defend their rights to control "the
means of cultural reproduction" (Oberschall, 1984) which are utilized
to socialize their own children and to reproduce their shared culture
and world view. Such groupings play a role in Hofstadter's (1955) concept of *status politics*—that is, political and legal conflict based not strictly
on economic or class distinctions, but instead on a sense of threatened
lifestyle.

Early studies employing the notion of status politics tended to point
to psychological "strains" as propelling individuals into extremist or reactionary movements.[1] However, Ann L. Page and Donald A. Clelland
(1978) have criticized these formulations as conveying the impression
that moral crusades are largely populated by status decliners, tradition
enforcers, status inconsistents, or individuals suffering from social marginality. In other words, the view was one of status politics as being
driven by emotional anxieties within individual adherents. Page and
Clelland instead suggested that among those in social movement organizations associated with defending a lifestyle, most are well off mate-
rially and in no immediate danger of a personal loss of status. Instead,
they stressed a more sociological view, suggesting that large special interest groups (in this case, vertical status groups protecting their way of
life and world view) are likely to develop systems of norms and values
that they wish to pass along to their children through control of the
means of cultural reproduction.

One illustration of Page and Clelland's point is that while there was
considerable furor in the 1920s over the issue of evolution in the public
schools, after the Scopes "monkey" trial of 1925 in Tennessee, little was

heard from the creationists until the 1960s. Why this should be so becomes apparent when we note that, despite the embarrassments suffered by creationists in the case, anti-evolution laws stayed on the books in Tennessee and other states, while coverage of evolution in biology textbooks almost disappeared after 1925 (see Nelkin, 1982). Creationists got most of what they campaigned for in the 1920s.

However, in 1957 the launching of Sputnik set off considerable anxiety among Americans about the effectiveness of U.S. science education. In the wake of Sputnik, the National Science Foundation sponsored several projects to improve secondary science education, including the Biological Sciences Curriculum Study (BSCS). The BSCS developed a series of new high school biology textbooks that featured evolution as the key concept in teaching biology. Appearing in 1963, the texts were soon in use in nearly half the nation's schools. It seems an unlikely coincidence that this is just when anti-evolution forces began a militant remobilization. Rather, conservative Christian parents felt compelled to defend against a loss of control over their "means of cultural reproduction." Suddenly they had been confronted with an ideological assault on the values they wished to inculcate in their offspring. They perceived the new federally sponsored scholastic materials as emphasizing rationalism, cosmopolitanism, secularism, humanism, and ethical flexibility. Such values are, of course, the very antithesis of those of creationists.

Indeed, this system of cultural modernism (to use Page and Clelland's terminology) even uses different tests for determining the truth of things than did the "cultural fundamentalism" typical of conservatives. Whereas the cultural fundamentalists "know" (in the sense of social psychological "constructionist" theory) that things are "true" by reason of tradition, authority, revelation, and faith, the cultural modernists emphasized validation by means of hypothesis testing and rationalized planning (often accomplished by large-scale organizations and the use of data collection and the scientific method).

THE "REASONABLENESS" OF CREATIONISM

Because creationism is not so much based on ignorance or personal aberration as on a rational defense of a world view based on theology and outdated versions of science,[2] it would seem that creationism is "logical" (if one is willing to recognize its assumptions) and even "plausible" (in the sense that there is no a priori reason it could not be true in the absence of evidence to the contrary). It does, however, appear to fail certain tests of "credibility," such as its inability to provide well-tested propositions *about the formation* of geological strata, radiometric dating of fossil remains, and so on (for a more complete discussion of this terminology, see Cavanaugh, 1983). However, for those not well trained in modern science, creationism may seem a plausible, reasonable, internally logical, and coherent defense of the world view of one status group facing a hostile external world.

SCIENTIFIC CREATIONISTS AND "THE NEW CLASS"

Anti-evolutionists can be safely considered to also be "cultural fundamentalists," in Page and Clelland's terminology. It seems necessary to observe here, however, that not all anti-evolutionists are pure cases of cultural fundamentalists. That this is so can be seen in the case of scientific creationists who in some ways fail to fit the mold of "cultural fundamentalists." Some of them are members of what Alvin Gouldner (1976) has called the "New Middle Class." Members of this class are neither owners of production, nor traditional businessmen, nor even laborers in the traditional sense. Instead, their capital lies in their expert scientific or technical knowledge or in the ability to create and manage information. In one important way, however, scientific creationists differ from the general category of cultural modernists; specifically, they tend to be biblical literalists who accept Genesis as a factual account. Because of their conviction that the Bible is literally true, they are compelled to conclude that mainstream science *must* be incorrect about evolution.

So there is much to join creation scientists with other members of the new class, but because of their belief in literalism and inerrancy, they are unlikely to find favor in the scientific institutions at the center of modern society. They must consequently form their own organizations (like the ICR) as they produce a brand of creationism that claims to be true to scientific principles. Fellow creationists, both in and out of the "New Middle Class," can point to scientific creationism to show that in rejecting evolution one need not reject science; one can be a modern thinker at home in a high-tech world *and* a Bible-believing Christian. Thus, a number of evangelical Protestants who embrace scientific creationism are known among the ranks of such a high-tech organization as the National Aeronautics and Space Administration (NASA). Most prominent of them was the late astronaut Jim Irwin, who once participated in an expedition to find remains of Noah's Ark in Turkey.

SCIENTIFIC CREATIONISM AND MOVEMENT TACTICS

Scientific creationists, particularly those in the Institute for Creation Research, have provided both the ideology and most of the tactics by which the creationist movement has waged its campaign. This campaign has been conducted at several levels.

Courts and Legislatures

After 1968, when the Supreme Court overturned state laws prohibiting the teaching of evolution (in *Epperson v. Arkansas*), creationists first attempted, unsuccessfully, to use the courts to prohibit federal support for the display or teaching of evolution on the basis that evolution was part of a religion ("secular humanism") and that teaching it in public schools therefore violated the "Establishment Clause" of the Constitution (Larson, 1985). There were also attempts to use the state legislatures to require "equal time" for creationism in science classes when evolution was presented. These efforts also quickly failed in the courts, rejected as attempts to teach religion in public schools.

Creationists then switched their tactics to present creationism, not as religious dogma, but as a *scientific theory* which on grounds of academic freedom, equal time, and fair education deserved to be presented alongside evolution. By 1981, over twenty bills based on this model had been introduced in state legislatures. Most died in committee, but two were enacted, in Arkansas and Louisiana, in 1981. They represent the high-water mark of creationist legislative efforts, and of national publicity for the movement. Both, however, were ultimately overturned in the federal courts on the grounds that they were in fact attempts to teach religious doctrine in public schools (Eve and Harrold, 1990: 147–55; Larson, 1985). In the aftermath of this setback, many creationists are convinced that the legislative arena is unproductive. Even those who support legislation have retired to produce new strategies rather than to support more laws requiring equal time for creation science.

Boards of Education

Another tactic can be seen in creationist attempts to influence state educational bodies. State governments play an important role in financing and regulating education. When their boards of education and other regulatory bodies select textbooks and set curriculum guidelines, creationist activists try to influence the process and thus to defend and promote their interests. Some state boards of education are elected and others are appointed by elected officials. In either case, they are seldom immune from political pressure. Since relatively few people are politically aware and active concerning educational issues, the support or opposition of a small group can be decisive.

Creationists frequently try to curtail evolution or promote creationism in public schools by influencing general curriculum guidelines. Getting the board of education to require inclusion of scientific creationism in biology courses may be nearly as effective as getting a law passed by the legislature, and it is less likely to be overturned in a court.

Creationists also try to influence textbook selection. Particularly important in this struggle are the two largest "adoption states," California and Texas. In these (and twenty other) states, the state board of education adopts a list of approved textbooks, and then subsidizes their purchase by school districts. Since Texas and California each represent huge markets, textbook publishers tend to tailor their books to these states' adoption criteria (Stacey and Shupe, 1984). In the 1970s creationists managed to have "anti-dogmatism" policies implemented in several states. Such policies typically required that biology texts carry a disclaimer to the effect that evolution is not a "fact" but "only one of several explanations of origins." In the 1980s, thanks to efforts by anti-creationist "countermovement" organizations like the National Center for Science Education and People for the American Way, evolutionists have rebounded. They have managed not only to eliminate most anti-dogmatism requirements, but to require the coverage of evolution in high school biology classes in both Texas and California. Nonetheless, evolution still tends to receive much more gingerly applied treatment in both curriculum policies and textbooks than other scientific theories. Gravitational theory, for instance, is never required to be balanced by "alternative theories" in physics classes.

Grass-roots Level

Currently, the most effective creationist campaigns against evolution are being waged at the level of local boards of education and individual schools. Here one finds pressure being applied by conservative Protestant parents, congregations, or clergy to try to affect curriculum decisions, textbook selection, and even teacher behavior in the classroom. Creationist appeals to elected local officials, and to principals and teachers who are their neighbors, can be very effective.

To what extent does creationist grass-roots effort actually pay off? For example, how many school teachers agree that creationism should be taught in public school science classes? Previous studies indicate that the proportion in favor of this practice ranges from a low of about 30 percent in Georgia and Illinois studies, to a high of about 69 percent in Kentucky (see Eve and Harrold, 1990: 163–67). Let us go one step further and ask how many teachers actually report teaching creationism (or downplaying evolution) in their own classes. Here the figures in various studies range from about 12 percent to 29 percent. Another indicator that the creationist grass-roots campaigns are not ineffective comes from data indicating that between 12 and 29 percent of teachers report pressure from parents or school administrators to teach creationism or to downplay evolution.

On a related topic, researchers have typically assumed that de jure decisions by federal or state courts or educational agencies will be directly translated into de facto behavior in the classroom. We have, however, considerable anecdotal evidence that such official decisions may have relatively little influence on many individual teachers. Our conversations with many students make it clear that, for instance in our area (Dallas–Fort Worth), evolution is considered a touchy subject in high schools, one that many teachers avoid, underplay, or "balance" with creationism, whatever official state or district policies may be.

As the creation/evolution conflict has progressed, creationists have advanced their case in different arenas, gradually concentrating their efforts in those that have shown the greatest successes. In the process, their approach has evolved from a more expressive (emotion-laden) phase to a more strategic, disimpassioned one as they have found the tactics that work best: pressing for equal time in local and state arenas, and advocating "fairness" and compromise rather than coercion. They are adapting to the reality that, at least for the present, they can appeal with far more success to some "bystander publics" (e.g., school administrators, teachers, and the general public) than to others (judges, legislatures, the media). Persuasion, facilitation, and compromise, the hallmarks of a more strategic orientation, are increasingly apparent in creationist literature. The new trends can also be seen in the "soft" creationist line of the newly prominent Foundation for Thought and Ethics, which eschews terms like "God" and "creation" in favor of "intelligent design" and "abrupt appearance." Even at the ICR, where rhetoric tends toward the zealous and even strident, the second edition of *Evolution? The Fossils Say No!* was given the less polemical title *Evolution: The Challenge of the Fossil Record* (Gish, 1978, 1985).

AMERICAN CREATIONISM IN LARGER PERSPECTIVE

Although creationism in its American form is not a major social movement elsewhere in the world, the creation/evolution debate reflects one aspect of a major structural and phenomenological dialectic in contemporary Western culture that arises out of declining ruralism and traditionalism along with increasing cosmopolitanism, rationalization of production, and secularization. This latter constellation of traits has often been called *modernism*. Modernism is psychoanalytic in its view of the mind and existential in its ethics. It furthermore takes a deterministic and materialist view of nature, no longer demanding the subordination of scientific inquiry to scriptural orthodoxy. It is easy to see how its offspring, such as secularism and hedonistic consumption, have been perceived by cultural fundamentalists as antithetical to everything they believed in. In the words of Frederick Turner "Modernism's adolescent masculine temper despised both the traditional matriarchy of family life and the traditional patriarchy of the old customary public institutions. It attacked the wisdom and the achievements of the West.... It was obsessed with power, for good or ill, as the fundamental human reality" (1991: p. 117).

Currently, however, for cultural fundamentalists the situation grows even more fraught with tension as the world witnesses the rise of *post-modernism*. In the first half of this century, conservative Christianity had almost made its peace with modernism. Glamour and sexuality had been accepted so long as they were kept within the bounds of traditional monogamy, and in a return to Weber's conception of the Protestant ethic, even conspicuous consumption needed not embarrass one but could be seen instead as a sign of God's favor. However, during the second half of the century, especially since the 1960s, many persons have become disillusioned by modernism and its consequences of secularism, consumerism, colonialism, urban growth, the rationalization of production—and the pollution and other ills such processes entailed. Many have begun to cry "Enough!" For them, modernism's reliance on rationality, science, and technology has failed (e.g., Hadden and Shupe, 1988: 55–73).

One result of this spreading disillusionment has been an outpouring of intellectual activity designed to *deconstruct* the rhetoric and imagery of modernism. Deconstructionists began to ask serious questions about whose interests were being served by modernism and its attendant emphasis on rationality in general and scientism in particular. Deconstructionists have been convincing to many in their arguments that modernism served primarily big government, big industry, big media, and associated members of the new class (scientists and technical workers). Deconstructionism has succeeded for many in delegitimating modernism, but there remains one "small problem"—it has led some to abandon modernism, but so far, in the view of many, it has failed to propose anything with which to replace it other than anomie and nihilism. Traditionalists, rejecting both modernism and what they see as barren postmodernism, have reacted with a wave of "fundamentalism" in both the Christian and Islamic worlds, seeking to reinstate the old certainties in place of existential uncertainty (Turner, 1991).

Incidentally, the analysis presented here is also suggestive of the origins of the "New Age" movements seen in American society. Like creationism, New Age beliefs probably arise out of a rejection of modernism and seek an alternative form of "empowerment" for a culturally alienated group.

CONCLUDING REMARKS

The creation/evolution debate is not primarily one over the scientific status of various accounts of origins. In the scientific research community, these issues were settled long ago. Instead, creationism provides cultural traditionalists with a raison d'être that can bring coherence to their opposition to a wide range of sociopolitical trends such as abortion rights, gay rights, drug use, pornography, equal rights for women, and so on. After all, creationists argue, if one accepts that scripture may not be literally accurate, then how is one to know that salvation can be obtained by adherence to a revealed divine plan? For these persons, belief in evolution becomes the first step down the slippery slope to secular humanism, with its emphasis on flexible ethics derived out of social interaction. Therefore, creationists argue that acceptance of evolution will lead to all the social problems and moral vacuousness seen in contemporary society. From such a perspective, even devout fellow Christians, if they accept evolution, are nearly as bad as secular humanists.

In a time of anomie brought on not by a collapse of values but by exposure to too many competing value systems, the problem for any group wishing to preserve control over the means of cultural reproduction is how to legitimate its own worldview better than can any other group. Ironically, creationists who accuse mainstream science of being elitist and morally barren do not hesitate to turn to science to seek legitimation for their own worldview.

Cultural modernists have been predicting the demise of creationism for decades, and they are still waiting. Because creationism represents the focus of conflicting worldviews, there is every reason to believe that their wait will continue for decades to come.

NOTES

1. See, for example, Joseph Gusfield's (1963) analysis of the temperance movement or Louis B. Zurcher's (1971) study of antipornography campaigns.

2. Scientific creationism draws heavily on Scottish realist philosophy, which in turn is descended from Baconian inductivism. In such systems, widely popular until the later part of the nineteenth century, the task of science was seen as the collection and arrangement of "facts," leading eventually to self-evident conclusions. Terms like "theory" and "hypothesis" were mistrusted as indicating mere speculation. This is sharply different from modern conceptions of the scientific method, in which theories are testable structures of ideas meant to explain data.

9

EXPLAINING PROTESTANT FUNDAMENTALISM IN CENTRAL AMERICA

Michael Dodson

Writing in the late 1980s, journalist Penny Lernoux (1988: 51) observed: "Every hour 400 Latin Americans convert to the Pentecostals or other fundamentalist or evangelical churches." At that rate of conversion, membership in Protestant churches was growing by more than 10 percent per year. This phenomenal rate of growth, which David Stall has aptly compared to the periods of intense religious revivalism that have occurred in North American history, is a relatively recent phenomenon in Latin America (see, e.g., Stoll, 1990: 22). Consider the case of Central America, which is the focus of this chapter. In 1936 there were fewer than 120,000 Protestants in all of Central America, or less than 2 percent of the population (Martínez, 1989: 34). Religious affiliation in the region was overwhelmingly Roman Catholic, despite fifty years of Protestant evangelizing. In the last three decades, however, the Protestant competition for converts has been amazingly successful. The experience of two quite different countries in Central America, Guatemala and Nicaragua, will illustrate this success.

The Presbyterian Church is the oldest Protestant denomination in Guatemala, having been founded in 1882. When Guatemalan Presbyterians celebrated their "Diamond Anniversary" in 1957, the country was still less than 2 percent Protestant. Twenty-five years later this figure had increased to over 22 percent (Burnett, 1991: 4), and by the end of the 1980s one study showed that membership in Protestant churches was nearing one third of the population (Sywulka, 1989: 46). By far the largest percentage of these conversions were to fundamentalist, and especially Pentecostal, churches. Today, the Assemblies of God is the largest single denomination in Guatemala, with well over 100,000 members (Burnett, 1991: 4). The same remarkable growth of evangelical Protestantism that took place in Guatemala, which was subject to right-wing authoritarian rule (including seventeen months under a "born-again" evangelical president, Efrain Rios Montt), also occurred in revolutionary Nicaragua. For example, during the first seven years of the revolution the country's population grew by 17.8 percent, while the number of Protestant congregations grew by 116.4 percent. Costa Rican sociologist Abelino Martínez estimates that by the mid-1980s more than 500,000 of Nicaragua's 3 million people were Protestants (Martínez, 1989: 27). In 1980 just over half of these Nicaraguan Protestants were Pentecostals, and by 1986 the proportion who were Pentecostals exceeded 70 percent (Martínez, 1989: 62)!

These data merely underscore what is increasingly obvious to those who study Central America: the region is experiencing a dramatic growth of evangelical Protestantism, and especially of Pentecostalism. The question is, why is this growth taking place now, and what accounts for the equally impressive spread of Pentecostalism in such different countries as Guatemala and Nicaragua? We might also inquire as to the religious and political implications of rapid evangelical growth for Central America's future. In response to these questions, I want to discuss the following: the role of aggressive fundamentalist churches and parachurch groups based in the United States in planting churches abroad; the theological and ecclesiological features that render Pentecostalism attractive in the Central American setting; and whether Pentecostalism is a reaction to the wave of popular, prophetic mobilization that took place in postconciliar Roman Catholicism. I will argue that these issues are most fruitfully discussed against the backdrop of four decades of frustrated "development."

MODERNIZATION AND MISERY: CENTRAL AMERICA FROM 1950 TO 1980

The political elites of Central America entered the post–World War II era by committing themselves to policies of economic modernization and industrialization. They were encouraged in this commitment by officials of the newly created United Nations Economic Commission on Latin America (ECLA), by the establishment of the Organization of American States, which strongly embraced these economic development goals, and by the general climate of enthusiasm for "modernization." Under the influence of ECLA a broad scheme took shape, which some writers have called the strategy of *progressive modernization* (see, e.g., Wynia, 1984: 111–17). This strategy tried to promote industrialization through the process of import substitution, while simultaneously en-

couraging agrarian reform and increased economic integration among
the nations of Central America. Foreign investment and technical assistance were welcomed, and indeed eagerly sought, on the assumption
that they would contribute to achieving these objectives. When President
John F. Kennedy launched the Alliance for Progress in 1961 to promote
a "democratic revolution" in Latin America, he embraced each of these
modernizing tasks.

Over a period of three decades this modernizing strategy was, in certain respects, enormously successful. Between 1950 and 1980, for example, Central America enjoyed one of the highest economic growth
rates in the world, averaging between 5.5 percent and 8.0 percent per
year. In several Central American countries the industrial base was expanded impressively, and throughout the region roads, bridges, hy-
droelectric power, and communications systems were upgraded.
Agriculture also underwent a process of modernization, primarily
through a dramatic expansion of the acreage devoted to new cash crops.
For example, the acreage committed to cotton and sugar production
increased almost tenfold (Barry, 1987: 7). At the same time, land set
aside for pasture also increased sharply so that in the early 1980s twice
as much land area was being used to graze cattle as was used for agriculture per se (see Barry, 1987: 10).

These data only begin to suggest the stark consequences that modernization, as it was actually pursued in Central America, had on the
majority of the region's people, most of whom were poor and dependent
on agriculture for their livelihood. The distribution of farmland, already
skewed heavily toward a landed oligarchy in the 1950s, became even
more sharply concentrated. A 1979 report by the U.S. Agency for International Development (AID), which had played an important role in
carrying out this modernizing strategy, showed that in Guatemala
1 percent of landowners controlled 78 percent of the nation's farmland.
What is more, this land was used increasingly to grow crops for export
rather than for consumption at home. Thus, Guatemala's landed elite
produced coffee, cotton, sugar, and beef, rather than beans, corn, or
rice. As a consequence, countries that had been self-sufficient in basic
grains in 1950 were, by 1980, major importers of grain. The practical
effect on Central America's poor was widespread hunger and malnutrition. In 1980 ECLA reported that 67 percent of rural Central Americans lived below the poverty line and that 42 percent of them were in
"absolute poverty" (Barry, 1987: 16).

In a sense, the tale told by these facts and figures is a simple one.
Although impressive levels of economic growth were achieved in Central
America over a period of three decades, the social reforms that might
have distributed the increased wealth more equitably never took place.
In the countryside, where most people still lived, wealth became even

more concentrated. As one writer has put it, the drive toward economic modernization "served to strengthen the hold of landed property over the economic and political life of the region. When industrialization came, it was managed and directed in a manner subservient to landed property, and its modernizing effect on the social system was thereby minimized. In no part of Latin America has the landlord class been as successful in holding back social and political change as in Central America" (Weeks, 1986: 44–45).

Central America was a particularly glaring case of what is sometimes called "growth without equity."[1] Its development model actually increased the suffering of a growing mass of marginalized people. Eventually, the desperation caused by such marginalization poured forth into the political arena. During the 1970s popular groups emerged throughout Central America that were mobilized to press for change. In time, some of these groups merged with guerrilla movements and took up armed struggle. Initially, however, they merely tried to find organized ways to improve, however marginally, their position in the socioeconomic order. The political repercussions were far-reaching and were already being felt throughout Central America by the mid–1970s. The mobilization of popular groups challenged the essential legitimacy of those regimes that had presided over the modernizing project, the effect of which was to challenge the legitimacy of oligarchical control over economic development. Lines were thus drawn that led to a profound escalation of political conflict. In 1979 a popular uprising in Nicaragua, led by the Sandinista Front of National Liberation (FSLN), overthrew the Somoza dictatorship; similar popular movements threatened the regimes in El Salvador and Guatemala. By the 1980s the political violence associated with revolution and counterrevolution had pervaded every aspect of life in Central America. The Christian churches, Catholic and Protestant, were deeply involved in these events and were strongly affected by them. Church involvement in popular struggle bears heavily on the issue of evangelical growth in Central America.

ROMAN CATHOLICISM TURNS LEFT

How did the Roman Catholic Church respond to the suffering and dislocation caused by rapid economic change in the 1950s? Prior to the Second Vatican Council (1962–1965), the church had little to say in the face of growing economic hardship and the breakup of rural communities. In theological terms, the church taught passivity in response to suffering; in pastoral terms it had lost the means and the will to minister effectively among the poor. Especially in rural areas, a popular, or "folk," Catholicism was widely practiced that had relatively little substantive base in Roman Catholic traditions. The poor were only nominally members of the church. Writing in the late 1960s, Ivan Vallier described the situation this way:

The Church has not been able to gain access to or control over many types of religious inclinations. Many of the members' spiritual needs came to be focused on and satisfied through extrasacramental practices, private devotions, "contracts" with divine personages, and by participating in festive, religiously toned social activities. In short, Latin American Catholicism, although strong in its own way, is typically extrasacramental. Consequently the official Church stands separate from habitual religious practice and has been unable to draw on existing religious loyalties for purposes of fostering ethical and spiritual strength. (Vallier, 1970: 26–27)

However, the great watershed events of Vatican II and Medellín stimulated sharp changes in the church's outlook, with fateful consequences for the region.

At Vatican II the Catholic Church opted to reach out more aggressively into the modern world and assert its presence there. The new attitude evinced at Vatican II reflected a growing acceptance of the increasingly secular and pluralistic character of modern society. At the same time, in making this decision the church implicitly relinquished its long-held view that grace was available only inside the Roman church itself. In effect, Vatican II turned this view inside out—grace was everywhere and the church had to be a sign of that grace through its pastoral presence. Local churches were encouraged to seek greater cooperation across diocesan lines and also to adapt their evangelizing practices to local conditions. In other words, they were encouraged to be more self-reliant at the local level but also more integrated at the national level. These innovations encouraged a great deal of experimentation. The Vatican Council gave special attention to the need to evangelize the poor. When put into practice in Central America, where the majority of the people *were* poor, this decision committed the church to a "preferential option for the poor," an option that was embraced officially by Latin America's bishops at Medellín, Colombia, in 1968.[2]

The historic meeting of Latin American bishops at Medellín stimulated a period of vigorous renewal in Central American Catholicism. One remarkable aspect of that renewal was that it had a decidedly Protestant or Reformational character. For instance, Medellín authorized the saying of Mass in Spanish, while encouraging distribution and study of the Bible. Women in particular, as well as the larger laity, were allowed to take a broader and more active role in the pastoral work of the church. Delegates of the Word were trained to lead worship in the priest's absence, a practice that spread rapidly across the countryside. Perhaps most vitally, a movement developed to create local-level religious communities organized and maintained largely by the poor themselves. As they developed these ecclesiastical base communities (*comunidades ecle-*

siales de base, or CEBs), the poor increased their religious self-awareness and deepened their political consciousness. In settings where worker organizations were legally banned, violently repressed, or tightly controlled from above by political elites, CEBs provided the only institutions available to the poor where reflection could take place on the causes of their suffering and where they could organize for making demands (Berryman, 1986: 45–79; Dodson and O'Shaughnessy, 1990: 116–39). Succored by a prophetic interpretation of the Bible, poor Christians throughout Central America began to speak out in the public arena and to push for change. In short, to a significant degree the popular mobilization of the 1970s was inspired and sustained by religious initiatives generated within the Roman Catholic Church.

Seemingly overnight the Catholic Church was transformed from quiet apologist for the status quo to raucous critic of an unjust order. The church became a vehicle by which the long-abused popular sectors could struggle to find a legitimate foothold in the political arena. One result of this politicization of the popular classes through religion was a growing wave of violence against the church. Although this violence fell most heavily on the poor, it also struck at the church hierarchy, as in the assassinations of numerous clergy, including the archbishop of San Salvador, Oscar Arnulfo Romero. Some church leaders came to feel that the option for the poor had gone out of control, threatening the integrity of the institutional church. By the 1980s a strong reaction had set in to reassert hierarchical control and direction, and to "depoliticize" the CEBs (Berryman, 1986: 77–79; Dodson, 1990).

Meanwhile, in the international arena the Central American church had acquired an image of extreme radicalization. Liberation theology, which sought to articulate gospel values from the vantage point of the poor, was stridently accused of being a form of religious Marxism. Priests, nuns, and Delegates of the Word were seen as "guerrillas," or as mere tools of guerrilla movements. This image helped fuel vigorous mission efforts on the part of the most conservative evangelical churches and parachurch groups in the United States, efforts that were supported and complemented by right-wing political groups eager to pursue their own political agenda in Central America (Diamond, 1989: 148–60, 208–24). As I have suggested, the surge in fundamentalist mission efforts in Central America occurred at the same time that the Catholic Church hierarchy began trying to rein in the popular church movement that had galvanized the poor so powerfully for more than a decade.

PROTESTANTISM TURNS RIGHT IN THE UNITED STATES

At the same time that the Catholic Church worked to reduce its high profile prophetic stance in the late 1970s and early 1989s, another dramatic process of religious activism was taking place. Central America was experiencing an explosion of growth among evangelical churches professing fundamentalist theologies. These churches were gaining adherents not only among the poor, but also among the middle and upper middle classes. In the analysis that follows I will examine the theology of evangelical fundamentalism as it has found expression first in the United States, then in the context of Central America. My purpose is to understand why churches of this sort have had such dramatic success penetrating a region that was long considered a safe bastion of Roman Catholicism.

In the most general sense, evangelicals are "born-again" Christians who have "rediscovered the gospel of the early church" (Nash, 1987: 23). They are found within most, if not all, major Protestant denominations, as well as among Pentecostal and other "independent" churches. Evangelicals share a common core of theological principles and, broadly speaking, a common style of worship. They are typically dedicated to promoting evangelism through revival campaigns, missions, and the distribution of Bibles and other Christian literature. One of the most pronounced features of evangelicalism is its transdenominational character. This aspect of the movement is illustrated by the large number of independent churches that was established after the great fundamentalist-modernist split of the 1920s (Hunter, 1987: 31–32). It is also evident in the proliferation of parachurch agencies dedicated to promoting an evangelical world view, including youth ministries, radio and television ministries, Bible institutes, and mission societies (Marsden, 1987: 63).

Whether mainstream, fundamentalist, or charismatic (as in Pentecostalism), evangelicals have traditionally held to a common core of theological principles, including the divinity of Christ, his atonement for sin, and his bodily resurrection. They also anticipate a literal return of Christ in history. According to evangelicals these central precepts are all to be found in scripture, which is the sole authority in spiritual matters.

Within the broad stream of evangelicalism, fundamentalism has been distinguished by the great emphasis given to Christ's second coming. Some evangelicals believe that the second coming will occur after a 1,000-year reign of Christians on earth, as predicted in the twentieth chapter of Revelations. This view, called postmillennialism, predominated in the first half of the nineteenth century, but gave way to premillennialism toward the end of the century. Premillennialists insist that Christ will return before the establishment of the earthly millennial kingdom.

As the premillennialist view became dominant at the turn of the century it also became identified with a doctrine called "dispensationalism," which was first promoted in the United States and Canada by an Englishman named John Darby (Hunter, 1987: 25). *Dispensationalism* divides history into distinct eras, or dispensations, each governed by a unique and dominating principle. This approach makes sharp distinctions among the ways God deals with human beings at different stages of history. According to Darby there were seven dispensations, but contemporary millennialist theologies require three.

The Dispensation of the Law describes the period from Moses to the beginning of the Christian church at Pentecost. This period corresponded to the history of Israel as told in the Old Testament. For that period salvation was attained in a way unique to the Hebrew people. The Dispensation of the Law lasted until the people of Israel failed the divine test by crucifying Jesus. A second era, called the Dispensation of Grace, began at the Pentecost. That era corresponds to the age of the Christian church and will last until the period of the great tribulation. During that era, which has not yet ended, the institutional church will degenerate into apostasy. The end of the period will be marked by the Rapture of the Saints and the onset of the tribulation. Following the period of tribulation, the third of the vital dispensations, the Dispensation of the Millennial Kingdom, will begin.

A fundamentalist will typically take a premillennialist position on the second coming of Christ. The dispensationalist will be both premillennialist and pretribulationist. That is, he will embrace the notion of the rapture in which Christ captures all born again Christians, living and dead, into the air at the same time that he ushers in a seven-year period of tribulation. During the great tribulation the antichrist will control the world and all persons who subsequently convert to faith in Christ will be severely persecuted. At the end of the seven years Christ will return, good and evil will do battle at Armageddon, and the millennial kingdom will be established when the forces of Christ prevail (Nash, 1987: 23).

Evangelicals who hold these dispensationalist, premillennialist views have emerged into prominence in the leadership of interdenominational fundamentalism. They tend to be anti-ecumenical and take pride in working independently of denominational controls. They are a major force within the independent churches, including Pentecostal churches. What Pentecostalism adds to fundamentalism, as we have defined it here, is an emphasis on the power of the Holy Spirit in the life of the believer. Pentecostalism is thus a charismatic tendency within evangelical Protestantism. Pentecostals believe that the charismatic gifts, which were originally seen among the first generation of Christians, are still available. Pentecostal liturgy stresses "baptism in the holy spirit" and "speaking in tongues." Theologically it tends to be fundamentalist (Nash, 1987: 78).

Historically, the premillennialist outlook in Protestant fundamentalism had the effect of discouraging believers from taking an active part in political life. Indeed, this outlook was indifferent or even hostile to the temporal world. Political action to make the world a better place, to relieve suffering caused by a lack of power, for example, was regarded as futile and pointless. If anything, widespread suffering was apt to be seen as confirmation that the era of tribulation was at hand. In this way the premillennialist eschatology became a "rallying call to support missionary activity and to personal evangelism—to use these last days to save souls" (Poloma, 1986: 337).

Beginning in the early 1970s, the traditional tendency of fundamentalist evangelicals to avoid politics underwent a sudden and dramatic shift. Evangelicals began to speak out on political issues and to mobilize their followers to act in the public arena. Two factors seem to underlie this remarkable change, both of which can be traced to federal government policy. The first factor concerned changes in Federal Communications Commission (FCC) regulations governing the air time committed to religious programming. In the early 1970s, the FCC allowed radio and television stations to begin charging for religious broadcasts. Most mainline churches refused to purchase air time, but fundamentalist preachers, who used the broadcasts themselves to raise money, were willing to do so (Reichley, 1987: 75). In this manner the audience for religious programming, almost all of it informed by fundamentalist theology, expanded astonishingly. Between 1970 and the early 1980s religious programming more than doubled its air time. Seventy percent of the religious radio programming and 90 percent of the television programming was produced by evangelical and Pentecostal groups (Hudson, 1987: 393).

The second factor was closely connected to the first. This was the rise of *parachurch* groups, some of which have achieved great notoriety in recent years, such as Moral Majority, Religious Roundtable, Christian Voice, and the Praise the Lord (PTL) Club (Wuthnow, 1987: 100, 177). With the fund-raising that was possible through broadcast ministries, these groups were no longer dependent on any denominational ties. They could raise their own funds, which they did prolifically, and go their own way, unaccountable to any church or denomination.

During the 1950s and 1960s many fundamentalist evangelicals were alienated from the mainstream denominations and their more liberal leadership because of the latter's heavy involvement in the civil rights movement and protests against the war in Vietnam. They were further estranged from public policy by the 1973 abortion decision in *Roe v. Wade*, by the drive to pass the Equal Rights Amendment (ERA), and the growing movement for gay (homosexual) rights. These movements and actions in the political arena created the perception among evangelicals that public policy was a threat to the Christian family and to the most basic personal morals of the Christian faithful. The Supreme Court decision limiting prayer in public schools only added fuel to the fire. This spreading and deeply felt sentiment against government policy found a forum in the special purpose groups and the broadcast ministries. After the failure of the born-again president, Jimmy Carter, to take up this agenda from the fundamentalist point of view, this sentiment was increasingly mobilized and articulated by "New Right" political organizers such as Paul Weyrich, Kevin Phillips, and Richard Viguerie, who had no roots at all in evangelical Protestantism (Reichley, 1987: 79).

In short, evangelicals became an active part of the strong rightward shift in American politics, fighting to stem the tide of moral decay at home and to resist the subversion abroad that threatened the American way of life. In this manner, religious fundamentalism became a potent element of the New Right's foreign policy toward Central America. The New Right's political perspective certainly spilled over into evangelical mission efforts in Central America during the 1970s and 1980s. As I maintain, however, the rapid growth of religious fundamentalism in Central America responded to indigenous causes that, while in some ways parallel to what occurred in the United States, are also independent of it. While penetration of U.S. missionaries and money may account for some of the growth, it cannot account for all of it.

THE GROWTH OF PROTESTANT FUNDAMENTALISM IN CENTRAL AMERICA

Evangelical protestants have been winning converts at a steady pace in Central America since the 1930s. Originally this effort was based entirely on the work of U.S. missionaries. In the 1950s the first evangelical radio stations were established in the region, at about the same time that the number of Pentecostal missionaries began to increase rapidly. Everett Wilson points out that in Guatemala, where Protestant growth has been the most significant, there were just five "pioneering" missions before 1930. By 1956 twenty-one new missions or national churches had appeared, and since then an additional thirty-four established a presence in the country. Wilson attributes much of this growth in new churches to a fragmentation of those already present, a point we will examine more fully below. Only 5 percent of the Protestant churches in Guatemala today are historic churches, such as Lutheran, Baptist, or Presbyterian. About "seventy percent identify with the Pentecostal or Holiness traditions." And, while they may have friendly relationships with North American mission agencies, "they essentially operate independently without organic coordination of their activities" (Wilson, 1988: 68–69).

These observations call for further analysis. They suggest an explanation of evangelical growth in Central America rooted in two causes. Up to a certain point these causes are complementary to each other, but at another point they are in competition, and ultimately they are irreconcilable. One cause is the vigorous promotion of evangelicalism by U.S.-

based churches and parachurch groups, and by international mission
bodies in Latin America. The other cause is more specifically indigenous
to Central America and includes the social setting of church growth and
the personal motives of evangelicals. We will discuss each of these causes
in turn.

The impact of foreign missions on the growth of Protestant evangelicalism in Central America can be illustrated by two programs, Evangelism-in-Depth and Campus Crusade for Christ. The former was
organized in the early 1960s by Latin American Mission (LAM), an
interdenominational faith mission based in San José, Costa Rica, and
funded largely from the United States. From the beginning the program
had a strong element of anti-communism, but its theological basis was
the biblical injunction to spread the gospel (Matthew 28: 19–20). Evangelism-in-Depth targeted such groups as students and workers, using
the evangelizing techniques that had been developed in the United
States. These included an aggressive use of the media, as well as retreats,
revivals, and small "prayer cells," within which converts were encouraged
to become evangelizers themselves. These campaigns were carefully
planned and marketed, rather than being allowed to spread spontaneously. In this manner Evangelism-in-Depth reached literally millions
of Central Americans during the 1960s and 1970s.

As I have indicated, the use of media played an important role. During
this period the number of evangelical radio stations in Central America
increased threefold and were producing over 200 programs per week
by the end of the 1970s. In the 1970s the religious programs produced
by such television evangelists as Pat Robertson, Jim and Tammy Bakker,
and Jimmy Swaggart also became regular features in Central America
(Dominguez, 1984: 18).

The work of Campus Crusade for Christ paralleled that of the Latin
American Mission. Initially established in Guatemala in 1964, even before it had achieved large-scale success in the United States, Campus
Crusade subsequently established branches throughout Central America. Campus Crusade's worldwide "Here's Life" campaign has had considerable impact in various countries in the region. The experience of
El Salvador is illustrative. Between 1978 and 1980 Campus Crusade
mobilized 120,000 Christians in 120 towns for door-to-door evangelizing,
claiming 64,000 new converts at the conclusion of the campaign. This
carefully planned and sophisticated program "to sell Jesus Christ" is
largely financed from the United States, with much of the funding coming from American corporations (Huntington, 1984: 24).

One goal of such programs as Evangelism-in-Depth and Campus Crusade is certainly to convert Central Americans to the gospel. They have,
in other words, a spiritual mission. But they also have a more purely
ideological function. Their millennialist theology has the effects of dis-

couraging the faithful from protesting against the abuses of repressive regimes and of inhibiting organizing to overcome the gross economic inequities that cause so much suffering among their members. What is more, some of the more prominent evangelical leaders give this theology an explicitly political twist. Campus Crusade's regional director for Central America has stated explicitly that the region is embroiled in an ideological struggle. An important goal of Campus Crusade is to combat liberation theology, whose exponents "are nothing more than masked Communists." On the other hand, Campus Crusade proclaims that "the American system is the expression of Christian ideas" and describes the founding of the United States as the "single most important event since the birth of Christ" (Huntington, 1984: 31). This direct incorporation of political ideology into theology is shared, even if less obtrusively, across a broad spectrum of evangelical churches and parachurch groups doing mission work in Central America today.

Having insisted on the role of mission agencies, however, we must also take account of forces within Central America that contribute to evangelical growth. It is essential to recognize that much of the church growth in Central America today, even if originally initiated by missionaries, is now largely self-sustaining and even self-reproducing. This is because the millennialist theology of evangelical Protestantism does in fact speak effectively to the situation and personal needs of the marginal poor. Specifically, evangelicalism responds to the needs created by the disintegration of community life among rural people, whether they be Indians in the Guatemalan highlands or campesinos in rural El Salvador or Nicaragua. By the hundreds of thousands these people have been uprooted and demoralized by economic developments and changes over which they have no control. This is quite apart from the violence that has been inflicted on them when they have organized to protest against, or exert some control over, these changes.

Everett Wilson (1988: 97) argues that the earliest evangelical churches in El Salvador and Guatemala "took form from the remnants of rural organizations fallen into disuse." That is, they filled the space created by the destruction of traditional forms of association among Indian communities. The nuclear family and village relationships were broken down by the loss of land and forced seasonal migration. This is a phenomenon that has continued, and indeed was even accelerated in recent decades, producing large-scale rural to urban migration. The shantytowns of Guatemala City, San Salvador, and Managua are filled with recent arrivals who have lost traditional ties to older communities and who are not only steeped in poverty but are also surrounded by crime and personal immorality such as alcoholism and drug addiction.

In such a setting the evangelical form of worship is successful. The absence of a centralized structure of bureaucratic control is an asset. In a typical scenario, a national evangelist visits a village and organizes meetings in private homes. Persons attending are encouraged to visit neighboring villages or plantations. A local patron donates land for the building of a small church. The church thus formed is a voluntary organization in which many members are "participating in a system of acquired rather than ascribed status for the first time" (Wilson, 1988: 100). Anyone who wants membership can have it. Once formed, such churches provide members with strong emotional support and a sense of shared identity. They also occupy the members' time in a variety of meaningful pursuits, including further evangelizing efforts. New leaders can emerge within these churches and then spin off to establish churches of their own.

This aspect of evangelical growth contributes to the fragmented character that evangelicalism exhibits in Central America. At the same time, fragmentation is due to the fact that evangelical growth is occurring among popular groups whose conditions of life are highly unstable. In Guatemala and El Salvador particularly, these groups are not only caught up in a cycle of migratory labor that undermines village and family life, they are also enveloped in undeclared but deadly shooting wars. The extremely rapid expansion of evangelical Protestantism that began in the 1960s was concentrated among these popular, typically impoverished groups. Even when located in urban shantytowns, the members of these groups are all essentially rural in outlook and lifestyle.

Evangelical Protestantism in Central America is a cross-class phenomenon. "Health and wealth" churches (i.e., those whose leaders preach that Christians may expect a full blessing of prosperity and good health as a reward for faith) with a fundamentalist bent are flourishing among the middle and upper classes in Guatemala and are spreading to the other countries of Central America. Nonetheless, Pentecostalism has spread most rapidly among landless campesinos, including those who have migrated to urban shantytowns. This means that evangelical Protestantism is growing in the same social environment that fostered Catholic base communities two decades ago. Although they rest on sharply different doctrinal foundations, the liberation theology of the Catholic CEB and the millennialist theology of the Pentecostal sect have the same capacity to bring a sense of meaning, dignity, and hope to the lives of the poor. In Catholic CEBs the function of theology is to integrate concern for material well-being and spiritual salvation. This has lead to a systematic denunciation of poverty, which is seen to grow out of societal injustice. By contrast, in the Pentecostal sect one draws closer to God not by seeking to create his kingdom on earth, but by renouncing material benefits. This theology tends to encourage political passivity, just as the other lends support to political activism. In both cases, the individual joins a community that has a special relationship to God, a relationship that can be attained even when material well-being is not.

CONCLUSION

To recapitulate, postwar programs of modernization in Central America had some, but not all, of their intended effects. They promoted economic growth and diversification, for instance, and also raised people's expectations. These programs failed utterly, however, in overcoming the obstacles to equitable distribution. At the same time, modernization encouraged a deepening of political consciousness and helped stimulate organized demand-making among the poor. One of the most fascinating aspects of the period was the emergence of the Roman Catholic Church as a source of support to the popular sectors as independent political actors. The demand to participate carried a high price, however, in countries where elites have yet to accept that popular groups have a right to their own voice in the political arena. In fact, national and even international power was mobilized against the popular sectors, provoking appalling levels of political violence.[3]

In this setting, where all the old sources of stability, community, and meaning are destroyed violently, what remains available to the poor? One answer is clearly the Pentecostal sect. The sect professes to explain all this suffering, while at the same time offering the promise of salvation on the near horizon. The premillennialist, dispensationalist theologies that are dominant in Central America today respond directly to the insecurity, fear, and sense of hopelessness that accompany widespread poverty and political violence. The churches that preach this theology offer a valuable membership to the "born again" person, a special status that is denied all others in society. The large majority of these churches, which are Pentecostal, also offer ample opportunities for affective release to persons who are silenced socially and politically. In other words, Pentecostalism gives the powerless a sense of personal efficacy that they can attain no other way; it liberates them psychologically and emotionally. Finally, there is no overarching bureaucratic authority among Pentecostal churches to control the process by which they spread.

One of the most intriguing features of evangelical growth in Central America today is that it has been as impressive in the revolutionary setting of Nicaragua as in the counterrevolutionary setting of Guatemala and El Salvador. In the latter countries reactionary governments have found the fundamentalists and charismatics congenial because their form of church organization and their theology represent an effective self-disciplining of the poor. Pentecostals, in particular, discipline themselves politically by eschewing political involvement, a posture that serves to reinforce a repressive status quo through acquiescence. We noted earlier in the chapter that the political passivity of evangelicals in the United States was reversed in the 1970s because evangelicals reacted against public policies that were seen as attacks on basic Christian values. Similar conditions have not, up to now, been obtained in Central America, where middle and upper class converts to evangelicalism are not adversely affected by the drift of public policy. (Indeed, there is some evidence that membership in an evangelical church can enhance one's career mobility in such major institutions as the armed forces.) While the lower classes, especially where they are ethnically distinct as in Guatemala, are adversely affected by public policy, they have no effective means of opposition available to them. For these groups, affiliation with an evangelical church may at least provide a margin of physical security.

In Nicaragua under the Sandinistas such sects were more congenial because, in a society that had little to offer the poor in material terms due to the Contra war and the U.S. economic embargo, their members disciplined themselves economically. The Sandinista policy of religious toleration created an open field for evangelical proselytizing in Nicaragua. That activity was reinforced when New Right religious programming and Pentecostal mission efforts were vigorously pushed in Nicaragua as part of the Reagan administration's war against the Sandinista government. The practical effect of such activity was probably felt most keenly in remote rural areas traditionally suspicious of the central government where Contra activity was the strongest.

In Guatemala and El Salvador, as well as in Nicaragua, Pentecostals have tended to support the government passively and the government has generally left them alone, allowing them to do their work of evangelization. That, of course, is the highest priority these groups have, given their premillennialist outlook on the world.

NOTES

1. The "equity" issue has been a dominant theme in the development literature for two decades. The phenomenon of rapid economic growth *and* increasing immiseration among the poorest sectors is found not only in Central America but throughout the Third World. For a good overview see Wilber and Weaver (1979).

2. For a concise analysis of the church's thinking at Vatican II and Medellín, see Dorr (1983: 117–38, 157–62).

3. The so-called "low-intensity" wars of the 1980s, which have cost more than 100,000 Guatemalans, Salvadorans, and Nicaraguans their lives, are the most obvious illustration of this point (see *NACLA Report on the Americas,* 1986).

10

ADVOCATING NONVIOLENT DIRECT ACTION IN LATIN AMERICA: THE ANTECEDENTS AND EMERGENCE OF SERPAJ

Ronald Pagnucco and John D. McCarthy

The modern world system is characterized by sovereign, territorial nation-states. But, while the nation-state may be the most important actor in the world system, there are other important transnational actors that link people with one another across countries and that may have an important influence on the domestic and international behavior of those nation-states.

Historically, religious organizations and churches have been transnational in scope and have been important transnational actors in many circumstances. In the twentieth century the growing interdependence of the world system, driven by developments in communication and transportation technologies among other factors, has facilitated the phenomenal growth of other transnational organizations. In 1909 there were only 176 international nongovernmental organizations (INGOs); by 1985 there were 18,000 (Boulding, 1988). Although the structure and goals of INGOs vary, many focus on fostering international understanding and peace, development and human rights, and are organized into national sections with local chapters. These organizations provide information on international issues to their members, facilitate international exchanges, and sometimes mobilize their members to take action on common problems (Boulding, 1988; Willetts, 1982a, 1982b). We call INGOs with the aforementioned goals and activities *transnational social movement organizations* (TSMOs). Amnesty International, the Fellowship of Reconciliation (FOR), and Servicio Paz y Justicia en América Latina (SERPAJ-AL) (Service for Peace and Justice in Latin America), the foci of this chapter, are examples of TSMOs.

Such transnational actors, especially those with networks in the resource-rich countries of the North, can play important roles as midwives to developing social movement organizations (SMOs) in the resource-poor South. Churches and TSMOs can provide financial assistance, skilled individuals, bodies of knowledge and experience, and international contacts to resource-poor social justice activists in politically repressive nation-states.

As we shall see, the Protestant and Roman Catholic churches and the Christian pacifist Fellowship of Reconciliation played major roles in the emergence and development of SERPAJ, itself a TSMO. Like the FOR, SERPAJ grew out of a transnational network largely composed of religious activists, many of whom were church professionals. European and U.S. FOR activists, together with indigenous Latin American religious activists, created SERPAJ and developed the philosophy and tactics of nonviolent direct action—a tradition that was, for the most part, absent from Latin America. As we shall see, SERPAJ's transnational web of support was important for its very survival.

Although there are other Latin American groups committed to nonviolence (C. Maciel, unpublished), SERPAJ-AL is without question the most important organized advocate of principled nonviolent direct action in Latin America.[1] Formally constituted in 1974 at a meeting in Medellín, Colombia, its General Coordinator from its founding until 1986 was the internationally famous 1980 Nobel Peace Prize winner, Adolfo Pérez Esquivel. A cadre rather than a membership SMO, SERPAJ acts to coordinate and communicate among groups seeking progressive change, and it provides training in the theory, philosophy, and methods of nonviolence. A faith-based TSMO, with chapters in several Latin American countries and ties with supportive SMOs and churches in Europe and North America, SERPAJ is part of a transnational web of interaction that enables it to mobilize resources beyond the confines of any particular nation-state. Formed out of a transnational network of religious activists, SERPAJ differs from some TSMOs in that it was not the result of "a small number of individuals coming together in order to put pressure on their own government and then later deciding to engage in transnational contacts bypassing the government" (Willetts, 1982: 179).

We will examine how this organization was built, noting especially some important antecedents; how the theory and philosophy of nonviolent direct action, relatively unknown in Latin America, came to be adopted by SERPAJ; and how this small organization was able to survive and successfully advocate human rights while operating under repressive military dictatorships. This chapter begins with a discussion of several theoretical issues central to our analysis of SERPAJ. We then sketch the emergence of the FOR and its work in Latin America and describe the sequence of events that directly led to the founding of SERPAJ. After characterizing its strategy and structure generally, we conclude by illustrating many of our points in an account of the premier SERPAJ chapter, SERPAJ-Argentina.

Until recently a social movement in the Latin American context referred to "large organizations calling upon a nationwide constituency and aiming to influence government policy along the lines of social class" (Lehmann, 1990: 149). However, the last few decades have seen the emergence of many new social movement forms, such as ecclesiastical base communities (*comunidades eclesiales de base*, or CEBs), neighborhood organizations, women's groups, and human rights organizations (Jelín, 1987; Mainwaring and Viola, 1984; Slater, 1985). Both Latin American and North American observers of these new movements have struggled to find ways of understanding them, realizing, as had their European counterparts, the inadequacy of traditional class-based approaches to explanations. The new social movement theory, popular among European and Latin American analysts of movements, emphasizes identity transformation; decentralized, participatory movement group structures; and cultural and noninstitutionalized forms of collective action in its framework for investigation (see Jelín, 1985; 1987; Mainwaring and Viola, 1984; Slater, 1985; but see also Eckstein, 1989).

We depend instead on resource mobilization theory (Jenkins, 1983; Zald and McCarthy, 1987), which provides the framework for our analysis of the emergence and development of SERPAJ as a TSMO. We will focus on several factors: preexisting networks and organizations; the religious and political opportunity structures; the sources of tangible resources (i.e., people, finances, meeting space), and intangible resources (skills, commitment, legitimacy); the processes by which these resources were coordinated, developed, and mobilized; and the cultural opportunity structure (e.g., the values and beliefs of the population that activists are trying to reach).

We will also examine the processes of tactical choice and tactical diffusion by which SERPAJ came to adopt the philosophy and practice of nonviolent direct action, which was relatively unknown in Latin America. Collective actors typically draw upon a rather narrow selection of tactics when they act. Such tactical repertoires (Tilly, 1979) change slowly, with communities sometimes trying new forms while at the same time letting others fall into disuse. Many factors may influence the choice of particular tactics: organizational characteristics, such as degree of formalization and centralization; goals, such as policy change, structural change, or individual transformation; available resources, such as number of members and amount of finances; ideology or belief system; and the political opportunity structure, which includes the institutionalized means of political participation, degree of state repression, and the configuration of political alliances (McAdam, 1982; Tarrow, 1988). There is no scholarly consensus on the role these factors play in tactical choice (see Freeman, 1979; Staggenborg, 1991). However, there is some evidence that faith-based protest groups may be more likely than others to use nonviolent direct action (see Epstein, 1991). This stems from the religious values of personal responsibility, individual transformation, moral witness, and the sacredness of life that many such groups embody (Holsworth, 1989).

Coherent repertoires of tactics that are embedded in abstract webs of justification that rationalize their use and their harmony with one another probably depend more on face-to-face communication and written texts than on the mass media for their diffusion than do the simpler and more easily mimicked tactical elements such as the sit-in (McAdam, 1983). So in our search for clues to the diffusion of the nonviolent direct action repertoire we will be especially alert to transnational communication networks.

ANTECEDENTS TO SERPAJ

The Fellowship of Reconciliation, a relatively small group of Christian pacifists in the United States and Europe, played an important role in the development of SERPAJ and the spread of the philosophy and techniques of nonviolent action in Latin America. Largely Protestant and not formally a part of any church, the FOR used its international network of ministers, missionaries, and lay people to advocate Christian pacifism and nonviolence in various countries. In the United States during the 1940s, 1950s, and 1960s, some FOR members worked with African-American civil rights leaders to develop nonviolent direct action techniques that successfully challenged racial injustices. In the 1960s and 1970s, FOR members as social movement "midwives," so to speak, brought to Latin America the lessons they learned from the civil rights movement.

The Emergence and Spread of FOR

The International Fellowship of Reconciliation (IFOR) and its national chapter in the United States, the American Fellowship of Reconciliation (AFOR), both had important roles in the developments that eventually led to the founding of SERPAJ. For many years representatives from both these groups had worked with limited success to plant seeds of the pacifist principles of nonviolent direct action across the nations of Central and South America.

The IFOR had its beginning on the eve of World War I in Europe, although it was formally established in 1919 at a meeting in Bilthoven, Holland. On August 3, 1914, Friedrich Siegmund-Shultze, the German

Kaiser's Christian pacifist chaplain, and Henry Hodgkin, the secretary of foreign mission enterprises for the British Society of Friends (Quakers), made a pledge in a Cologne railroad station to extend the "bonds of Christian love unbroken across the frontier" (quoted in Barton, 1974: 1). Both men had been involved in the Church Peace Union and the World Alliance for Promoting International Friendship through the Churches. In December 1914, through the efforts of Hodgkin, the British Fellowship of Reconciliation, the first national chapter, was born.

The FOR came to America through the efforts of Hodgkin and some of his British associates. Hodgkin was part of a trans-Atlantic church network that facilitated his efforts to organize an American branch. With the help of American pacifist churchmen, such as the Episcopalian priest John Nevin Sayre, the AFOR was founded in November 1915.

In October 1919, fifty Christian pacifists from ten countries, including FOR members from Britain and America, gathered in Bilthoven, Holland, and formally organized the IFOR. The IFOR and AFOR immediately began an energetic campaign of international organizing. The attempts to organize FOR chapters in Latin America were just one part of these efforts.

The founders of the AFOR did not intend to establish a radical, action-oriented group; it began primarily as an informal fellowship of Christian pacifists motivated by spiritual concerns (Barton, 1974). The FOR's first statement of purpose stated that the

distinctive note of the Fellowship is its repudiation of war and commitment to a way of life creative of brotherhood. . . . Membership implies such a dedication to the practice of the principle of love as the inviable law of personal relationships and the transforming power of human life that any use or countenance of the war method by those who belong is impossible. (Quoted in Barton, 1974: 3)

Although in the 1920s some FOR leaders began to take an interest in Mohandas K. Gandhi's nonviolent direct action campaigns, most FOR members in the United States and Great Britain continued to have a passive view of nonviolence, eschewing even nonviolent conflict and confrontation (Sharp, 1979). However, several FOR members, including Howard Thurman, Muriel Lester, and Richard Gregg, went to India to learn what Gandhi was doing. They returned as ardent supporters of Gandhi; Gregg's *The Power of Non-Violence* (1934), based on his four-year experience in India, became the bible for such FOR advocates of nonviolent direct action as James Farmer and Rev. Glenn Smiley. It was not until the 1940s that some pacifists in the AFOR began actively experimenting with aggressive nonviolent tactics. With the support of some important AFOR leaders, black FOR member Farmer, a friend of Howard Thurman, helped organize a national interracial nonviolent action organization, the Congress of Racial Equality (CORE), and recruited many local FOR members into the organization (Chatfield, 1971). CORE and some members of the FOR continued to innovate in the use of unruly nonviolent tactics for civil rights. For some FOR members the philosophy and technique of nonviolent action was becoming a central part of the organization's message. The FOR was literally becoming a midwife—assisting the birth of nonviolent collective action as it provided nonviolence trainers and organizers. In 1956 the leader of the Montgomery Improvement Association (MIA), the Rev. Martin Luther King, Jr., sought the assistance of AFOR's Rev. Smiley and Bayard Rustin as his group planned and implemented the famous Montgomery bus boycott (A. Morris, 1984). Reflecting on his work with Martin Luther King, Jr., Smiley observed that his role was "to carry the mail of the organization [e.g., the FOR] and that mail was the method of nonviolence" (quoted in Morris, 1984: 160). That mail would also be carried to Latin America. The successful experience of the civil rights movement, the writings of King, and the Latin American organizing efforts of Smiley and other FOR civil rights veterans would play a role in the development of SERPAJ and its adoption of nonviolent direct action.

Early Advocacy of Nonviolence in Latin America

The AFOR was active in Central and South America as early as 1919. A driving force behind these efforts by AFOR was the Rev. John Nevin Sayre, an Episcopalian priest who helped establish AFOR and IFOR and who was a key leader in both organizations for nearly six decades. According to Sayre's (1961) invaluable summary of FOR activities concerning Latin America from 1919 to 1960, the first South American FOR group was formed in Montevideo, Uruguay, in 1941 through the help of the Methodist church network. At the prompting of FOR member the Rev. Earl Smith, an American Methodist missionary in Montevideo, Sayre arranged for Muriel Lester of London, Travelling Secretary of the IFOR, and Margaret Campbell of the AFOR, to make a South American tour. Smith arranged their schedule. Lester and Campbell held meetings, developed two prayer schools, and had many person-to-person contacts in Peru, Chile, Argentina, and Uruguay. With the help of Smith and the Uruguayan Methodist Bishop Enrique Balloch, Lester and Campbell organized in Montevideo the first South American FOR group. Lester and Campbell then went to Buenos Aires, where they organized another FOR group (Sayre, 1961: 2; see also Deats, 1991).

Other FOR organizers, including Sayre, continued to make short trips to Latin America throughout the 1940s and 1950s. However, all these FOR organizers were Protestant, a number being Methodist, and worked largely through the Protestant church network. While there was a significant and growing Protestant population in Latin America, the countries were overwhelmingly Roman Catholic. Sayre saw the difficulties this might pose for the organization of FOR and reported to the IFOR North American Committee in 1944 after his visit to Mexico: "The outstanding weakness of our position is that we have no Roman Catholic assistance for the planning and development of pacifist work in a predominantly Catholic country Mexico" (Sayre, 1961: 3). Commenting that this statement applies to the FOR throughout Latin America "right up to the present day [February 28, 1961]," (Sayre, 1961: 3), Sayre saw the need to have Roman Catholic organizers sent to Latin America to help recruit Catholics to the FOR and its pacifist message, otherwise the pattern of nearly total Protestant membership in Latin American FOR chapters—a pattern also present in Great Britain and North America—would continue (Sayre, 1961: 7). In his report Sayre recommended that as soon as possible the IFOR send from Europe to Latin America two accomplished Roman Catholic advocates of nonviolence, Jean and Hildegard Goss-Mayr. This was insightful advice, as the Goss-Mayrs went on to play a crucial role in the emergence of SERPAJ. The Goss-Mayrs went to Latin America in 1962; they were the first non–Latin American FOR organizers to make an extended, concerted effort for active nonviolence in Latin America. Although they were executive secretaries of the IFOR, they did not go with the exclusive intention of organizing FOR chapters (although they did organize several), but primarily to try to convert the Roman Catholic Church in Latin America to active nonviolence, which could, in turn, be an instrument for nonviolent liberation of the oppressed in Latin America (Chartier, 1980).

The Goss-Mayrs especially wanted to recruit the clergy to the creed of active nonviolence, believing that their leadership was uniquely important in Latin America. Once recruited, this cadre of priests and ministers would be able to reach people at all levels of society (Goss-Mayr and Goss-Mayr, 1966). The Goss-Mayrs were very aware that, as Europeans and foreigners, their ideas concerning nonviolence could not be imposed from outside; they recognized that all they could do was help sow the seed, give the example and the initiative. From their perspective it was absolutely essential that Latin Americans take leadership roles in the nonviolent movement and adapt nonviolence to the concrete situations in their countries.

The articulated, active nonviolence advocated by the Goss-Mayrs was, indeed, on the whole, relatively new for Latin America, although peasants, Indians, and others had nonviolently resisted oppression for centuries and there had been some nonviolent "civic strikes" attempting to remove dictators from power (see Eckstein, 1989; Parkman, 1990). On the whole, these forms of nonviolent action were pragmatic, not rooted in a philosophy and general strategy of nonviolent direct action. Richard

Chartier, a Methodist missionary and FOR member in Argentina from 1959 to 1973, described the Latin American situation:

For years nonviolence was virtually unknown—restricted to a few familiar with its theory and practice elsewhere—or regarded as alien or irrelevant to the harsh realities of Latin America. For many, it connoted passivism, emphasis on democratic and decent deportment privately and publicly, mild reformism or the resolution of insignificant conflicts. (Chartier, 1980: 9)

Thus, before the Goss-Mayrs came in the 1960s, nonviolence was virtually unknown in Roman Catholic circles (Cornell, 1977). Even those few groups in Latin America committed to nonviolence did not advocate direct action. FOR groups throughout Latin America tended to have a more passive, nonconfrontational view of nonviolence (Chartier, 1980; McManus, 1991a). In this they resembled the orientation of many AFOR members, most notably Sayre. The predominantly Catholic Lanza del Vasto groups throughout Latin America practiced a spiritual nonviolence and "tend[ed] to withdraw themselves from life" (Goss-Mayr and Goss-Mayr, 1962b: 2). The reconceptualization of nonviolence taking place in the United States, largely under the impetus of the civil rights movement, had yet to take place to any significant degree in Latin America.

In the course of their efforts in Latin America, Jean and Hildegard Goss-Mayr interacted person-to-person with bishops, priests, and ministers; spoke in seminaries, both Catholic and Protestant, and in various intellectual and labor groups, both leftist and conservative. They also met with various lay leaders and groups such as Catholic Action, an organization established to promulgate Catholic social teachings that had chapters throughout Latin America and that was especially important in the Brazilian church (Bidegain, 1985; Chartier, 1980). The Goss-Mayrs organized study groups and training seminars on nonviolence and went to groups involved in resistance efforts, such as land occupations and strikes, to talk about nonviolent techniques. Among the bishops and church officials they met with was Dom Helder Cámara, former national chaplain of Brazil's Catholic Action, when he was an auxiliary bishop working with the poor in Rio de Janeiro. According to Cornell (1977) and Chartier (1980), Jean and Hildegard helped convert Cámara to nonviolence through the writings of Martin Luther King. Cámara was to become one of the most prominent nonviolent leaders in Latin America and eventually Archbishop of Recife, Brazil.

However, not everyone was receptive to the Goss-Mayrs' message of active nonviolence. Just War theology, which some used to justify revolution (Goss-Mayr and Goss-Mayr, 1962a), dominated Catholic thought and the Latin American church was becoming polarized between conservatives and leftists. Latin America was in a revolutionary situation. But the Goss-Mayrs worked undeterred, trying to convert conservative and leftist alike to the Gospel message of justice and nonviolence.

THREE STAGES OF SERPAJ'S DEVELOPMENT

We have seen the important role that the Rev. Earl Smith, Jean and Hildegard Goss-Mayr, and the AFOR and IFOR played in laying the foundations of SERPAJ. We can now investigate the sequence of events that directly led to the founding of SERPAJ. This sequence can be divided into three stages: (1) 1966–1971: outreach and coordination; (2) 1971–1974: the founding of a transitional organization; (3) 1974–1985: the establishment and growth of SERPAJ (see SERPAJ-AL, 1987; Goss-Mayr and Goss-Mayr, 1984; Muñoz, Maciel, and de Souza, 1986). In each of these stages there was significant participation by leaders of various North American and European nonviolent groups as well as Latin Americans. There was also significant participation by church professionals, including the clergy.

Stage 1: Outreach and Coordination (1966–1971)

While the FOR in Latin America had their own limited continental meetings for several years, the first major gathering on nonviolence in Latin America was a FOR "consultation" held in 1966 at Montevideo, Uruguay, followed by a "continental meeting" in 1971 at Alajuela, Costa Rica. These early meetings were "concerned with adopting the intellectual tradition of nonviolence and pacifism received from Europe and the United States" while paying equal attention to the Latin American situation (Antoine, 1983: 8). The Goss-Mayrs and Rev. Earl Smith played important roles in these meetings (Cornell, 1977).

Although the "consultation" at Montevideo was organized by the Latin American FOR, it was supported by other groups. The meeting was largely Protestant, though there was some Roman Catholic involvement. Among those speaking was Lanza del Vasto and AFOR member James Lawson, a Methodist minister and associate of Rev. King, who gave the keynote address on "Nonviolence: The Revolution that Matters." King sent a message of support (see South American Committee of the IFOR, 1966). Among the Latin Americans present was Adolfo Obieta, who in 1973 would help Adolfo Pérez Esquivel start the newsletter *Paz y Justicia*, and FOR member Herberto Sein, a Mexican Quaker who worked with AFOR civil rights veterans Glenn Smiley and Brady Tyson in Justice-Action-Peace Latin America (JAPLA).[2] Significantly, the participants at the meeting resolved to actively reach out to other groups and to collaborate with them if possible. Various organizing efforts were made

134 Ronald Pagnucco and John D. McCarthy

during this period to spread the message of active nonviolence and to build continental and global ties among advocates of nonviolence. For example, in March 1970, Tyson, a dynamic Methodist minister who had been a missionary in Brazil, an associate of Dr. Martin Luther King, Jr., a SCLC executive board member, and an FOR member, introduced the Rev. Ralph Abernathy, who succeeded King as head of the SCLC, to Dom Helder Cámara in Recife, Brazil. Together Cámara and Abernathy issued the "Declaration of Recife" calling for a worldwide movement of nonviolent protest against the unjust structures that maintain poverty, racism, and war, concluding with the statement that "we look forward to other contacts with each other, and with others of other nations" (Tyson, 1970: 722). During this first stage we see such civil rights movement veterans as Tyson, Smiley, and Lafayette contributing to the nonviolent movement in Latin America through JAPLA. (Tyson would continue to play a role in all three stages.) The Goss-Mayrs, Smith, and others continued their organizing efforts, contributing to the success of the meeting in Alajuela where a new organization that superseded the FOR was founded.

Stage 2: The Founding of a Transitional Organization (1971–1973)

The next continental meeting took place in 1971 in Alajuela, Costa Rica. Jean and Hildegard Goss-Mayr helped organize the conference, and, again, international networks were important. Smiley helped with the program, invitations, and financing of the Alajuela meeting (Goss-Mayr and Goss-Mayr, 1971), and he attended the meeting, as did Lafayette, a staff member of SCLC who had been an early leader in SNCC. At this meeting, representatives from groups working nonviolently for change in Latin America, including such church leaders as Dom Helder Cámara, Dom Antonio Fragosa, Msgr. Valencio Cano, and Bishop Federico Pagura, met for the first time (Deming, 1978).

A new Latin American nonviolent organization was born at this meeting. Named "Servicio para la Acción Liberadora en América Latina—Orientación No-Violenta," this continental organization, the precursor of SERPAJ-AL, was comprised of FOR members and others. Smith was chosen to be the coordinator. Servicio was not created to be a mass movement organization, but, rather, a service group that would provide information and help other groups in communication, planning, coordination, and nonviolent training (Muñoz, Maciel, and de Souza, 1986). To help fulfill these tasks, Servicio established a newsletter, *Boletin del Servicio para la Acción Liberadora en América Latina Orientación No-Violenta*, with Smith as editor. Organizing and coordinating efforts were expanded, with the goal of developing a stronger continental organization.

Stage 3: The Establishment and Growth of SERPAJ (1974–1985)

It was during the continental meeting at Medellín, Colombia, in 1974 that SERPAJ was formally created. Smith and Hildegard Goss-Mayr organized the meeting. A few months before the meeting, Hildegard made an extensive trip during which she visited almost all of the delegates to the meeting. Both she and Smith raised enough money to pay the travel expenses and living expenses of all who needed help. Richard H. Post of the U.S. War Resisters' League (WRL) wrote an invaluable report on the Medellín meeting (unpublished meeting minutes). Both the IFOR and the WRL were among the endorsers of the meeting. The 1974 meeting had a distinctly Latin American character, and the newly established SERPAJ became a truly Latin American organization.

Only Latin Americans could vote at the meeting. According to Post: "Conscientization was the watchword of the conference. All the delegates were familiar with the works of Paulo Freire, whose classic 'Pedagogy of the Oppressed' . . . became the conference bible" (Post, n.d.: 2). The churches provided much support; the meeting was held in the Roman Catholic major seminary in Medellín, and a large number of Latin American church professionals participated:

The delegates included twelve Catholic clergy—two of them bishops and a third an archbishop—and six Protestant clergy—one [an] active bishop, another a retired bishop. Six of the fourteen women are nuns. Some ten percent are engaged in social service for Indians. About one third are poor tenant farmers (share croppers) or urban industrial workers, all with some experience in nonviolent actions but none of them trained in theory. (Post, n.d.: 3)

In all, some forty-eight delegates from four Central American and eight South American countries participated. Four representatives from the United States and ten European delegates attended, continuing the invaluable transnational connections that would provide increasingly important support for SERPAJ.

THE OPERATIONAL STRUCTURE AND STRATEGIC APPROACH OF SERPAJ

The basic structure of SERPAJ was established at Medellín. Although there has been continual modification of SERPAJ's structure since its founding, its basic organizational features, as well as its strategic approach, has remained essentially the same throughout the 1970s and 1980s.

SERPAJ is a loosely structured, a relatively decentralized, and an informal transnational organization. The organizational form adopted by SERPAJ is not unique and bears much resemblance to those of many of the SMOs that nurtured it into existence. There is no rigid hierarchy or formal leadership structure. The general coordinator is limited in his or her power. National chapters have their own structures that vary from country to country. "Lines of action," providing a general orientation rather than concrete goals, are established consensually at the continental meetings, leaving national chapters broad discretion about which of the issues will be emphasized and exactly how the policies will be carried out.

SERPAJ is an autonomous organization, not directly tied to the church, political parties, or any other organization, even though it draws heavily on its links to the Roman Catholic Church in many countries. In this regard it is a relatively new organizational form in Latin America. Its autonomy has been important in allowing SERPAJ to maintain the integrity of its tactical message. Also, because SERPAJ is not bound to any special interests, it is better able to function as a mediating and coordinating organization (Pérez Esquivel, Personal Communication, 1985).

Attempting to be a catalyst of nonviolent change, SERPAJ functions much as a vanguard elite (Pérez Esquivel, Personal Communication, 1985). The national secretariats of SERPAJ typically are composed of a few paid staff, along with church-affiliated social activists such as priests, and volunteers. The typical national secretariat had ten to fifteen members. Several chapters, such as those in Brazil, Uruguay, and Chile, have priests in important leadership positions, although SERPAJ-Argentina, perhaps because of the unique situation of the church in that country, does not have any priests in prominent positions. Thus the actual number of people working for SERPAJ is small. However, SERPAJ was not intended to be a mass membership organization but, rather, a cadre service organization of *animadores*, or facilitators. Much like its predecessor, Servicio para Liberadora, SERPAJ helps nonviolent groups communicate with each other and publicizes and documents their actions; it organizes solidarity and support actions for these groups, organizes nonviolent training sessions, and provides literature on nonviolence; it helps mobilize groups for nonviolent action; and it helps organize new groups (see Schravesande, 1981: 3–8).

Mainwaring and Viola provide an excellent summary of the role of the animador as opposed to that of the *dirigente*, or director:

They attempt to develop leadership as *animador* (facilitator) and supersede leadership as *dirigente* (director). The animador stimulates autonomous popular action and mobilization. The logic of the social movement is not pre-established according to the animador's orientation. The animador respects and values the logic of the movement and attempts to establish a relation of mutuality and respect with the members of the movement. By contrast, the dirigente attempts to control the nature of popular mobilization and to orient this mobilization towards his/her objectives. The dirigente believes in expertise and technocracy. (Mainwaring and Viola, 1984: 37)

The animador tries to stimulate the full participation of group members and, rather than providing the answers, asks the right questions (McManus, 1991b). This approach is supposed to empower people, to help them build the organization and acquire the skills they need to be able to act on their own. The animador does not recruit members into SERPAJ per se, although the groups are invited to continue to work with SERPAJ.

The Transnational Dimension of SERPAJ

As has been made clear, SERPAJ has had very close ties with European and U.S. groups since its beginning, principally with FOR groups (AFOR and IFOR). SERPAJ-Europe was organized by Jean and Hildegard Goss-Mayr with the help of the IFOR. According to its 1984 yearly report, SERPAJ-Europe consisted of a variety of groups in fourteen countries, "most of them linked in one way or another to the Fellowship of Reconciliation, . . . the War Resisters International, or/and Pax Christi—in so far as they are interested in . . . SERPAJ" (SERPAJ-Europe, 1984: 1). The organization provides the bulk of SERPAJ-AL's financial budget and informs Europeans about the Latin American movement through speakers, literature, and its newsletter *INFO*, established in 1980. SERPAJ-Europe also organizes solidarity and support actions for SERPAJ-AL.

SERPAJ-AL relations with U.S. groups have been of a different form—there is no SERPAJ-U.S. for example. However, close ties are maintained with the AFOR—throughout the 1980s, Tyson was the official AFOR liaison with SERPAJ-AL—as well as through AFOR members such as Richard Chartier, and the AFOR Task Force on Latin America and the Caribbean, founded in 1983. Likewise SERPAJ-AL has close ties with the Resource Center on Nonviolence (which has several AFOR members on its staff), as well as the Committee in Solidarity with Latin American Nonviolent Movements (CISLANM), founded by two AFOR members in 1982 after a meeting with Pérez Esquivel. These U.S. groups provide information and educational materials to North Americans about Latin American nonviolent movements in general, as well as SERPAJ-AL in particular, organize support actions, and have helped arrange meetings for SERPAJ-AL members in the United States; however, U.S. groups have not provided SERPAJ with substantial financial resources.

The modern world system is characterized by sovereign, territorial

nation-states; the degree of governance provided by international institutions, most notably the United Nations, is minimal. INGOs, while providing "unofficial" linkages among citizens in these nation-states, are
limited in their abilities to directly influence national policies. Yet, indirectly, they can influence political leaders in nation-states by appealing
their local cases to international bodies, thereby seeking legitimacy for
their claims by going over the heads of those who control their own
states (see Nagel and Olzak, 1982; Smith, 1991). An exclusively state-
centric model is inadequate for analyzing SERPAJ; while national chapters engaged in various activities in their respective territorial nation-
states, SERPAJ actors regularly interacted with actors outside their state.
These transnational ties were crucial for the very survival of SERPAJ.
As Mainwaring and Viola (1984:30) write of human rights groups, including SERPAJ, in Argentina: "Without international support for the
human rights organizations, the Argentine state could have—and probably would have—destroyed the human rights organizations. Thus the
limits to state terror were set in part by the international community to
which the regime itself aspired to become a more central part." They
go on to note that "a movement with relatively few participants had a
significant international impact and became the major challenge to a
regime with an immense capacity to control civil society" (Mainwaring
and Viola, 1984: 31).

SERPAJ as Movement Midwife

Aldon Morris (1984) coined the phrase "movement halfway house" to
characterize the role of AFOR and SMOs like it in the 1960s civil rights
movement. SMOs of this type, he argued, specialize in aiding other
groups that are fighting for their own rights:

A movement halfway house is an established group or organization that is only
partially integrated into the larger society because its participants are actively
involved in efforts to bring about a desired change in society.... [They] develop
a battery of social change resources, such as skilled activists, tactical knowledge,
media contacts, workshops, knowledge of past movements and a vision of a
future society. What they lack is broad support and a visible platform. (Morris,
1984: 139–40)

We prefer instead the imagery of the term *movement midwife* since it
more clearly conveys the nature of the aid that such groups provide—
skill and knowledge to facilitate creations that are ultimately out of their
hands. SERPAJ has functioned as a movement midwife, as we have seen
above and will illustrate in more detail below. It has created a distinctive
form of midwifery adapted to its cultural and political context. The

development and legitimation of the role of animador beyond the efforts of SERPAJ no doubt facilitated its work much in the same way that Marxism paved the way for a central role for intellectuals in the struggles of the working classes. Yet the activists of SERPAJ, as we have seen, do not envision a long-term leadership role for themselves in the movements they encourage and support.

SERPAJ AND THE LATIN AMERICAN CHURCH AND STATE

For most of its 500-year history, the Roman Catholic Church in Latin America has identified with dominant elites, although there have been some exceptions to this pattern (see Salinas, 1990; Smith, 1991). Social, economic, and political changes in the nineteenth and twentieth centuries somewhat diminished the political power of the church, which for centuries had been a key actor in the power elite in Latin America. Commenting on religion and politics in contemporary Latin America, Thomas G. Sanders observed that "the principal political actors are political parties, the military, and economic groups. Religion plays a role, but a secondary one" (Sanders, 1987: 115). The church's important, if not central, role in Latin American society and politics was amplified during the 1960s, 1970s, and 1980s as a wave of repressive military regimes hit many Latin American countries. Religious activists, and in some cases church leaders, became vocal critics of regime repression as political parties, labor unions, and other possible sources of organized opposition were silenced. Broader changes in the church contributed to the emergence of this new religious activism on behalf of human rights.

Vatican Council II (1962–1965) marked an important turning point in church-society relations, calling for greater efforts to achieve political, social, and economic justice on the part of the church. The Latin American bishops responded to this call in a widely known conference in Medellín, Colombia, in 1968 (see Smith, 1991). The bishops produced a document condemning the violence of social structures that doom many to misery, criticizing the economic dependency of the developing world on the developed world, and supporting the newly emerging ecclesiastical base communities (CEBs), including many small lay-led groups of poor people who support each other and pray and read the Bible together, as well as several other typical forms (Smith, 1991). The document put the church in solidarity with the poor and oppressed, and it opened up the church to greater opportunities for lay leadership. These changes created "religious opportunity" akin to the political opportunity that scholars of movements in rich nations view as increasingly important to understanding their emergence and vitality (Smith, 1991).

In a variety of ways organized religious structures may facilitate social movements.

It was in this new context that SERPAJ was formed. The importance of the Medellín CELAM conference for the reorientation of the Latin American church toward social justice advocacy was summed up best by Pérez Esquivel when he said, "we are all the children of Medellín" (quoted in Antoine, 1983: 4). However, not all of the national episcopates stood with the oppressed and their middle-class supporters, and some doubt the depth of commitment to liberal, individual human rights of those that did (Garrett, 1988).

The twentieth century has seen a cycle of military dictatorships interspersed by periods of less oppressive governance in most of the countries of Latin America (Skidmore and Smith, 1989). The first eight national chapters of SERPAJ, established between 1974 and 1982, were formed in countries with military dictatorships. Our case study, SERPAJ-Argentina, was established in 1974; its predecessor was formed in 1973 during a brief turbulent period of civilian rule between the military regimes of 1966–1973 and 1976–1983. In general, the military dictatorships eliminated or severely repressed the civil associations that might have opposed them, though the degree of repression varied by country. Under such circumstances the church hierarchy in some countries came to actively oppose the dictatorships, whereas in others, such as Argentina, it did not.

SERPAJ-Argentina

The development of SERPAJ in Argentina has a special place in the history of SERPAJ-AL as its key organizer, Adolfo Pérez Esquivel, recognized for his work, was elected general coordinator of SERPAJ-AL at its formal establishment in 1974. In the 1960s Pérez Esquivel joined one of del Vasto's "Friends of the Ark" groups in Buenos Aires and met and befriended del Vasto. There were many such groups in Argentina, and del Vasto visited Argentina regularly (Chartier, 1980; McManus, 1991b; Pérez Esquivel, Personal Communication, 1985). Committed to Gandhian nonviolence, the groups were small, predominantly Catholic, and very spiritual, and they fostered prayer and study rather than engaging in nonviolent direct action (Chartier, 1980; McManus, 1991a). Pérez Esquivel also met and befriended Jean and Hildegard Goss-Mayr in the 1960s and became a part of the network that they were building (Maciel, 1986).

In 1972, Pérez Esquivel, Chartier, and others participated in a public fast to protest the increasing violence of the left and right in Argentina. Perceiving a need for a publication to inform Argentines and other Latin Americans about nonviolence and the various nonviolent efforts throughout the world, in April of 1973 Pérez Esquivel, with a team of five assistants including Adolfo Obieta, a Catholic Friends of the Ark member, began publishing the monthly newsletter *Paz y Justicia: Acción No-Violenta Latinoamericana*—hereafter called *Paz* (Pérez Esquivel, Personal Communication, 1985; see also *Paz*, April 1973). Pérez Esquivel's group in Argentina at this time was called "Acción No-Violenta Latinoamérica." This group cooperated with the Friends of the Ark in Buenos Aires as well as the local FOR chapter. The Friends of the Ark have a place of prominence in the 1973–1974 issues of *Paz* and clearly played an important role in the developing nonviolent community in Buenos Aires and in the emergence of SERPAJ-Argentina.

Among the broad range of issues addressed in the 1973–1974 issues of *Paz* were the right to conscientious objection in Argentina; the ecology; human rights; economic development; French nuclear testing in the Pacific; and Argentina and nuclear weapons. The newsletter also carried stories about peace groups and nonviolent campaigns in numerous countries, listing the names and addresses of groups throughout the world. It also had essays on nonviolence by Europeans, North Americans, and Latin Americans. In 1974 when SERPAJ was formally established, *Paz* became its official publication, merging with the *Boletin* edited by Earl Smith in Montevideo, Uruguay.

Besides publishing *Paz*, Acción was involved in other activities. In one of the first major campaigns noted in the newsletter, Acción, the Friends, and the local FOR issued a statement protesting France's planned nuclear test in the Pacific (see *Paz*, August 1973). On August 3, 1973, Acción and the Friends, but not the FOR, sponsored a march in front of the French embassy to protest the nuclear test. Nine of the protestors, including Pérez Esquivel, were arrested by the Argentine federal police.

As can be seen, the precursor to SERPAJ-Argentina was not exclusively a human rights organization but, rather, a group of religious activists committed to nonviolence and pacifism. They addressed many peace and justice issues within the framework of religious, usually Christian, faith. These issues continued to be of interest to all of SERPAJ-AL, although work for human rights, the source of SERPAJ's and Pérez Esquivel's fame, became a more central concern. However, Pérez Esquivel traveled to Europe and North America to talk about disarmament and conditions in Latin America and was known to peace activists before the 1976 coup. These contacts, already evident in the 1973 issues of *Paz*, were to prove invaluable.

As noted, the Argentine church hierarchy was quite conservative politically and theologically (Lehmann, 1990; Mignone, 1988). The church did not support SERPAJ and may have welcomed its suppression. One significant example of the hierarchy's conservatism occurred in 1975 as the political horizon was growing ever darker. At that time there was a

lack of work in human rights in Argentina (Acuna, Personal Communication, 1985; Pérez Esquivel, Personal Communication, 1985), the only
human rights organization was the Communist-dominated Argentine
League for Human Rights, founded in 1937. In 1973 civilian rule was
returned when Juan Perón was elected president; however, he gave his
approval to crackdowns on leftist rallies and publications. After he died
in 1974 the vice president, his wife, Isabel, succeeded him, but she was
unable to stop the chaos in Argentina. Many believed that a military
coup was inevitable; the future of human rights looked bleak. In March
1976 the military took power in "Argentina's best predicted coup" (Skidmore and Smith, 1989: 102). According to Carlos Acuna, a SERPAJ-
Argentina staff member, Pérez Esquivel and SERPAJ-Argentina had
proposed in 1975 that the Argentine church strengthen its Justice and
Peace Commission and work on human rights. The bishops refused.
Consequently, in February 1976 Pérez Esquivel helped start the Ecumenical Human Rights Movement, a group of religious and lay workers
from several denominations. At the end of 1975, Pérez Esquivel and
SERPAJ helped start the Permanent Assembly for Human Rights, a
group of trade unionists, politicians, and intellectuals. The strategy of
Pérez Esquivel and SERPAJ was to organize two human rights organizations with different constituencies and to coordinate their activities
with those of SERPAJ (Acuna, 1985; Jelín, 1987).

In the March–May 1976 issue of *Paz*, SERPAJ announced, in the face
of the military junta that seized power on March 24, a two-year campaign
to get the United Nations General Assembly to hold a special convocation
on human rights and to strengthen the enforcement of human rights
throughout the world. Included in the issue was the entire Universal
Declaration of Human Rights and a petition for people to sign and send
to the Secretary General of the United Nations. On March 29, 1976,
Pérez Esquivel began an international tour to drum up support for the
campaign.

In spring 1977, Pérez Esquivel helped form the Mothers of the Plaza
de Mayo, which appeared as a distinct group on April 30, 1977 (Acuna,
1985; Navarro, 1989). The Mothers were women who had children who
"disappeared" and had good reason to believe the government was responsible. They gathered regularly in the plaza and marched in front
of government offices demanding an account of their children. The
Mothers became one of the most celebrated human rights groups in
Latin America, and they continued to march regularly throughout the
tenure of the military regime.

Also in spring 1977, SERPAJ arranged to hold the International Seminar for Training in Nonviolent Action during July in Cuernevaca, Mexico. As Pérez Esquivel prepared to travel throughout Latin America to
recruit participants for the seminar, on April 4 he went to central police

headquarters to get a passport. He was detained. Police told inquiring friends that they did not know where he was. He became one of the "disappeared."

An international campaign for the release of Pérez Esquivel, largely organized by the IFOR, was begun immediately. The response was quick and widespread; many groups in Europe and North America promptly joined the campaign. Amnesty International adopted him as a prisoner of conscience, and when Patricia Derian, the U.S. State Department's human rights coordinator, visited Buenos Aires in August, she formally inquired into Pérez Esquivel's case, signaling the Carter administration's concern. Pérez Esquivel was imprisoned for fourteen months, during which time he was tortured. He was released from prison in June 1978 as the World Cup soccer championship in Argentina drew the international spotlight there. He remained under house arrest for another fourteen months. After his release, he resumed his activities in Buenos Aires as general coordinator of SERPAJ.

It was during Pérez Esquivel's imprisonment that Jim Forest of the international headquarters of IFOR informed Maeread Corrigan and Betty Williams, the 1976 Nobel Peace Prize winners, of Pérez Esquivel's plight. Corrigan and Williams subsequently nominated Pérez Esquivel for the Nobel Peace Prize, which he received in 1980 (Ready, Tyson, and Pagnucco, 1985). Using its international network, SERPAJ arranged for Corrigan to visit Buenos Aires for a one-week speaking tour late in August 1979. At that time she publicly praised Pérez Esquivel for his work and stated that she wanted to see him get the Nobel Peace Prize (see *Paz*, October–November 1979). SERPAJ strategically used its international network to criticize the military regime right before its eyes.

The news of Pérez Esquivel's receipt of the prize was greeted critically by the military regime and ignored or downplayed by the Argentine media. The Argentine Catholic Information Agency simply stated that SERPAJ was not associated with the church's Peace and Justice Commission (Ready, Tyson, and Pagnucco, 1985). In spite of such responses, Pérez Esquivel believed that his receipt of the prize strengthened the social movement for democracy in Argentina and gave him an international forum to talk about human rights abuses in Argentina and Latin America as a whole (Pérez Esquivel, 1985). According to the Argentine sociologist Elizabeth Jelín, the September 1979 visit of a delegation of the Organization of American States' Inter-American Commission on Human Rights, which resulted in criticism of the Argentine regime, along with Pérez Esquivel's receipt of the prize in 1980, helped create in Argentina an opening for public debate of human rights (Jelín, 1987). Part of a trend of awarding the prize to leaders of movements for domestic reform, the Nobel Committee expressed the hope that the award would assist Pérez Esquivel in his work (Ready, Tyson, and Pagnucco,

1985). Pérez Esquivel (1985) and Acuna (1985) both believe that the prize made life safer for SERPAJ-Argentina workers, as well as for other human rights activists. It would appear that the Nobel Committee's hopes were fulfilled.

CONCLUSION

IFOR and AFOR, social movement midwives themselves, were instrumental in nurturing the birth of SERPAJ, the TSMO that became the Latin American midwife to countless new collective efforts to bring about social change across the nations of central and south America. The Protestant and Roman Catholic churches, with their transnational organizational structures and networks, also played an important role in the emergence and growth of SERPAJ. Earlier, less successful efforts by IFOR and AFOR to midwife Latin American social change efforts were superseded by more successful SERPAJ efforts that grafted indigenous ideas, such as that of the animador, to the more abstract commitment to a more aggressive nonviolence in pursuit of justice for oppressed peoples.

The early organizing efforts of the FOR helped provide a transnational base for the eventual emergence of SERPAJ, but it was the work of Jean and Hildegard Goss-Mayr that proved especially valuable. Working in the changing political and religious opportunity structures of the 1960s, the Goss-Mayrs played a very important role in developing the Latin American network of Catholic bishops, priests, nuns, and lay people advocating the philosophy and technique of nonviolent direct action. It was largely this network, combined with the Protestant network cultivated by the FOR, that became the core of SERPAJ.

While SERPAJ mobilized a number of Latin American Catholics to work for political goals, it differed from earlier twentieth-century Catholic political action organizations. One such organization was the Christian Democratic Party, a political party embodying Catholic social principles, with Catholic lay people as political candidates. Established in Latin America during the 1930s, by 1949 the Christian Democratic Party had spread to several countries on the continent, contending for political office when and where it could.

SERPAJ took a different approach, however. Like many of its contemporary Latin American SMOs, SERPAJ strove to maintain its autonomy from political parties, trying to operate outside the realm of partisan politics as it worked for peace, social justice, and the empowerment of the popular classes. Also like its contemporaries, SERPAJ advocated "new ways of engaging in politics" as well as "new forms of social relations and social organization" (Jelín, 1990: 3; see also Lehmann, 1990; Munck, 1989). On the one hand, such an orientation is not surprising, given the limited structure of political opportunity in which SERPAJ was born. On the other hand, SERPAJ's ideology led it to advocate social and political transformation and to reject the centralized structure and dirigente approach of political parties in favor of a decentralized structure and animador approach. Likewise, SERPAJ wanted to preserve the integrity of its message by avoiding its identification with partisan politics. Indeed, given the continuing legacy of manipulation and corruption in Latin American politics, it is not surprising that SERPAJ chose autonomy. A key question for autonomous SMOs such as SERPAJ after the democratic transition was whether or not they could have any political impact without working with a political party in some way (Bidegain, 1985; Jelín, 1987). Under the dictatorships, the channels of political participation were closed; such conditions, combined with SERPAJ's ideology, provided a context for SERPAJ to advocate nonviolent direct action. Now that the political channels have opened somewhat, will SERPAJ adopt more conventional means of political action?

As we have seen, the transnational character of SERPAJ is important in understanding its success in several respects. First, it is based on transnational networks of faith-based communities. Religious communities are naturally transnational. As a result, there is an element of transnational solidarity among them that can be translated into pressure by a faith community, such as AFOR, upon the leaders of one state, such as the United States, to pressure the leaders of another state, such as Argentina, to take action in support of comrades in faith, such as SERPAJ. The advantages of this strategic approach may be summarized as (1) the creation of solidarity across national boundaries, (2) the communication of new ways of doing things, (3) the development of mechanisms of mutual support, (4) the creation of international legitimacy for local claims and action, and (5) international mobilization in support of local activists. The leaders of core states where religious freedom is a norm tend to be diffusely supportive of such freedom for members of such communities in non-core states. Second, the many other advantages of transnational SMO structures that we noted above allowed a cadre organization with few resources made up of a very small number of activists to exert telling pressure on parochial and repressive regimes.

The history of SERPAJ has been brief, tumultuous, and inspiring. It has now entered a new phase in which the tactical advice and principled commitment to nonviolence of its several national groups may become less central to the affairs of their political and social landscapes. The SERPAJ we have described existed mostly under military regimes. The transition to democracy in the mid- to late-eighties has caused changes in the structure and role of SERPAJ, as well as of other social movement organizations (Cardoso, 1989; Jelín, 1986; (Pérez Esquivel, Personal Communication, 1985). If the experiences of North American "move-

ment midwives" are any guide, however, SERPAJ has many new opportunities ahead to be of service to progressive causes, as both political
and religious opportunity are likely to remain fleeting.

NOTES

We are deeply indebted to the following: Dr. Brady Tyson, longtime AFOR
liaison to SERPAJ and other Latin American nonviolent groups; Adolfo Pérez
Esquivel; Creuza Maciel, executive secretary of SERPAJ from 1982 to 1986 and
general coordinator from 1986 to 1990; Richard Chartier of AFOR, who worked
with nonviolent groups and activists (including Adolfo Pérez Esquivel) in Latin
America, particularly Argentina, from 1959 to 1973; Fr. José Alamiro Andrade
da Silva, president of SERPAJ-Brazil (1982–1984); and Timothy Ready. All of
these were available for interviews and provided materials on various aspects of
SERPAJ's history and structure and function. Scott Mainwaring, Michael Foley,
Susan Eckstein, Jackie Smith, and Bob Edwards provided helpful advice on
earlier versions of this manuscript. An earlier version of this manuscript appeared in the July and December 1986 issues of *Solidarity Solidaridad*, the newsletter of the Committee in Solidarity with Latin American Nonviolent Movements
(CISLANM) and the Task Force on Latin America of the Fellowship of Reconciliation.

Our description of FOR's work in Latin America and the emergence and
development of SERPAJ through 1985 draws heavily on key FOR organizing
reports and SERPAJ documents, interviews with several principal FOR and
SERPAJ activists, and a variety of secondary accounts of the activities of SERPAJ.

1. In SERPAJ's terminology, it advocates "active nonviolence," which is a new
way of engaging in politics that seeks not only political but social transformation.
McManus and Schlabach define active nonviolence as:

A means of struggle for social change based on an unswerving commitment to speak the
truth and a willingness to put oneself at risk in the process while refusing to harm others.
Major components of nonviolent action include reflection, dialogue, education, challenging
existing power relations, and building alternative structures to create a just and compas-
sionate world. (McManus and Schlabach 1990: 300)

In this essay we focus on how a central component of active nonviolence, the
philosophy and methods of nonviolent direct action, became part of SERPAJ's
repertoire of contention. For a succinct summary of SERPAJ's approach to
nonviolent direct action, see Goss 1974.

2. JAPLA shows the interest that civil rights veterans had in spreading the
methods of nonviolent direct action in Latin America. Described as "a group of
Methodist inspiration which gives instruction in non-violent action techniques"
(Richardson Nute 1974: 22), JAPLA was founded in the late 1960s by Glenn
Smiley, who achieved fame for his work with Martin Luther King, Jr., at Montgomery in 1956. As early as 1968, JAPLA held a seminar on the strategy of
nonviolent action at Medellín, Colombia. In the early 1970s, JAPLA sponsored
seminars in Mexico. By the early 1970s, several former colleagues of Martin
Luther King, Jr.—Andrew Young and AFOR members James Lawson, Brady

Tyson, and Bernard Lafayette—had joined JAPLA, with Lafayette replacing Smiley as executive director. Lafayette was a member of the Nashville, Tennessee, Sit-In Steering Committee in 1960–1961, the precursor to the Student Nonviolent Coordinating Committee (SNCC), and was a co-founder of the Raleigh, North Carolina, SNCC chapter. He later became a national staff member of the AFOR and the Southern Christian Leadership Conference (SCLC). In 1968, he was the national coordinator of the Poor People's Campaign. In 1971, Lafayette joined Smiley at the Alajuela, Costa Rica, meeting in which the Servicio para Liberadora was created.

Part IV —————————————————————————————

THE FUTURE OF RELIGIOUS FUNDAMENTALISM EAST AND WEST

11

RADICAL RELIGIOUS MOVEMENTS: A GLOBAL PERSPECTIVE

Anthony B. van Fossen

Words such as "prophetic," "millennial," and "messianic" have been used loosely and interchangeably (cf. Burridge, 1969: 11–12; Fuchs, 1965) or incorrectly (Barkun, 1985), and yet each has a precise meaning and social implication. A *prophetic movement* is a radical (i.e., nonmainstream) religious movement oriented around an utterance that is supposed to have derived directly from a sacred or inspired source, is concerned with the immediate and ultimate future of the people meant to hear it, and is confirmed as decisively important by the earnestness of its bearer(s) (see, e.g., Trompf, 1977: 1). The *millennial movement* is a radical movement without a saving messiah specifying imminent paradise for its adherents and/or extraordinary punishment for unbelievers. The *messianic movement* is a radical movement proclaiming its living leader to be God or some ultimate principle in human form, or at least to be guided directly by God or this ultimate principle.

In this chapter I identify the principles of formation, organization, time, and symbolization in prophetic, millennial, and messianic movements, and also the situations in which these radical movements are suppressed, absent, or extremely limited in scope. Prophetic, millennial, and messianic movements are based on progressively more critical attitudes toward existing modes of production and rewards, while *anti-radicalism* is primarily a defense of these.

There is a profound historical connection between the emergence of radical religious movements and conflicts between traditional and new modes of production that challenge traditional (not necessarily hereditary) religious specialists who may be inclined to lead such a movement. The radical religious movement is not so closely tied to its sociohistorical context that it does not have substantial similarities to other movements of the same type in other times and places. There are similarities or universal qualities in human experience and everyday life out of which these ideological organizations arise. There are also great differences, with which I shall not be concerned here. Much of religion's undifferentiated influence has been declining in a slow and uneven manner with the advance of science, capitalism, socialism, and secular social movements, but there are clear similarities in theme between, for example, the messianism of Apolosi Nawai in Fiji in the first half of this century, early Christianity, and the contemporary movement of Georges Roux in France. In Fiji, Israel, and France, people dream and wake, they become ill and die, a division of labor is in place, and alongside it exists a system of domination and subordination, production, appropriation, exchange, and consumption, which often have been the objects of religious legitimation and repudiation; this has been so since ancient times. Human beings have common problems, although they may have very different interests, perceptions, and solutions. The members or opponents of radical religious movements are solving immediate problems, but this does not mean that those problems and solutions do not relate to other immediate problems and solutions in other times and places. I reject the watertight compartments of extreme cultural and historical relativism. Movements in not-fully-capitalist societies are treated as having some important similarities to those in capitalist societies and not as being in some cultural apartheid or ethnogeographical time warp. Barriers of economy, technology, history, culture, and language are important, but there are larger common deep structures in humanity's response to alienation in religious terms. Here I do not attempt to outline exactly why some movements of the same type have become more powerful than others, but instead I point to their common qualities. It is not necessary for any actual group to have all features in common to be classified as the same type, but only a majority of attributes.

ANTI-RADICALISM

Resistance to radicalism is most likely to come from rulers who enforce a view of strict continuity between past, present, and future, the relevant past being marked by their rise to ascendancy. Ruling elites have labored to classify and entrench people within unchanging hierarchical ideologies and cosmic systems, against which radicalism seems absurd. Thus, regardless of how much oppression Tongans or Hindus suffer, they rarely resort to prophetism and almost never to millennialism or messianism. How widespread anti-radicalism is within a society can tell us a great deal about how much support that ruling class has among the many distinct groups in society.

In very different class systems such as our own, where people spend considerable time and energy negotiating class roles and never seem quite sure of what is normal and who they are and who other people are, there are inconsistent attitudes toward radicalism. When it is attacked it is generally because it ruins careers and families and because the prophet or messiah seems authoritarian, violent, exploitative, or too sure of himself, with a message that is far too simple, unscientific, and religious in a complicated, ambiguous, and secular world. It is not so much because radical change or a drastic upheaval in the ruling elite are considered impossible or inconceivable or that cosmic reality is fixed, hierarchical, and undisplaceable. There are, of course, fragments of prophetism, millennialism, and messianism in advanced capitalist societies. Fears of imminent nuclear annihilation may have religious overtones, and millennialism and messianism are present in some fundamentalist churches and new religions. State power and physical force may be directed at such movements. In societies where the sense of a normal, unchanging, and hierarchical world is stronger, humor is often an adequate weapon.

At the most immediate level, pressure will come from family members committed to established ideologies. These will often appear to be the foundation of anti-radicalism, especially when the radical religious movement attracts little general public attention, and they may be supplemented by a *lumpen* element of hired deprogrammers [i.e., vigilantes who forcibly abduct, detain, and verbally browbeat religious converts until they recant (see Shupe and Bromley, 1980)]. Broader opposition will come from established religions and even the state if the group is sufficiently threatening or visible. The dangers may be fabricated and the visibility enhanced by established groups seeking definition and advantage (such as a general mobilization of religious fervor). More liberal anti-radical elements may support research, publication, and counseling concerning the new movements (Bromley, Shupe, and Busching, 1981).

To the degree that the ruling class of conventional society notices the new radical religious movement, it usually regards it as absurd and infantile or, particularly with millennialism and messianism, immoral or shocking. The movement, for its part, is likely to regard conventional society's elite as an enemy to be subdued, either wholly or in part,[1] but milder prophetism, which conventionals regard as merely eccentric, is more inclined to reformism. Elites usually distinguish between movement leaders (who may be crankish, fraudulent, or dangerous) and their disciples (who are pathetic dupes or even slaves). In Europe of the Middle Ages, leaders were often killed as witches; today, disciples are coercively "deprogrammed" of alleged "brainwashing."

Faced with opposition, the movement may become introverted or inconsequential, and both the ruling classes and its "grass-roots" opponents may regard this as a victory unless the movement becomes passively resistant in inconvenient ways. Elites may incorporate some of its ideas or leaders into agencies under their control, which they see as cleansing them of their absurdities and retaining whatever is valuable. But, more commonly, elites suppress movements, sometimes ferociously, especially where there are state churches or repressive states. The frequent imprisonment of leaders is designed partly to show that they are common people with few, if any, of the powers they claim. The intention is to create so many problems for the movement that it disappears or to encourage it to reduce its claims and accept conventional ruling class power. The movement, by necessity, becomes extremely concerned with internal organization and its relation to the outside. If it persists in taking extreme actions, rulers are likely to harass it continually and to imprison or, in a few cases, to execute its leaders. Rulers generally recognize the danger of martyrdom and attempt to present the prophet or messiah as sinister or dangerous.

PROPHETISM

Prophetism, in contradistinction to millennialism and messianism, emphasizes deliverance from some problem of far smaller magnitude than the immediate end of the world. It may be witchcraft (in New Caledonia or central Africa), sickness (in healing movements throughout the world), or personal frustration [as in est (Erhard Seminar Training) or other manifestations of the human potential movement]. The prophecy is the focus of the movement, and the means for fulfilling or testing it may be quite impersonal. Magic potions, devices, or rituals are often as important as the prophet, who is nevertheless superior to his followers, though inferior to a deity or the powerful cosmic forces for which he is the conductor.

The prophesied deliverance is often assumed to come automatically and inevitably to those following the rituals of the movement correctly, and the rituals may have something of the air of a scientific experiment. Christian Science, Werner Erhard's Forum, and New Caledonian Kanak witchcleansing propose efficacious rituals often designed to automatically or technically improve personalities. Failures of prophecy are usually attributed to incorrect performance of rituals.

The movement attacks the mode of production and class structure for their inadequacy on a single point (e.g., the failure to deliver health or self-realization), and the conflict that is formed is rather simple compared to the more complex critiques by millennialism and messianism. Like them, prophetism often sees the ruling elite as ignoring it, opposing it, or using law against it to defend its power in the existing mode of production, which prophetism is attempting to transcend. The prophet sees himself/herself as at least equal to members of the dominant class, and repression of the movement will likely lead to assertions of moral superiority. However, the emphasis is not so much on morality as on how the ruling mode of production and elite hinder the understanding or realization of some innovation or larger, but specific, improvement in cosmological process, social relations, and personal welfare. These conflicts constitute the most crucial process of history, as the prophetic movement sees it. The opposing elites may never meet the prophet or his/her followers. They may merely use the police, or they may be protected from any realization or challenge by the apathetic intransigence of the populace. However, the tendency of the prophetic movement is to isolate and diminish the ruling elite and mode of production through promulgating its vision of the proper society of the future.

The critique may be from the right, the left, or the apolitical anywhere, but in all cases there is a greater explicit opposition to existing technology, work processes, career objectives, and consumption and their social results (as experienced or perceived by members) than exists within the larger population, although investigators of these movements have not always given this fact proper emphasis. As the prevailing mode of production obviously does not offer the historical transformation the prophet is envisioning, it is tolerated only insofar as it allows the prophet to assume the paramount position. On the other hand, the movement's opposition to the mode of production may dissolve if the wider society accepts the prophet's claims and techniques. The fact that many new religious movements in the West appeal to the more privileged sectors of society than Third World movements of the poor means that they tend to either less radical forms of prophetism (e.g., those focusing merely on self-improvement or a more innovative capitalism) or more symbolic rejections of the existing mode of production if they are millennial or messianic [e.g., through valorizing adventures in outer space and reincarnation, as in Scientology (e.g., Wallis, 1977; Whitehead, 1974)]. Atrocity tales about "cults" are generated when affluent parents see their children abandoning or compromising promising careers, or contributing heartily to unconventional religious movements (Barker, 1989: 41–42), although very little of the condemnation may be expressed in direct, economic terms.

Leadership and organization tend toward greater impersonality than in the messianic movement. The prophet is the central figure, whose authority rests on new, efficacious, and socially unifying rituals rather than merely on personality. Although proselytism is usually present, the basic concern is often with the individual, family, or local group. The prophetic movement may be a "client cult" (Stark and Bainbridge, 1985), expressing gregariousness more than the social cohesion and the center that messianism demands. Enemies of prophetism are more likely to regard it as foolish or slightly dangerous than as subversive to the fundamental structures of society (as is the tendency for enemies of equally widespread millennialism and messianism).

Prophetism promotes a distinctive sense of time. It begins by refusing to concede to some localized oppression in the present and by predicting its abolition in the immediate, reformed future. The prophet proposes new rituals, which form the basis of a movement requiring a new form of education for young and old alike. The movement encounters opponents and predicts that they will be punished or deprived. It narrows its sense of time and history so that they are defined by its rituals, which are elaborated to attempt to encompass a more differentiated reality. It does not propose that time has an end, as millennialism does, and the movement may have a very long life, doing very much the same things.

MILLENNIALISM

Millennialism predicts the imminent and total transformation of society. For the Jehovah's Witnesses, the "Plain Truth" movement, the early (and many contemporary) Mormons, the Children of God, and Oceanian "cargo cultists," the current holders of power are illegitimate. A new redeemed society will form around adherents. Their rituals promote the advent of salvation, and they serve as a prototype for it. When compared with prophetism, millennialism tends toward greater proselytism—that is, toward including the maximum number in the redeemed society. The principal actions of adherents are directed toward surmounting hindrances to salvation. These are usually conventional authorities and, in the Third World, particularly during the colonial period, they often included Europeans. Resistance to authority, in truth, frequently calls forth suppression, perhaps even infiltration of the movement, by agent provocateurs of the state.

While prophetism aims to isolate and diminish the existing mode of production and ruling elite, millennialism attempts to overthrow and supplant them to produce a completely new kind of society, although one that often has a family resemblance to a proper and legitimate society of the past. As in "cargo cults," the new mode of production often seems magical and ritualistic. Millennialists are more prone to violence or civil disobedience against the powerful than are prophetic movements as rulers are generally perceived as far more cruelly committed to absurd, repressive, and outmoded forms of control and societies that exclude and repress them. Rulers are often thought to be hiding the secret of the mode of production that grants them power or to be willfully ignorant of it and fooling themselves about the harm and suffering it causes. Some rulers may be sympathetic and eligible for salvation, but the elite as a class is doomed, as are the social relations and in many cases even the technologies on which their power is based. But millennialism can also draw away from political and economic reality altogether and subordinate them to mythical principles of control while awaiting the collapse and disintegration of the existing mode of production and ruling elite. Natural plain living may express dissatisfaction with the prevailing mode of production, even when it leads to great commercial success (e.g., in marketing health food) and when adherents proclaim the advent of miraculous high technology from another world as essential for redemption (e.g., Trompf, 1990).

Money is usually an image of exploitative power, which will pass away or be radically transformed when the movement triumphs.[2] Money and other possessions have been stolen from their rightful owners, and violence and militarism are particularly likely when land has been appropriated by foreigners. However, there is frequently an attempt to convert antagonists into members furthering the goals of the movement—as when, in Melanesian "cargo cult" myths, plantation owners miraculously reveal themselves to be "moral Europeans" aiding the millennial prophet in distress (Burridge, 1960, 1969).

Millennial *movements* (as opposed to popular sentiments of apocalypticism or loosely organized activities such as parading "The End Is Nigh" on sandwich boards) are more likely to emphasize salvation than destruction, although this is not always the case. The millennial movement makes promises to its adherents, not just impersonal prophecies. Among these is often the promise of universal reconciliation in a redeemed society. If enemies can be converted into participants, so much the better.

The strength and frequency of conversion are related to the supposed validity of the millennial prophecy. The proponents and enemies of the movement engage in a debate that is supposed to be settled in the near future when the prophecy comes due. There are numerous subsidiary claims to miraculous powers, such as healing, amazing personal transformations, or spectacular escapes from martyrdom, that contest conventional expectations. These also buttress the movement's power when people swear to their validity.

The movement may define itself primarily in terms of its enemies. In most accounts of Third World millennialism, the movements appear primarily anti-European and there is little attention to indigenous class structures, modes of production, or the organization of adherents, who often seem to function too simply as colonized beings (as in Adas, 1979), rather than as reformulating complicated systems of indigenous ideology (as viewed in the writings by Burridge, 1960, 1969). In descriptions of Western movements, members are less schematized and more complicated, but are also portrayed as more foolish for believing in absurd and extreme prophecies while they live in a scientific culture (as in Festinger, Riecken, and Schachter, 1956).

These observed differences partially reflect the standpoints and biases of authors. Yet a recurrent theme of millennialism throughout the world reported by researchers is that enemies are materialistic and weighed down by incessant lust for wealth and power, forcing others to do their bidding while they repress them. They dominate the society that the millennium will supersede. They use the law of that society against those attempting to redeem it. Millennialists often believe that the law merely expresses their enemies' despotic will. Thus, liberation is the primary millennial image. Frequently this is the working out of a well-known historical process—such as the long-anticipated return of a good or sanctified state of being.

The organization of the movement proceeds from its millennial goal. It postulates several types of people. The struggle between the movement's leaders and enemies is central. Leaders and enemies threaten one another, either verbally or physically or both. Violence is highly moralized, clearly separating good from evil. The leader is the prophet, but in the millennial movement he is not given the power of the messiah. He may receive messages from redeemers, but he is usually not the redeemer himself. Other leaders are administrators who collect resources and organize and even design movement activities, but seldom claim inspiration not deriving directly from the visionary leader. Ordinary members form the movement but contribute little to its organization and message. They provide resources and an atmosphere of urgency, practicing extreme millennial rituals that dramatize the movement and extend its influence through spectacle and proselytism. The last group is composed of those who are suitable for membership but who refuse it. The disposition of these people is extremely important as the typical movement's members try to account for the mass publics' less-than-enthusiastic response. They are often accused of complicity with the enemy. Particularly in movements that promise victory in radical or ethnic conflicts, these "collaborators" indicate the limits of the movement's appeal. Movements may concede that there can be one or more neutral observers, although the possibility seems remote in a cosmos polarized between good and evil.

The sense of time is dominated by the threat of death, which is the fate of the conventional society. The continuing battle between the movement and its antagonists promotes a sense of urgency as the day of judgment draws near. Attacks on the movement are countered by miracle tales of leaders or members narrowly escaping death. Frequently there is the promise of immortality or rebirth into another identity. But there is also the threat of imminent disaster for outsiders and even insiders who do too little for the movement. The present is in violent transformation and crisis, and a sharply critical stance is mandatory for demystifying the illusion that the evil and deadly conventional order may have any permanence. The past is dead and there will be a victory over death in the immediate future. The perplexing multiplicity of conflicting times will resolve into a new kind of clear, unified time. From this higher and more comprehensive perspective, adherents gain a keen sense of their superiority to their contemporaries. The oppressive society will soon die, and they will live forever in perfectly harmonious groups of the like-minded.

MESSIANISM

A weak form of messianism has great influence in the world today, since all Christians are at least nominally committed to it and tend to identify their interests with it. This generally staid messianism is different from the new and revolutionary messianism with a living messiah and millennial urgency that I examine here, although one influences the other. The center of early Christianity, Charles Manson's Family, the contemporary French Rouxists (van Fossen, 1984, 1988),[3] the Unification Church, or "Moonies" (Bromley and Shupe, 1979), and the Fijian movement of Apolosi Nawai (van Fossen, 1986) is the extraordinary life of the messiah—a series of miraculous events that define his mission.[4] The messiah continually opposes wicked enemies and defies death. Frequently the messiah is arrested, imprisoned, or threatened with imprisonment, and a strong aura of power clings to the messiah if he dies or if she is killed while a captive of the state. When he dies, his disciples often believe that he is immortal in one or another form. His resurrection or reappearance, in the flesh or in visions, are clearly aligned with millennial expectations.

The messiah comes to fulfill what was missing in previous envoys and their predictions. The messianic movement tends to have the fullest ideology and cosmology since it encompasses and reinterprets all references to significant gods, persons, events, places, and things in previous movements, which serve as counterpoints to it. Even if it claims scientific status (such as Scientology does), it is furthest from the current scientific view because it centers the destiny of the entire universe on the life of a single person on earth rather than on more limited and impersonal statements, although, as in millennialism in the strict sense, some may actually occur—as, for example, in a nuclear holocaust. The messiah claims much greater power of action than the millennial prophet, who displaces it on larger forces, such as God, gods, ancestors, spacemen, or even the forces of history. Disciples identify with the messiah more than with the prophet, and they try to model their behavior on his.

The forces of good and evil are more individualized than in the relatively impersonal millennial movement. The fate of the universe is determined by the outcome of the conflict between the messiah and her enemies, and it is frequently not as keyed irrevocably to specific dated prophecies. Enemies accuse the messiah (even more than prophets) of duplicity and exploiting disciples to gain wealth, power, or sexual advantage. The messiah's final victory over her enemies, who may even seek her death, is the millennial victory that ends conflict, poverty, oppression, and illness. Thus, the messiah is a guide in a confusing world and is able to alter his or her movement as need arises. These features, among others, such as the ability to innovate quickly and inconsistently, give the messianic movement a greater ability to survive failures of prophecy than the millennial movement (cf. van Fossen, 1988).

Leaders of a messianic movement are likely to have more power than millennial leaders since messianism is more disposed toward hierarchical organization, albeit under messianic command. They are more inclined to claim superhuman abilities such as healing or telepathy imparted to them by the messiah to aid his mission. Since the messianic movement is more personal, there is greater fear of betrayal, and traitors (particularly leaders who surrender to conventional reality) are a constant threat to the movement's unity. The messiah or her agents may take extreme measures against those accused of betraying her.

If the movement experiences prophetic failures, strong opposition, internal crises, or loss of purpose, the messiah may want to withdraw from his disciples, whom he considers unworthy of his mission. They become defined as mediocrities, and they attract other mediocrities to what should be a most important activity. It demeans him to associate with them, but they often have the gall to contest his orders. There are apostles who have done admirably. But the movement is not what the messiah intended it to be. The problem is least when the messiah actively directs the movement. But this often requires delegating responsibilities to disciples or organizational talents or interests that he does not have or want. The messiah may tire of his role or decide to reject his disciples before they reject him. Often eminent apostles assume leadership at this point.

The struggle for the overthrow of the ruling class and mode of production is most clearly seen in the messiah, who will presumably rule at the head of a new elite. The goal is most clearly *not* complete equality but, rather, spectacularly productive relations (which may in fact turn out to have an equalizing effect), under the master of the universe, whose advent makes any previous mode of production or class relations obsolete. This may lead to violent confrontation if the doomed order resists or even persecutes the messiah or her movement. But the hierarchy of the people within the movement is assumed to correspond to the ultimate hierarchy of the cosmology, and this can permit escapism from political and economic concerns, as well as hostility to their present configurations, without having to confront them. Just as the messianic movement creates its own ruling elite, it may also develop its own mode of production, as when the Shakers under Ann Lee formed communities with radically innovative work relations and technologies that were to prefigure the redeemed world. Relatedly, there is a greater tendency in messianism than in either the prophetic or millennial movements for disciples to pool property or simply to give it to the leader. Abdication of private property and individually driven career trajectories also threatens the dominant mode of production and outrages numerous outsiders—from disappointed friends and families to religious and political elites.

Almost all messianic movements resemble millennial movements in that they entertain a similar view of time. However, the focus is more on the messiah's life than on the death of the conventional society. The messiah is born under miraculous circumstances, which indicate the beginning of a new era. During his youth the messiah discovers divine powers and acquires disciples, but no movement as such develops. The messiah seeks the "clarity" of his "intended path," performs miracles, and gradually a movement crystallizes around him. There is millennial expectation, but the movement differs from pure millennialism in doing more to redeem the world in the present through imitating the messiah rather than waiting for this to be accomplished in the future. Thus, there is a greater emphasis on the unity of the movement, under strict control by the messiah, who demands great sacrifices to strengthen the mission. The messiah is likely to claim ever greater powers and create a more elaborate and definite hierarchy, particularly if the movement is to survive failures of significant prophecies (van Fossen, 1988). This indicates his conquest of time. Finally there is the death of the messiah, which defines just who his real disciples are and sets apart the traitorous and dubious. The anticipated reappearance of the messiah will initiate the end of time, and meanwhile it is the responsibility of the select group to spread the word.

In sum, the main theme of messianism is the progress of the messiah's life and endeavor. In millennialism, on the other hand, the emphasis is more teleological and sequential, focusing on immortality, rebirth, and a return to origin. It is less individualized than messianism, and the state of redemption and the steps for reaching it may be less defined. Although leaders of both types of movement may be courageous and persistent, it is the messiah who takes more responsibility for his/her own destiny.

CONCLUSION

The continuum from prophetism to messianism is marked by progressively greater tension with the larger social environment. The motifs by which these religious movements appeal to followers are not the same, however. Prophetism embraces history. Millennialism is closer to a dream that drastically transfigures time relations according to a large impersonal time schedule. Messianism emphasizes the messiah's personal triumphant and episodic struggle to transfigure power, time, and human destiny. In very broad terms the appeal of these radical religions increases progressively as the alienation from the prevailing mode of production increases, although this may come from disillusioned social "dropouts" and radical rightists, as well as from class-conscious peasants and proletarians.

Each of these radical religious movements seeks primarily to contest existing power relations by identifying them as incompatible with a future cosmological order ruled by deities or superheroes and other extraordinary human beings. And, not unexpectedly, anti-radicalism emerges in the former of rejecting, even repressing, resistance to the goals of the radical movement. These can range from simple apathy (which may indeed be the factor that ultimately accounts for the demise of most unconventional religious movements) to violent official suppression. Ironically, there is evidence to suggest that once a movement offers a significant enough threat to elements of the status quo it actually enters into a sort of *symbiosis* with anti-radical forces, mutual sacred-secular opposition that shapes their strategies of survival-propagation and repression (Shupe and Bromley, 1985: 169).

Sociologists Stark and Bainbridge (1985) have likened religion to a system of "compensators" or this-worldly assurances of other-worldly benefits. Given the unlikelihood of science or any political philosophy ever dealing adequately and fully with theodicies of injustice, inequality, and disease-death, they do not see an "end" to religion via secularization that some, like Wallis (1984) and Wilson (1987b, 1973) somewhat simplistically do. And, clearly, while radical religion faces increasing competition from capitalist, socialist, feminist, and environmental ideologies in proposing solutions arising from class conflict, it may also form alliances with any of these.[5] In the course of religious evolution, its various forms, like radical religious movements themselves, perhaps could be likened to the science of any era: destined to be challenged and even superseded by new "pedagogies," or inspirations. The three classic "types" of radical religion examined here are as old as recorded history, and there is no reason to think their appeal is slackening.

NOTES

A version of this paper was presented at the 12th World Congress of Sociology, August 1990, Madrid, Spain.

1. In the wake of Jonestown, the Manson Family, and Ananda Marga, it seems odd to claim, as Beckford (1988: 260) does, that "none of today's groups is avowedly (or covertly) hostile to the State."

2. Money and other earthly possessions have been given away or destroyed in countless movements—from the Jehovah's Witnesses and flying saucer millennialists in the United States (Festinger et al., 1956) to the Vailala Madness in Melanesia (van Fossen, 1979; Williams, 1923). The destruction of property seems paradoxical in "cargo cults" promising material abundance.

3. The Rouxists are interesting in having gone from prophetism (1947–1950), to millennialism (1950–1951), and then to messianism (1951–present), while facing the forces of anti-radicalism.

4. Particularly in the consideration of messianism, where imperial expansion has imposed Christianity in widely separate parts of the world, Galton's problem appears. The problem raised by Francis Galton, a late nineteenth century anthropologist, is that if one assumes that there are fixed stages of cultural or organizational evolution, the borrowing or sharing of culture makes it impossible to demonstrate the certainty of this evolution.

5. For example, radical religion has often been seen as proto-Marxist by Marxists (Engels, 1950; Worsley, 1968), as well as by anti-Marxists (Cohn, 1970; Lasky, 1976), although Marxists usually distinguish between progressive and regressive radical religions.

12

THE CONFLICT BETWEEN "DENOMINATIONAL STATE" AND "STATE OF LAW"

Bronislaw Misztal

State autonomy cannot be taken for granted; it must first be created
and then, since it can be lost, maintained.

John A. Hall, *States in History*

With the dismantling of the political construction of state socialism, one
of its previously unshaken foundations—the officially marginal role of
the church in the secular political environment—became a passé matter.
Religious beliefs of the people resurfaced, the churches either reopened,
as in the Soviet Union, Czechoslovakia, and East Germany, or came to
the fore of social, political, and intellectual life, as in Poland. The role
of the clergy, their social position, importance, and influence were rapidly enhanced since they filled the gap in the previously lay public space.
The matters of faith, religion, and consistency of individual moral views
with the doctrine of the church, as well as those of the consistency of
the state policies with the church's current policies, gained new significance. Previously repressed and frequently ignored, the bureaucratic
structure of the church, along with the pool of intellectual potential of
its cadre, started playing the role of a determinant of political and social
policies.

Nowhere was this role to be better seen than in Poland, where traditionally the Roman Catholic Church conceived of its position as crucial
for the nation's existence. It was best summarized by Cardinal Wyszynski:
"In Poland the hierarchy has always had the nation's interest close at
heart.... No one is more of the people and for the people than we priests,

and in no political or class sense. We are the emanation of the nation itself" (Goodwyn, 1991: 317).

This clearly religious-nationalistic stance was a distinctive feature of Polish Catholicism, and it played an instrumental function in protecting the institution of the church from erosion intended by the authoritarian secular state (Goodwyn, 1991). Therefore, the disappearance of the secular Communist state had made it likely that the church, with its history of religious nationalism, would have crucial importance in any future post-Communist etatistic arrangement. By the same token, the role that the institution of the state can and will play in post-Communist societies came into question.

At the core of these ruminations lies the concept of *political space*, which refers to the "range of issues over which general, universal decisions are made within a given political unit, particularly decisions which are seen by political actors to affect overall social order" (Crouch, 1986: 180). Normally, public space is monopolized by specialized political institutions, including the legislative, executive, and judiciary branches. Several studies (Poggi, 1978; Crouch, 1986) suggest that there is a certain form of the zero-sum game logic that applies to the occupation of public space: if certain vital functions are not performed by the state, they are taken over by other groups, in particular by groups that constitute the civil society.

THE RISE OF THE DENOMINATIONAL STATE

For several decades of Communist rule the state has been effectively cannibalized by the political party, thus yielding to the Leviathan of the party-state. Under the authoritarian arrangement provided by communism the state was weak, yet extensive. The repressive and dominating Communist ideology exercised by the party apparatus was able to penetrate it effectively. The state's institutions were appropriated and subdued to overwhelming political yet extra-legal control. The state had become an outlet for implementation of the over-ideologized policies of the Communist Party. Until the very end of communism, state functionaries were selected by party apparatus (Wasilewski, 1990), and the state legislature was subjected to full control by the executive body of the Communist Party.

With the state yielding to extra-legal claims of the party, the public space had been appropriated and dominated by one political actor. If the civil society had existed it would have taken the state in defense, thus protecting access to public space and demanding state autonomy. But such an experience was not available to any of the Communist countries and, even in Poland, a truly civil society was absent until the early 1980s (Frenztel-Zagorska, 1990; Frentzel-Zagorska and Krzysztof,

1989; Misztal, 1992; Szelenyi, 1990b). Subsequently, the state neither withered away nor grew autonomous, remaining enslaved in the hands of party bureaucracy.

In the absence of avenues of interest intermediation, state socialism had been lacking essential mechanisms that would allow ongoing democratization and reform, and thus it became obsolete as a system of social organization. In order to continue its existence it had overextended itself, allowed politicization of social life and of the economic relations, and intervened in the newly emerging organization of civil society. Rather than restrict itself to being able to carry out functions essential to the social order, the state had been systematically ill positioned between the growing claims of the civil society, on the one hand, and the demands of the party, on the other.

The major systemic restraint on the state ceased to exist with the dismantling of the legal foundations of communism. Yet the role of the state in the newly shaped system is far from clear. In this chapter, I will discuss the prospects for establishing the autonomous state of law as a replacement for the Communist state. By the *state of law* I understand the set of institutions and arrangements through which the public space is effectively controlled by the legislature and the judiciary, with the executive branch being constitutionally unable to introduce the extra-legal, ideological, and religious values into state policies. By the *denominational state* I mean the arrangement through which the religious, and thus extra-legal considerations, can determine the course of state policies, can penetrate into the contents of the legislative activity, and affect the overall operation of the state, including personnel recruitment. Under this definition, the Socialist state was a form of secular denominational state, with the dominant Communist ideology playing the role of extra-legal considerations.

I argue that in the wane of state socialism there exists a historical and political likelihood for the emergence of nationalistic-religious fundamentalism that might become a new dominant ideology. I refer to the empirical evidence of the nature of the late stage of the socialist society, to accumulated theoretical and historical knowledge of the states, and to revolutions and political breakdowns. Finally, I look into the existing political processes of post-communism to advance the argument that the breakdown of communism has brought about freedom, but not democracy; that it has done away with the circumstantial aspects of regress, but has not created structural conditions conducive to progress; that it has done away with the dominant ideology of state socialism, but not obliterated the ideological vacuum left after such holistic ideology. Subsequently, I argue, the state remains vulnerable to the attempts of appropriation by religion and the church.

CONTRADICTIONS IN THE BRAVE NEW WORLD

Political breakdown always poses important questions with regard to the future of society, its organization, and its ability to create an autonomous, democratic state. In the case of post-communism, the most pertinent issue is whether the essentially nondemocratic, totalitarian (as in Poland), or authoritarian (as in the former Soviet Union and Romania) type of social order, which for the past several decades had been based on the monocentric structure with the Communist party-state playing the core role, can be now replaced by a somewhat more progressive (by Western standards) and more democratic sociopolitical system, or whether the state will remain essentially a dependent institution. In the latter case, the church, by the means of religious control, will assume a role similar to the one that had been once played by the Communist Party.

The fall of communism awakened hope (Misztal, 1985) that has been long absent from the lives of the people. With hope came optimism that life would change rapidly for the better. Such optimism, however, does not reflect the structure of ongoing processes and merely connotes the surface events that brought about social change. Below the level of enthusiasm generated by the semirevolutionary episodes there remain looming questions about the future of this fragile entity that has been freed by the recent revolutionary political and economic processes: the future of the state and of the public space.

The interest in the future of the state in post-communism is legitimized by several concerns. First, recent and indeed revolutionary change came about as a result of the rapidly diminishing state capacity to wield economic and political control—that is, to govern. The command economy had been proven to become an ineffective method of administration of the national resources, thus producing a considerable level of waste, both in the sphere of material and nonmaterial (social, intellectual, cultural) assets (Misztal, 1990a, 1990b; Morawski, 1980; Pickvance, 1988; Stark, 1990). Post-communism, therefore, is marked by penury and shortages which are no less extensive than those that had characterized state socialism. This is because the current change consisted mostly in doing away with the "shell" of Communist etatistic apparatus and not in changing the structural conditions that prevailed in society. Consequently, the prevalence of the conditions of penury results in the fact that the struggles over the appropriation of public space will have a practical influence on one's position in the currently emerging system of inequality.

Second, the Communist state ideology, based on a warped intrepretation of Marxist ideas, also possessed an ineffective method of shaping civic attitudes (Rychard and Sulek, 1988; Staniszkis, 1988, 1989). Therefore, state socialism failed to produce the "socialist personality" (Jasinska and Siemienska, 1975) and allowed the public sphere to penetrate into the private sphere of life. Eventually, the private sphere was subjected to considerable erosion, and then, especially in the 1970s and 1980s because of the continuing inability of the state socialist system to satisfy individual human economic and spiritual needs, the greatly eroded private sphere repenetrated the public space, thus contributing to the further erosion of the latter. Once public matters were subjected to private manipulation, the state lost its ability to control the public space.

Paradoxically, the process of forced socialization under Communist domination rendered a type of personality that is now called *homo sovieticus* (Tischner, 1991). One can say that *homo sovieticus* is the by-product of the aborted processes of Sovietization. It has yielded a type of person full of contradictions: rejecting socialism and yet supporting the welfare program of the socialist system; looking at the West with envy and yet unwilling to undertake the risk brought about by free market economy; characterized by considerable levels of learned helplessness or the inability to act independently (Marody, 1991), and yet willing to see implemented social change that would force one to be independent. Tischner put it this way: "During the period of totalitarianism the role of intellectuals was mostly reduced to the attempt to change the world. Today one has to understand it in the first place, and only then to transform it. The post-totalitarian mentality is characterized by the primate of change; everybody would like to change something, yet few understand it" (Tischner, 1991: 11–12). This description is similar to the view of the "true believer" as portrayed by Hoffer (1951: 142)

Freeing the political and economic system from the restraints of communism has left individuals still bound by the habitus of the past, and therefore not adequately equipped with experiential knowledge in order to deal independently with the two now-free spheres: the public and the private. As Hoffer put it, "it is not the wickedness of the old regime they rise against, but its weakness; not its oppression, but its failure to hammer them together into one solid, mighty whole" (Hoffer, 1951: 142).

Third, the production of civil society and of the subsequent public space under communism had been undermined by the phenomenon of role reversal (Misztal, 1991) that has eroded basic social roles yet left intact the role of a believer. Routinely, the postindustrial social order depends on three roles: those of citizen (member of a community), consumer (actor on the market), and producer (organizer of social relations of production). The system of state communism had claimed that it can match or, ideally, exceed the organization of capitalist industrial society. Henceforth, it put itself in the situation where the same essential roles were crucial for its survival, as they were under the conditions of liberal capitalist market economy. At the same time, however, the constitutive principle that normally leads to role configuration—clear definition of property rights—was conspicuously absent from the system by-laws. In East-Central Europe, property rights had been won by the nobility in the fifteenth century, prior to the establishment of core citizenship rights. The Communist doctrine had denied an active role to property in the organization of political and productive activity of society, assuming, contrary to past historical experience and to common sense as well, that the disowned masses would demonstrate unparalleled growth of virtues and citizenship responsibilities. Instead of property rights, political servitude was expected to play a constitutive role in social order. State socialist social order had eliminated property as the essential determinant of collective action and reversed basic social roles so that it rendered citizens powerless, consumers helpless, and producers unchastised (Zawislak, 1988).

The resulting social, economic, and political chaos is a distinguishable element of post-communism in which the three roles were never consistently incorporated into the system. The knowledge of how to play those essential roles, and therefore the ability to utilize the newly freed public space independently of the private one, did not immediately arrive with the breakdown of the Communist state. Amidst all the changes and rapidly disappearing state institutions, one institution stood solidly and intact: the church. The erosion of social roles did not affect one other fundamental role, however—that of a believer. As noted by Hoffer (1951: 143), chaos produces "the strong men of action" on the one hand, and the fanatic "true believers" on the other. The former attempt to take over the state apparatus; the latter take the church into their possession.

In brief, the imprint that the late stage of communism had on (socialist) society has allowed, or even expedited and forced, institutional change, but not social change. The two types of changes have different and frequently incompatible paces. While reality forces people to concentrate on institutional transformations, the everyday practice of action is and will remain shaped by habits that crystallized under conditions completely different from those that characterize the environment of such new institutions (Marody, 1991: 258). A society of "real socialism" as it had existed during the last years of the Communist formation will not, therefore, become overnight a society of "real capitalism," and its structural features may interfere with the process of social change (Marody, 1991: 259). The eroded roles cannot turn into social skills.

Progress in dismantling the state apparatus of communism makes it obvious that, rather than to seek the "third way" or try to build on the institutional and structural elements of the socialist welfare state, the former socialist countries are attempting intensive emulation of the Western model of democracy, as if they were seeking—unachieved to date—

modernity. Analysis of the "Western model" suggests (Feher, 1991: 5) that modernity was somehow born during and due to the French Revolution. This historical process, however, becomes completed only where the two inherent trends of this cycle—that is, political freedom and management of the social question—become reconciled. Goldstone argues that the Western model is in reality based on a false interpretation of historical processes, since the latter trend has never found realization in the aftermath of the revolution. Capitalist organization, which became the vehicle of social change and the tool of industrial economic success, had "exacerbated social conflict and deprived and exploited the working class" (Goldstone, 1991: 483). He further argues that revolutions tend to produce authoritarianism instead of democracy, that there is no proof that revolutionary endeavors are capable of removing blockages to economic development, and that what they offer instead are some incentives and opportunities for propagating democratic ideologies by previously marginal elites.

The processes that follow dismantling of the state socialist system are therefore unlikely to produce by themselves greater democracy or even freedom. Research indicates that "a decade or two after state breakdown . . . all the elements for a reemergent absolutism are in place" (Goldstone, 1991: 480). Immediately prior to and following the state breakdown, all former Communist countries showed a dramatic increase in the components of the "political stress indicator" (state fiscal crisis, elite alienation and competition, rising mass mobilization potential) that are intrinsic elements of the revolutionary situation (Goldstone, 1991: 482n).

The more the former Communist countries attempt to emulate Western models of democracy, the more rapidly are their public spaces vacated by dismantled state structures. Those countries represent the combined tradition of weak, overextended states and the ability of state apparata to accommodate authoritarian corporatist ideology (they used to yield to the Communist domination). In some cases, as in Poland, Hungary, Lithuania, and Romania, there is also a tradition of powerful, nationalistically oriented Catholic churches that for the past four and a half decades have been shunned by the secular authoritarian state. In other cases, as in the Republic of Russia, Ukraine, and (to some extent) Czechoslovakia, the state is stronger and the church is weaker, yet the public space is also being rapidly vacated by the downfall of communism.

The claims to public space are made simultaneously by the newly emerging, liberalizing states, by the organized segments of the population (social movements), and by the ever-present church organizations. Mobilized constituency finds the immediate results of the downfall of communism unpleasant, unexpected, and frequently unbearable, with food prices rising sharply over 300 percent, shortages of previously state-distributed goods, devalued yet dear money, disappearance of the public assistance programs, and the overall fall of the living standards. "Bread" takes the place of "freedom" on the symbolic agendas of popular movements, and the unresolved social problems are piling up. Erosion of authorities leaves the church as the unchallenged object of popular moral and spiritual inquiry. In terms of the economic development of liberal capitalism the emulation attempt has put the post-Communist countries back to the stage where Western countries used to be in the eighteenth and nineteenth centuries.

The organizational, structural, and economic problems of post-Communist countries therefore resemble the two-centuries' old experiences of the West. Progress in implementing democracy in the latter was determined by the pattern of settling the relationship between state and church, in particular by the fact of whether the public space was "co-habited" peacefully by the former and the latter. In the countries where fundamental Catholicism had confronted militant, secular liberalism (Austria, France, Italy, Spain, and Portugal in Europe and in all of Latin America) the political actors have been both jealous and determinedly active about occupying public space (Crouch, 1986). With few concessions made by either actor, the mobilization of society to access public space has rendered its popular segments vulnerable to fundamentalist and nationalist, frequently even fascist, persuasion. Freeing up the public space by the capitalist, industrial, bourgeois, or even popular revolutions has therefore produced conditions conducive to extra-legal penetration of the public space. Fundamentalist bases of interest organization have proven to be a much more effective means of access to public space than democratic-legal forms. Until the mid-twentieth century, the growing and inaccessible liberal state offered few avenues for interest intermediation. The Latin American experience, on the other hand, demonstrates that displaced Catholicism is likely to generate an authoritarian corporatism of a fascist kind.

In general, there have been two different sets of causes that had, in the past, contributed to an emerging denominational state. Establishing such control of the public sphere was usually preceded by fundamentalist claims to the public space based on an authoritarian and/or a fascist form of interest organization. First, there was a Catholic hegemony, mixed with the practice of shared political space and authoritarian Catholic corporate tradition. Second, there was a contested Catholicism, combined with the conflict between the church and the state and followed by corporate-liberal conflict (Crouch, 1986). Such structural causes had led to the nationalist, fundamentalist, or otherwise fascist set-up of public space and to the production of the denominational state. Even with some democratic traditions present, as in Ireland, fundamentalism appeared to be the major form of claiming access to public space.

Emulation of the Western road to democracy may therefore signify that considerable segments of East European political constituencies, facing disenchantment with the negative aspects of institutional change that they have had initiated as a response to the Communist state's decreasing capacity, would turn to populist, nationalistic, fundamentalist, or otherwise extra-legal and extra-political opportunities to enter the public space. The apparatus and the institutions of the newly emerging "liberal" state could take one of two options in responding to such claims. They can either yield, thus allowing the populist/fundamentalist claims to dominate the state, or they can take a strong, noncooperative stance against such claims. In the former case the state may become vulnerable to the fundamentalist/populist claims, either because it is too weak to defend its autonomy or because its personnel and its legal by-laws are still formed under the conditions of dependency, and therefore it habitually would rather yield to extra-legal and extra-political pressures than try to generate legal mechanisms of self-protection. In Poland, where the church has always been strong and nationalistic, or in the former Soviet Union, where religion has always been based on fundamentalist attitudes, the discourse about the access to public space will inevitably include the religious context.

In various post-Communist countries the state and the church, respectively, can make either a strong or a weak claim to control the public space. Figure 12.1 presents possible scenarios for resulting models of interest intermediation and the type of political (state) order that may result. It illustrates the range of possibilities available with church and state in positions of strength or weakness. A weak church and a weak state will result in a denominational state, in the Belgian mode; a weak church and a strong state will result in an authoritarian state, in the Chilean mode; a strong church and a weak state will be denominational, in the Iranian mode; and a strong church and a strong state will be both denominational and authoritarian, in the Italian mode.

The claims to the public space made by the church and the state interact. Following Michael Mann (1986) one can say that the church exercises infrastructural power since it has penetrated the civil society; it has been enmeshed with it for the decades of the Communist rule; and it—at least in the case of Poland—helped establish the post-Communist order. Facing neither the problems of legitimacy nor those of renewal of consent by electoral procedures, the church is in a considerably more advantageous position to develop strong claims without actually having to confront society.

The situation is completely different for the state, because its position is much more vulnerable to the crisis of legitimacy. It is therefore confronted with a choice of either making claims based on some general concept of laws (that would include citizenship rights), or an attempt to access the public space based on certain despotic interpretations of values

Figure 12.1
Claims to the Public Space

by THE STATE

		WEAK	STRONG
		D	**A**
WEAK		liberal-corporatist regime; disorganized society; religiously based mass movements	bureaucratic-enlightened absolutist regime; mass mobilization for controlled reform
		BELGIAN MODEL	**CHILEAN MODEL**
by THE CHURCH			
		D	**D - A**
STRONG		religious fundamentalist regime; religion becomes state ideology and penetrates the state institutions	populist-statist regime; disillusioned society; protracted conflict over interests intermediation
		IRANIAN MODEL	**ITALIAN MODEL**

D = denominational state; A = authoritarian state

of centrality and globality. The former requires an elaborate conceptual and legal structure in place, but the legislative process to produce such a structure is long and is contingent upon the existence of an efficient executive apparatus. It is my argument that, in the absence of the former and the weakness of the latter, the state can easily become subjected to the globalist persuasion of religious fundamentalism. In other words, with intellectual elites playing a decreasing role in production of the etatistic infrastructure, the prospects for a strong claim to public space by the post-Communist state are bleak, and its vulnerability to the penetration of fundamentalist values is high.

That the fundamentalist-religious values find an easier way to the etatistic structure of the post-Communist state, rather than the conceptual-intellectual-legal checks and balances, can best be seen in Poland. One of the major points of the postwar Communist regime was that the state should be separated from the church. Consequently, religion and sacred symbols were purged from schools and state offices, and, although teaching religion was performed on the church's premises, the educational curriculum was completely laitic. One of the first moves by the post-Communist government was to issue a decree that would introduce religion to schools at all levels. Interestingly, the Ombudsman of Public Rights has found this decree to be unconstitutional and filed a protest with the Supreme Court. But the decision to allow religious (Catholic) education did not change the situation of society at large, since its bulk, being Catholic, was easily exposed to religious teaching in church. The move by the government reflected the fact that intellectually and organizationally it was unable to conceive and implement a much-needed educational reform, yet it had to demonstrate that it takes action. The church hierarchy came in handy with an idea of what to do, and the decree was enforced without ever being voted on by parliament. In a similar vein, the government decreed that divorce trials should be moved from local to district courts where the backlog of cases is much longer, although the process of granting divorce is already slow and ineffective. The decision was dictated by the church hierarchy and was implemented in lieu of reform of the civil code and of judicial structure.

The area where the etatistic legal and intellectual structure was most perforated by religion in all post-Communist countries is the administrative division of the territory of the state. The one that existed under communism was artificial and unrealistic. Likewise, the religious administrative structure was either incomplete or otherwise crippled by a priori political decisions. It remains to be seen whether the post-Communist states would be able to implement the new administrative territorial division prior to and independently of the new structure of diocesan powers. In the case of Poland, Czechoslovakia, and Hungary, at least, the latter might come prior to the former, thus influencing the state administrative system. With paralleled etatistic and religious administrations the church will gain further access to public space.

In conclusion, historical and sociological evidence demonstrates that the postrevolutionary, post-Communist state is especially vulnerable to the penetration of fundamentalist meanings, symbols, and contents. With massive mobilization and popular discontent and with lack of democratic legal traditions, any extensive claims to the public space by the state can either precipitate some type of fundamentalist assault on democracy or prompt authoritarian defenses of the etatistic apparatus. Restricting its own claims to the public space, on the other hand, the state does not affect or circumscribe the other party's claims, thus making it possible that religion will become fused with its own ideology, as shown in Figure 12.1. Allowing the protracted conflict over access to public space may produce a situation of ungovernability, with a weak executive branch and disillusioned masses. A cautious approach to interest intermediation, frequently referred to as corporatist arrangement, will debase social movements of their class origins and replace it with denominational-religious identity, thus allowing liberal, nonreformist persuasion to dominate. Finally, in cases practically different from those of Poland or Hungary, the fast moves by the etatistic structure to claim and appropriate public space prior to the organization of interests by the church can lead to the absolutist regime that would slowly, yet in a limited way, control the reform process.

In making history one seldom has any choices; therefore, the grid presented has little prophetic or social engineerial (manipulative) value. It should remain what it was meant to be—an intellectual analytical tool of reconnaissance that should help identify conditions conducive to the emergence of the denominational state in post-Communist society.

13

MOVEMENTIZATION OF SOCIAL CHANGE

Slawomir Jan Magala

Change appeals to us through its sudden, dramatic nature. The breakup of the Soviet state socialist empire, the explosion of Solidarity in Poland, the fall of the Berlin wall, the "velvet" carnival-revolution in Prague: all have caught the eye of the camera and the imagination of millions. However, sociologists maintain that social change is a process, not an event. It is wrong to assume that social history consists of long periods of relative stability very rarely separated by brief outbursts of explosive change. Rather, the roots of an explosion have to be found in the periods of relative stability, and the explanation of change has to be found in the accumulation of individual decisions, group networking, and macromovements.

Likewise, modern social movements are perceived as "bunches" of processes. They are seldom characterized from the point of view of their "stability-enhancing" procedures. For instance, the founding of a political party or a passing of a legal act are considered less crucial from the point of view of an explanatory description of a social movement than the study of the ways and means that are employed to create, sustain, and activate the movement "below" or "beyond" the threshold of institutionalization; that is, "outside" the solid shell of an established, recognized, and hierarchic organization. Sociologists try to describe modern social movements both in terms of agencies for "mobilization of resources" and in terms of expressive instruments, vehicles for "identity formation" and "identity guarding." They try to demonstrate that latent networking can turn out to be an influential and effective open "occupation" of some public space. As Alberto Melucci put it:

Social movements cannot be represented as characters, as subjects endowed with being and purpose, as acting within a scenario whose finale is predetermined. Such misconceptions can be rectified only by rejecting the assumption of collective action as a unified datum.... This problem cannot be resolved by considering collective action either as an effect of structural conditions or as an expression of values and beliefs. Collective action is rather the product of purposeful orientations developed within a field of opportunities and constraints. Individuals acting collectively construct their action by defining in cognitive terms these possibilities and limits, while at the same time interacting with others in order to "organize" (i.e., to make sense of) their common behaviour. (Melucci, 1989: 25–26)

The new theoretical approach toward an analysis of social movements can best be characterized as a refusal to impose a clear-cut model on an emergent social reality before certain investigative procedures have run their course. Alain Touraine (1988) and Melucci (1989) advocate a reconstruction of underlying networks and definitions of reality through participating research—that is, by letting a sociologist (or a team of sociologists) co-work with the participants in a social movement. Only when these procedures have been implemented and the findings of sociologists "cross-checked" with the "subjects-objects" of research can some tentative hypotheses be formulated. This suggestion has two weaknesses. First, since at least some social changes "surprise" sociologists as much as anybody else, chances are that some eruptions of new social movements will have to be studied after they have actually culminated in some form of collection action (which can also mean that they are busy disappearing, giving way to new forms of association). For instance, a wave of popular unrest swept Nicolae Ceauşescu away in Romania, but no programs to study the transformation of obedient and controlled crowds into the rebellious insurgents could have been made. Therefore, we have to reconstruct this process from personal documents and a general analysis of the definitions of reality ("The secret police are too strong"; "I am afraid of losing my job." versus "If I do not riot, I'll die of malnutrition and cold". "This cannot go on.") However, since post-Ceauşescu Romania is also a stage on which a former political elite quickly regrouped and renetworked, and since Romanian sociologists are part and parcel of this political game, it is hard to expect them to study the former elite's new networking in a "sharing" way.

Second, the participating mood of social inquiry, as suggested by Touraine and Melucci, must be based on an assumption of a reciprocal honesty ("fairness") of both the participants in a movement and the accompanying sociologists. However, this is easier said than done, especially because the politicization of some social issues, the public relations needs of movements, and the requirements of secrecy can prevent such reciprocity from emerging. This second problem appears to me to be much more vital than the former. The assumption of a nonpartisan or a non-policized nature ("neutrality") of social change is quite pervasive. This assumption is based on the belief that a change is like a genetic drift; that is, before the existing political parties adapt themselves to it, it is "neutral." This belief is expressed especially by representatives of the "resource mobilization" school of interpreters of social movements:

Social movements may, or may not, be based upon grievances of the presumed beneficiaries. Conscience constituents, individual and organizational, may provide major sources of support. And in some cases supporters—those who provide money, facilities, and even labour—may have no commitment to the values that underlie specific movements. (Zald and McCarthy, 1987: 19)

Melucci, who is much more sensitive to the politicization of issues than are the above-mentioned American authors, tries to avoid this problem by constructing the concept of transformation of the authoritarian regulations into political relationships. In a general trend toward the democratization of daily life, says Melucci, we tend to introduce reciprocity where asymmetric authoritarian regulations used to rule. We introduce "systems of exchanges and procedures of negotiation which, by means of confrontation and the mediation of interests, produce decisions, whereas before there were only mechanisms for authoritatively transmitting regulations by means of power" (Melucci, 1989: 165).

This general concept of the main thrust of new social movements also fulfills another theoretical role in the explanation of social change. It allows us to reconsider the limitations of our concepts of the public space. Since many modern social movements tend to defer the entrance on a political stage until a mass mobilization of support is needed (and not necessarily for much longer than it is actually needed), one often notices a preference for loose coupling rather than rigid structuring, for private contacts rather than public roles, and "invisible" (from the point of view of formal, institutionalized relationships) networking. Assuming that the thrust of the new social movements allows for the deregulation, depoliticization, and anti-authoritarian swing in patterns of decision-making, one can acquire a very good criterion for differentiating between new social movements on the one hand and traditional defensive networks of interests of the power holders (e.g., the Mafia, the Masonic Lodge, Nomenklatura, etc.) on the other. In the cases of ecological and feminist movements, the networking tends to remain invisible because a political party is not considered the most suitable instrument for articulating their demands. In case of a Mafia-like organization, the networking remains invisible because of a conscious effort at secrecy (linked to an attempt to generate options allowing for an illegal, even criminal behavior). Let us note in a historical aside that an invention of the professional revolutionaries' mafia coupled to a mass social movement of discontent seems to be at the heart of both the Bolshevik and Nazi political revolts in the twentieth century. According to our criterion, neither revolt can be classified as a modern social movement because both of them increased, rather than decreased, the authoritarian control of individuals and social behavior.

Finally, the way in which modern social change actually takes place presupposes the transformation of the agents of change and of their original designs and values. The actual threshold of a "change" means that the processes that brought this change about continue, and sometimes reveal a dramatic reversal of the concepts of "gain" and "loss." For instance, the attempt to increase the sphere of individual liberties prompted some groups of mainly Protestant medical doctors to promote voluntary euthanasia (especially in The Netherlands in the late 1980s). This movement promoted a new option that increased individual freedom of choice. In its eyes, a terminally ill patient should have the option of choosing a voluntary death administered as one legitimately offered medical service (in due course observed with respect to the medical, legal, and family circumstances). However, when the debate surfaced, many other groups, most notably Roman Catholic spokespersons and lawyers, came to see this option as an irreversible institutional intervention and a loss of individual liberty. Thus a successful raising of this issue to public attention transformed the apparent "gain" into an apparent "loss" in the eyes of the concerned constituencies.

SHIFTING SOLIDARITIES AND OPEN-ENDED SOCIALIZATION

Reading sociologists who have written on new social movements, one is struck by their reluctance to go beyond a formal description of the principles of association and to link an analysis of any given movement (or of a change caused by it) to a theory of social dynamics. I believe that the emergence of public spaces in modern society (and of the new social movements competing to occupy them) is linked to two underlying processes—arrested mobilities and an open-ended socialization.

The main thesis of this chapter is that social movements of the modern type (i.e., ecological, feminist, Solidarity-like) are emerging because of an open-ended socialization model that is gradually and slowly replacing rigid institutional socialization of the past based on such foci as the family, school, church, and the workplace. Moreover, they emerge as a response to an upward social mobility arrested after the latter had come to be regarded (as interactive "public spaces") as one of the rights of every human individual (on a par with a right to decent living conditions or personal liberties). The open-ended socialization of today means that a human individual encounters rival claims of various "clusters" of human organizations very early in his or her life cycle. These clusters are usually labeled according to the political sociology of institutions: one tends to speak of "states," "markets," "clans," or "civil societies." They may also be classified according to the types of dominating relationships—social psychologists speak, for instance, about human individuals being socialized into "communal sharing," "authority ranking," "equality matching," or "market pricing" forms of social relations (cf., Fiske, 1991).

Some sociologists represent a "weaker" version of Melucci's democratization hypothesis and claim that modern socialization processes have to be "open" because the "political" and "social" citizenship (the term was first introduced by Franco Ferrarotti) is being continuously extended (for instance, by including formerly excluded categories in some decision-making processes, such as voting rights being extended to women, youth, and foreign guest workers). However, no matter how this open-ended socialization is being interpreted, most sociologists agree that there are no "sacred" patterns of growth, no clearly defined institutional paths and institution-based identities in most modern educational organizations. A simple juxtaposition of "civil society" on the one hand and of a "market economy" or "state authority" (Cohen and Arato, 1982) on the other is one of many attempts to find a theoretical model for explaining the tensions, dynamics, and open-ended nature of modern socialization processes.

What has been accepted is the idea that there is no unimpeded transfer of values, attitudes, and identities; there is thus no reproduction of patterns of behavior and of systems of social action from generation to generation. Paradoxically enough, there is a growing awareness that it is this very intergenerational mutability which ensures a much better conditioning of future "consumers" and "citizens" who will be facing an accelerated and accumulating change. In a sense, Jurgen Habermas's (1989, 1990) well-known idea—that there is an ideal of undisturbed communication underlying our linguistic exchanges and our social "dialogues"—is a brave philosophical attempt to provide this open-ended socialization with a formal and negative model. (The model is formal and negative because it does not advise us to try and determine the "positive" solutions to problems, but it prompts us to eliminate formally "disturbing" procedures and to secure the continuity of open-ended discussion on decision-making.)

Italian sociologist Francesco Alberoni (1984) has suggested that modern forms of socialization are "volatile." Their volatility creates an indispensable condition of "value-free" and institution-free socialization. This observation is based on sociological investigations of value shifts in modern Europe (the so-called postmodern values debate). While it is by no means clear whether Alberoni is right to speak of value-free and institution-free socialization, one can safely assume that socialized individuals are exposed (due to the breakdown of "lasting" and all-round authorities and to the availability of information about alternative value systems in the media) to many more value systems than used to be the case. Although he does not speak of an open-ended socialization, he does mention "nascent states" of new social movements and looks for them in his analyses of the reproduction of social order through the upbringing of new generations (i.e., in the socialization processes). But Alberoni still appears to believe that there is a preferred, "balanced" approach toward socialization from which a modern imbalance "deviates." He claims that every upsetting of the "balance of forces" in relevant social subsystems leads to a nascent state and that, subsequently, some of these nascent states give rise to profound social changes—for instance, to religious reformations, political revolutions, economic reconstructions ("miracles"), and so forth. Therefore one has to conclude that his approach is still based on an underlying idea that some structure "yields" and "gives way" to a new structure, leaving a narrow gap or interval in which individuals are temporarily endowed with a power to reshape social order. The history of human societies is thus a history of "solid structures" with brief and dramatic shifts in between. As he himself put it:

Both aggregative and especially group collective movements also play a part in this progress. They alter solidarity by proposing alternative models or questioning the legitimacy of certain institutions, on the one hand, and by provoking reactions which reinforce the hold of institutions, on the other. The structural preconditions in the specific historical process must therefore be searched for in each case among those conditions which reduce the solidarity of a given subsystem without extinguishing it and which at the same time facilitate an alternative restructuring of it. In more general terms, the structural preconditions can be determined as those conditions which weaken the areas of solidarity and the corresponding lines of structural polarization in a given social subsystem and at the same time bring into being alternative kinds of interaction. (Alberoni, 1984: 42)

One should add that the "bringing into being" of alternative kinds of interaction happens today on a daily basis. Were it not so, all human groups would go on reproducing their patterns of behavior indefinitely. However, what makes the modern situation intuitively different from the premodern one is the degree of tolerance for the emerging alternatives. What had once been accepted as an exception to the rule has become a routine. What used to be a privilege of the Bohemian avantgarde in art has become a right of countercultural imagination in the mass social movements of the late 1960s and became subsequently incorporated in the concept of the "intelligent" or learning organization in the 1980s. Art critic and historian Kirk Varnedoe quotes the plaque commemorating a rugby player of 1823, one William Webb Ellis, who "first took the ball in his arms and ran with it, thus originating the distinctive feature of the rugby game" (Varnedoe, 1989: 9). The angry students of 1968 shouted *imagination au pouvoir* and "there are no normal people, only normalized ones" in front of a striking Sorbonne and in the occupied Odeon Theater. They made it clear that social intervention and generation of alternatives should not remain the prerogative of a selected, "star"-like minority. If organizations are to accommodate this battle cry, they have to become less closed and less repressive vis-à-vis innovative, unusual, "alternative" behavior. Thus we are presently dealing with shifting solidarities and alternative kinds of interaction that are valued for their own sake (very much like the innovation in European painting introduced by the impressionists was once considered valuable in itself, not because of a "new ideal" or a "new balance" of visual arts). And if such interactions are valued for their own sake, then there is no necessary, alternative ideological goal. In other words, instead of dealing with a brief revolutionary interval between long periods of stability, we are dealing with long periods of multidirected ("quasi-chaotic") change— a change, let us add, that can be triggered from almost any "locus" of change—technological, political, or moral. Should the triggering of change give rise to conflicts (we can imagine that William Webb Ellis might have been stopped and thrown out of the field for his attempt to change the rules of the game), the conflicts in question can arise in all walks of life. And since conflicts, which can eventually lead to a major transformation, do not have to be lodged firmly in a single, "privileged" sphere of behavior, there can be no "master blueprint" for social change. (Again, the Bolshevik and Nazi blueprints called for the recognition of either class or race conflicts as the principal ones, deriving their agenda for change from a solution offered to these conflicts.)

Open-ended socialization means that younger generations do not take institutional landscapes for granted. For instance, the technological invention of a personal computer (PC) killed an institutionally monopolistic network of computing centers based on an alliance of mainframe producers, university educators, and state bureaucracy. The idea of central computing centers was based on the assumption that all computing needs of society would be "laundered" through major centers. Individuals and companies were supposed to bring their "dirty laundry" of uncomputed numbers in, and they were supposed to receive printouts of ready-made calculations. The computing centers were thus supposed to be the major distribution centers of computer-based services. The invention of the PC killed this attempt to construct an equivalent of a central radio broadcasting system, very much like the personal car killed centralized railways as a privileged means of transportation. Victory was not achieved through a head-on political power struggle. The motto of PC users and suppliers could have been "if you can't beat them—make them irrelevant."

The open-ended nature of our socialization procedures is best visible in the continuous curricular change in most educational institutions. One attempts to educate the future Ellises rather than the perfect occupiers of a certain position within a company or holders of a certain finite sum of "knowledge." The way in which education is being developed (multiinstitutional, permanent, and "open," both from the point of view of the goals of education and from the point of view of access to the programs) testifies to the acknowledgment of *movementization*. Changes in our educational institutions are not short breaks between periods of stability. The recognition of turbulent environments results in an institutionalization of permanent organizational innovation (change of curricula, introduction of new forms of adult and permanent education, employment of the new techniques of electronic communication) and in stimulating an open ideal of an educated individual, capable of finding his or her way in an increasingly dense and uncertain ("chaotic") environment (cf. Broekstra, 1991).

ARRESTED MOBILITIES

Movementization of social change (i.e, the concept that social change increasingly takes the form of a social movement) and open-ended socialization do not emerge as one-sided processes without any resistance on the part of the organizations and individuals. If an alternative to a stable ideology and a closed institution appears, individuals have to be motivated to pick it up. Why should one be motivated to participate in an alternative rather than in the traditional, mainstream process? Why should one do so if changes of loyalties and shifts of solidarities did not bring about any reward? Among the most popular rewards for participating in an emerging alternative would be the promise of upward mobility. The recent history of markets, states, civil societies, and "cultural civilizations" (the term introduced by Alberoni) provides us with many instances of a mythology of upward mobility. The Nazi revolution promised a heaven of "the master race" and opened venues of upward social mobility in the Nazi party, army officer corps, and economic management (partly by earmarking professionals who could be dismissed and replaced, either by being Jewish, non-Nazi, or otherwise "unfit" to continue in their professions). The Bolshevik Revolution did the same, annihilating most of the professionals and building relevant bureaucracies (the military, the police, economic management, and the party) from scratch, offering upward social mobility in return for unwavering, blind loyalty to the top political elite. Some sociologists could object to the above interpretation of the success of two failed revolutions of the twentieth century. They could point out that upward social mobility did, indeed, take place, that both relative and absolute numbers of individuals enjoying decent standards of living and higher social rank than their parents had been growing, and that both slow and accelerated industrialization brought about many rewards.

Still, the concept of a mythology of upward social mobility appears to be justified on two grounds. First, a chance offered by a political elite to the rural masses can remain an attraction only for a limited period of time. The bureaucracies become saturated, and the access to attractive positions for the next generations becomes more difficult. One can try to open the channels of upward social mobility either by domestic purges (as Stalin did) or by an international war (as Hitler did), but both solutions are dysfunctional for the system even in a short run. Barring violent purge and war, the promise of massive upward social mobility is bound to remain an empty mythology in the situation of an authoritarian "closure" of the very bureaucracies at stake.

Second, since the system has to remain authoritarian if ideological goals are to be ruthlessly pursued (classless society demands an increased terror against class enemies, and a master race has to inflict a total destruction on other races even if it interferes with an overall war effort), the very value of the promised positions in bureaucracy diminishes. Authoritarian control deprives the holders of those positions of the benefits they could have reaped under a less authoritarian system. The phenomenon is well known to sociologists who studied upward mobility in state socialist societies. Polish sociologist Jadwiga Staniszkis notes that social space in state socialist societies has been perceived in terms of cultural signs. Group dignity, vis-à-vis other groups, became very important (as testified by various attempts to introduce a "code of conduct" for particular professions in postwar history of Polish or Hungarian societies), while conflicts acquired a slightly "theatrical" atmosphere. Quoting another Polish sociologist's study, she says that:

[Narojek the sociologist] uses memoirs to document that a measure of one's social promotion is how they relate to those defined as members of intelligentsia. According to Narojek, the main cause of tension for first generation white collar employees is the feeling that their advancement is not complete because they cannot fully acquire the mythologized status of the intelligentsia. This situation results in frustration even when the authors of the memoirs are aware of the intelligentsia's largely mythologized status. (Staniszkis, 1985–86: 71)

The attractiveness of alternative modes of interaction and of emerging organizational innovations (including an attractiveness of participation in social movements) is thus made easier by an open-ended socialization but becomes activated by frustrated expectations of upward social mobility. Arrested social mobility provides a motivational incentive for a search for alternatives. Once all bureaucracies are in place and there are limits to further expansion of their ranks, the young generation's aspirations are hard to channel and control. Personal emancipation, a symbolic search for "meaning" and "identity," and "consciousness raising"— all of these become alternatives to a former mainstream socialization pattern.

There are reasons to believe that frustrated hopes for upward social mobility generate generalized sympathy for alternative attitudes, behavior, and movements. By doing so, they reinforce the tendency, which we have tentatively described as the "if you can't beat them, make them irrelevant" principle. New social movements tend to disregard or avoid the institutional enemy, trying to "bypass" him until a point of "no return" is reached (i.e., until a relative balance between repression and citizen's protest tilts toward the majority taking to the streets, asking for a referendum, and instructing the deputies to the parliaments, and until repressive institutions become largely irrelevant). Some Polish and Hungarian sociologists try to explain the emergence of new social movements (which resulted in the overthrowing of the Communist regimes) by analyzing the "second sphere of sociopolitical interactions" outside of the political space controlled by the Communist Party. A Hungarian sociologist, Elmer Hankiss (1988: 31–33) mentions the reemergence of micronetworks, regeneration of local communities, improved chances for interest mediation, and a "resocialization" of some party and state institutions from below. A Polish sociologist, Bronislaw Misztal, stresses an incompatibility of the instruments of new social movements with the ones used by a traditional political agency and acknowledged in political theory:

Alternative, non-conventional social movements, as they appear in contemporary Poland, mark a new chapter in social life. They bypass the traditional areas of class politics, they ignore distinctions between commodified or non-commodified actors, they mobilize otherwise non-mobilizational resources, recruit enthusiasm rather than concern, and focus on universal qualities rather than on any immediate gains. Since they are not vindicative, they are not (so far) incorporated into the major movement of "Solidarity." . . . Unlike mass movements, they do not try to recruit large numbers of members; instead they rely on being able to influence audiences and to bring new and alternative values into everyday life. The social change they effect, if any, cannot be immediately linked to any particular movement's activity and results in increased awareness of large and loose segments of population. (Misztal, 1990a: 86–87)

All three movements analyzed by Misztal—underground educational and publishing activities, a pacifist initiative called "Freedom and Peace," and a surrealist "Orange Alternative"—are movements of young intelligentsia who are responding both to an open-ended socialization leaving "empty social spaces" and to the frustrated desire (failed mythology) for an upward social mobility within the established channels of advancement. The response is directed toward the new, unoccupied "social space." The new social space can be the space opened by the new media (for instance—interactive teaching and desktop publishing techniques in the case of alternative "flying university" and clandestine publishing), by acceptance of a spillover of the artistic experimentation to the areas of art reception and public forming (the Orange Alternative drifting between political happenings and artistic march-ins), and by a challenge to the most "closed" state bureaucracies (i.e., that of the military, as was the case with the Freedom and Peace movement). Access to the new public spaces is perhaps best exemplified by the pirate radio broadcasting ships, which provided youthful audiences with rock music at the time when conservative control of the established media limited access of rock musicians to their audiences. Needless to say, these pirate ships of the 1960s and 1970s have currently been replaced with professional high-tech satellite music stations, but a precedent was introduced, and monopoly of control over media is harder to achieve today than it was in the early days of this century. The control exercised by the opponents of rock music over the media was challenged, and then successfully made irrelevant.

MOVEMENTIZATION AND ITS DISCONTENTS

"Liberty, equality, and brotherhood was the war cry of modernity. Liberty, diversity, and tolerance is the armistice formula of postmodernity. And, with tolerance reforged into solidarity, armistice may even turn into peace" (Bauman, 1991: 98). Sociologists turn into wistful poets when definitions of the modern predicament are concerned. Movementization of social change ("All of us are always on the move within a rapidly changing environment"), open-ended socialization ("None of us knows which skills and which acquisition patterns will turn out to be relevant".), and arrested upward mobilities ("How can we take hierarchies for granted?") have led us toward the vision of social reality as an armistice, an uneasy cohabitation, a "round" table ("How can we turn tables against our enemy if we all sit at the round table?").

Modern organizations are less "closed" than the organizations of the past because of the pressure from the outside (because of the rapidly changing environment) and because of the pressures from within (because of the subcultures and individual struggles against the routinization and standardization of an organizational reality). A NATO official told my students in late 1989 that in view of the approaching end of the

Cold War, his organization's main claim to glory might very well be a by-product of their defense policy. He pointed out that in the 1960s and 1970s NATO had planted millions of trees in Lower Saxony, figuring out that tree trunks are a formidable anti-tank barrier even after a heavy artillery barrage. Now that the green ideology was in vogue and defense priorities became less pressing, the fact that NATO planted those trees might very well become a significant factor in assessing the organization's chances of survival. Pressures from within are usually conceptualized under the heading of "flexibility" and "empowerment." Some forms of this flexibility are easy to cope with, but some infringe on the very "core" of organizational identity. Soldiers may help man railway systems during a strike and they may rescue children in times of flood, but to question the nature of armed struggle in the name of a greater flexibility of the armed forces would certainly cause alarm. Students may score points in their long march of protest through academic institutions; they may even acquire a voice in an elected legislature of a university. But throwing all authority away and pronouncing the "cultural revolution" that replaces academic merit with political zeal invites a major disaster. How should one build up a consensus around flexibility if a flexible return to the "core" function (in our case—a deployment of armed forces in a war or a transfer of knowledge, skills, and experience at a university) can never be ruled out?

One of the ways of deciding this issue is to provide a theoretical background of a possible answer and to evoke an empirical case. The theoretical background can be drawn from a concept of an organizational agency (even if the agency is latent, as is the case with a networking that did not produce a movement or an institution), while the empirical case may be drawn from a quick march of "solidarity" through the institutions of state. Let us begin with a theoretical issue.

Melucci (1989: 66) tries to define the dimensions that are significant for the making of a new social movement and for a decision of the emergent social agency capable of collective action. He finds them for the youth, feminist, and ecological movements and describes them as follows. In the case of the youth movement, the participants have to decide whether to opt for a change of social structure (let us say, a radical reform of a university) or for a challenge of cultural codes (let us say, a new curriculum with a new balance of skills and knowledge), for their inclusion in broader organizations (careers) or for their exclusion from them (dropping out or creating alternative networks) and, finally, whether to become part of a mass society (as consumer and citizen) or to prefer a group/movement solidarity (withdrawal from a mass society either in a physical sense of establishing a communal life or in a sub-cultural, for instance, generational sense). For Melucci the options are empirically deduced from a participating observation of the youth groups in Milan, but they can be perceived in a number of other contexts (e.g., the West German "greens" or the Polish anti-Communist and countercultural groups). What matters is that individuals and groups can perceive, calculate, and represent the interests of their "constituencies" when making decisions that place them somewhere on the continuum between the poles of the above-mentioned dimensions. For feminists, the choices are between individual self-realization or feminine solidarity, between public or private space, and between "affective reflexivity" or feminine "otherness." Ecologists have to choose between an institutional action (political ecology) or a direct action (daily ecology), between acting on a social environment or focusing on a culture of group members, and finally between a preservation of individual/nature equilibrium or a transformation of a nature/society relationship.

It should be noted that most of these choices are in fact choices with respect to the kind of agency for collective action individuals want to create. Movementization of social change means that these choices are neither predetermined by the institutional environment of individuals nor easily polarized between major competitors (as was supposedly the case with the "working class" parties opposed to the "bourgeois" ones). Moreover, very different rationalities and criteria are being simultaneously applied. For instance, changing a repressive social structure may be a much preferred solution, but challenge of the cultural codes may turn out to be a less punishable, thus a more attractive and directly available option. Creating a female political party in the public space may diminish the attractiveness of the feminist cause for those women who would also like to preserve the private space without the political zeal of the feminist ideology. And, finally, the necessary compromises with other political agencies might prompt ecological activists to go for a daily direct action rather than for the overall blueprint for making whole societies sensitive to environmental destruction and deterioration. Choices are therefore made on the basis of the calculation of ends and means, costs and benefits, meaning and meaninglessness of potential action. They are not abstract choices made outside of local and temporary context. They are improvisations and they require knowledge (which always come with a professional supplier's price tag and a list of ingredients). Writes Stewart Clegg:

Organizational agencies may be individuals or they may be collective agencies of some sort which have developed mechanisms for both the calculation and the representation of interests. They are able to make these calculations through the various discursive forms available to them. In particular, one thinks of the articulation of the various scientific, technical, and other knowledges which constitute the primary occupational identities and resources of organizational agencies. Other sources of discursive availability will be drawn from whatever regulative (that is, political, legal, economic, accounting and so on) and local frameworks of meaning present themselves, as well as from many competing sources of value representation which surround any agency. What are constituted as local frameworks of meaning may be embedded in an infinite variety of contexts. "Local" refers to specific sites of organizations, sites which empirically offer a plentitude of possible meanings and memberships with which to organize or resist. (Clegg, 1990: 160–61)

The three comebacks of the Polish Solidarity movement are a case in point. The first comeback occurred after the lifting of martial law and a period of vigorous policy of the Communist government aiming at the breakdown of Solidarity. Since December 13, 1981, when martial law was introduced, the Communist Party tried to break Solidarity by barring the trade union from the public sphere, imprisoning the organizational elite, and creating government-backed trade unions. Facing increased mass resistance expressed by frequent demonstrations, clandestine publishing, and two huge waves of political strikes, the Communist power elite decided in late 1988 that it had to accept Solidarity within the public sphere. Lech Walesa was recognized as the leader of a successful social movement and a partner in round table negotiations. These round table negotiations brought the mass movement back to the public space for the first time since martial law had been introduced. Being unable to suppress the agency of Solidarity, the rival Communist power elite had to grant the movement a right to co-decide about the future political system in Poland. This first comeback of the mass social movement meant a return of the whole movement onto the public space—complete with the political elite, a network of trade union organizations, and supporting networks of experts, publishers, and other professionals.

The second comeback occurred in mid–1989, when the parliamentary elections, conducted according to agreements reached during round table negotiations, demonstrated an overwhelming support for Solidarity and a total rejection of the Communist Party by the electorate. The immediate results of this comeback were a new division of power and election of a Solidarity-backed prime minister, Tadeusz Mazowiecki. While Solidarity started running the government, the descending Communist power elite remained formally in power by nominating General Jaruzelski to the post of president ("head of state"). This second comeback split Solidarity into a mass organization, which then created a network of local political representations ("citizens' committees") and started preparing elections to local self-government for 1990, and a political elite that started to take over the central government positions in the state.

The third comeback of Solidarity took place in the second half of 1990, when local elections practically eliminated the Communists from power positions, Lech Walesa was elected president, and the Communist Party dissolved itself. The mass social movement had split itself into rival groups within the political elite (the Warsaw "professionals" around Mazowiecki, and the Gdańsk "professionals" and "trade-unionists" around Walesa), into various political parties and into different trade unions still linked by a common past and name but already differentiated with respect to the branch of economy, region of Poland, and political sympathies.

Three consecutive comebacks of Solidarity as a mass social movement were simultaneously three different outcomes of individual and group decisions as to the structuring of an agency for collective action. At the very outset a uniform and coherent agency has been needed to oppose the Communists still holding power. At the very end, the Communists left public space (those who dissolved the Communist party formed a social democratic one) and a very differentiated group of agencies was formed to claim this space.

The first comeback happened when the choices within Solidarity were by and large made by the first generation of activists either elected in the first "legal" period of the trade union's existence (1980–1981) and subsequently repressed or by the activists who emerged during the "delegalized" (partly underground) struggle (1982–1988). They managed to create a broad political network of "citizens' committees" and to involve the entire population in removing Communists from positions of power. Lech Walesa is the prime example of this generation of movement activists.

The second comeback happened in the course of a political struggle in the parliament, in the media, and on a local level. It meant that organizational resources allowing them to reach the entire population became much more important (and issues became more subtle and differentiated). The advantage of having the Roman Catholic Church as a network of places where a majority of people could be regularly reached and the importance of the media became clear. This second comeback was therefore "manned" to a larger extent by Catholic intellectuals (who had their independent base in the media and could immediately broaden it when Communist control broke down) or by activists who managed to secure the church resources for a political activity (K. Kosela, 1991). Tadeusz Mazowiecki, an editor of a Catholic monthly and a former adviser of Walesa, is a very good example of the people behind the second comeback of Solidarity.

It is more difficult to ascribe a type of an activist to the third comeback of Solidarity since the movement itself was transformed during its return to the public space. However, one can definitely see the difference in support offered to two presidential candidates. Mazowiecki was supported by the professionals who considered the second comeback of

Solidarity to be the true conquering of the public space. Walesa was supported by the broad coalition of those for whom the first comeback was the most important one (since it broke the postwar Communist monopoly) and by the younger generation, for which his past record was much more impressive than detailed intricacies of daily politics. The past image of the broad social movement able to break the Communist monopoly contrasted starkly with Solidarity splitting into divergent parties, lobbies, and potential political elites.

And this splitting was exactly what the young generation observed when entering public space and beginning to articulate their interests. The youngest generation felt that the professionals around Mazowiecki were not to be trusted. They were perceived as a new "nomenklatura" in the making. Walesa was a powerful charismatic figure, and he stated clearly that he wanted to rely on local citizens' committees to get rid of the last Communist deputies to the parliament. The latter survived because they were elected in June 1989, when the round table conference secured their positions. Later on, they survived because they refused to be loyal to the Communist Party and co-generated its dissolving. For Mazowiecki's professionals they were an interesting political partner (easy to manipulate in the parliament). For Walesa and for the youngest generation they were the remains of the Communist past. They had to be removed to turn a parliament into an instrument of radical policy (privatization, introducing the market economy, restructuring of the industries, etc.). Walesa's adversaries accused him of playing a populist— thus manifesting their refusal to accept the third comeback of Solidarity.

Professionals by and large expected the movement to come to a standstill after the second comeback. When it did not, they supported Walesa's opponents. In the 1991 parliamentary elections they had supported candidates who promised to keep the system of checks and balances on the president. But the movement's movement breeds as much satisfaction as discontent. There is no privileged outcome of the movement's successive "comebacks," nor is there a way to stop the movements differentiation, polarization, and change. Walesa's charisma and local citizens' committees provided an ideology and a network for the third comeback of Solidarity, already divided into Mazowiecki's professionals and Walesa's industrial workers and the youngest generation.

In view of this chapter's main thesis, we can explain Walesa's electoral success by evoking the young generation's frustration with arrested upward social mobility. A common feeling was that the pace of institutional reform is much too slow. The Communists have been removed, but professionals mobilized around the Catholic politicians and took over the vacancies. And massive participation in stormy political events meant that open-ended socialization of the young generation was conducted to a considerable extent within the newly discovered and cultivated public sphere. Does it mean that the next, or fourth, comeback of "Solidarity" will depend on the ability of Walesa, Mazowiecki, or citizens' committees to attract those dissatisfied young individuals whose loyalties will decide how quickly and in what direction the movement will move?

There is no clear-cut conclusion to be drawn from the above case. The Solidarity movement did succeed in abolishing the Communist power monopoly and in changing the political, social, and economic rules of the social game in Poland. But in doing this, Solidarity experienced the consequences of movementization of social change with respect to itself. It became divided, generated conflicts of its own, and designed a new blueprint for the making of agencies capable of starting a collective action. New social spaces and new social movements bring about as many ambiguities that breed discontent and as many chances for taming as the authoritarian structures of the past they tend to replace.

REFERENCES

Aberle, David, 1962. "A note on relative deprivation theory as applied to millenarian and other cult movements," in Sylvia L. Thrupp, ed., *Comparative Studies in Society and History*, Supplement II, pp. 209–14. The Hague: Mouton.

Adas, Michael, 1979. *Prophets of Rebellion: Millenarian Protest Movements against the European Colonial Order.* Cambridge, MA: Cambridge University Press.

Adorno, T. W., Else Freukel-Brunswik, Daniel J. Levinson, et al., 1950. *The Authoritarian Personality.* New York: Harper.

Alberoni, Francesco, 1984. *Movement and Institution.* New York: Columbia University Press.

Alexander, Jeffrey, 1991. "Bringing democracy back in: Universalistic solidarity and civil sphere," in Charles C. Lemert, ed., *Intellectuals and Politics: Social Theory in a Changing World*, pp. 157–79. Newbury Park, CA: Sage.

Alexander, Thomas G., 1986. *Mormonism in Transition.* Champaign, IL: University of Illinois Press.

Ammerman, Nancy, 1987. *Bible Believers: Fundamentalists in the Modern World.* New Brunswick, NJ: Rutgers University Press.

Antoine, Charles, 1983. "Introduction," in Adolfo Pérez Esquivel, ed., *Christ in a Poncho*, pp. 4–12. Maryknoll, NY: Orbis.

Arrighi, Giovanni, Terence K. Hopkins, and Immanuel Wallerstein, 1989. *Antisystemic Movements.* London: Verso.

Arrington, Leonard J. and David Bitton, 1979. *The Mormon Experience.* New York: Vintage.

AV Report, 1990. September. (Monthly newsletter from American Vision, Atlanta, GA.)

Bahnsen, Greg L., 1985. *By This Standard: The Authority of God's Law Today.* Tyler, TX: Institute for Christian Economics.

———, 1984. *Theonomy in Christian Ethics*, 2nd ed. Phillipsburg, NJ: Presbyterian and Reformed Press.

Bainbridge, William Sims, 1985. "Cultural genetics," in Rodney Stark, ed., *Religious Movements: Genesis, Exodus, and Numbers*, pp. 157–98. New York: Paragon House.

Bainbridge, William Sims and Rodney Stark, 1980a. "Scientology: To be perfectly clear," *Sociological Analysis* 41 (Summer): 128–36.

———, 1980b. "Superstitions: Old and new," *The Skeptical Inquirer* 4(4): 18–31.

Barber, Bernard, 1941. "Acculturation and messianic movements," *American Sociological Review*: 663–69.

Barker, Eileen, 1989. *New Religious Movements: A Practical Introduction*. London: Her Majesty's Stationery Office.

Barker, William S. and W. Robert Godfrey, eds., 1990. *Theonomy: A Reformed Critique*. Grand Rapids, MI: Academic Books-Zondervon.

Barkun, Michael, 1985. "The awakening-cycle controversy," *Sociological Analysis* 46(4): 425–44.

Barron, Bruce, 1990. *Re-Christianizing America: The Reconstruction and Kingdom Now Movements in American Christianity*. University of Pittsburgh: Ph.D. dissertation.

Barry, Tom, 1987. *Roots of Rebellion*. Boston: South End Press.

Barton, Betty L., 1974. *The Fellowship of Reconciliation: Pacifism, Labor and Social Welfare, 1915–1960*. Ph.D. dissertation. Florida State University.

Bauman, Z., 1991. *Modernity and Ambivalence*. London: Polity/Blackwell.

Beckford, James A., 1985. *Cult Controversies: The Societal Response to New Religious Movements*. New York: Tavistock.

———, 1983. "The 'cult problem' in five countries: The social construction of religious controversy," in Eileen Barker, ed., *Of Gods and Men: New Religious Movements in the West*, pp. 195–214. Macon GA: Mercer University Press.

Bell, Daniel, 1964. "The dispossessed," in Daniel Bell, ed., *The Radical Right*, pp. 1–45. Garden City NY: Doubleday.

Bellah, Robert N., 1967. "Civil religion in America," *Daedulus* (Winter): 1–21.

Belshaw, Cyril S, 1972. "The significance of modern cults in Melanesian development," in William A. Lessa and Evon Z. Vogt, eds., *Reader in Comparative Religion: An Anthropological Approach*, 3rd edition, pp. 523–27. New York: Harper and Row.

Berger, Peter L. and Thomas Luckmann, 1967. *Social Construction of Reality: A Treatise in the Sociology of Knowledge*. Garden City, NY: Doubleday.

Berryman, Phillip, 1986. *Liberation Theology*. New York: Pantheon.

Best, Marigold, 1982. *Information about Servicio Paz y Justicia en America Latina*. Buenos Aires, Argentina: SERPAJ-AL.

Bidegain, Ana Maria, 1985. "From Catholic action to liberation theology: The historical process of the laity in Latin America in the twentieth century," Working Paper no. 48. Notre Dame, IN: Kellogg Institute.

Bloom, Alan, 1987. *The Closing of the American Mind*. New York: Simon and Schuster.

Bociurkiw, Bohdan R., 1977. "The catacomb church: Ukrainian Greek Catholics in the USSR," *Religion in Communist Lands* 5(1): 4–12.

———, 1975. "Religious dissent and the Soviet stage," in Bohdan R. Bociurkiw and John W. Strong, eds., *Religion and Atheism in the USSR and Eastern Europe*, pp. 58–90. London: Macmillan.

Bolczyk, Henryk, Rev. and Pawel Wieczorek, 1987, "Oazy" [Oases], *Wiez* [Bond] 2–3: 22–29.

Borowski, Karol H., 1986. "Religion and politics in post–world war II Poland," in Jeffery K. Hadden and Anson Shupe, eds., *Prophetic Religions and Politics*, pp. 22–32. New York: Paragon House.

Boulding, Elise, 1988. *Building a Global Civic Culture*. Syracuse, NY: Syracuse University Press.

Bourdeaux, Michael, 1979. *Land of Crosses: The Struggle for Religious Freedom in Lithuania, 1939–78*. Devon: Augustine.

Bourdieu, Pierre, 1991. *Language and Symbolic Power*. Cambridge, MA: Harvard University Press.

Brodzki, Krzysztof and Jozef Wojna, 1988. *Oazy: Ruch Swiatlo-Zycie* [Oases: The Movement 'Light-Life']. Warsaw: Ksiazka i Wiedza.

Broekstra, G., 1991. "Chaos, the fifth environment and the revolution of inter-organizational cooperation," in G. Zeeuw, ed., *Problems of Support and Culture*. Boston: D. Reidel.

Bromley, David G., 1985. "Financing the millennium: The economic structure of the Unificationist movement," *Journal for the Scientific Study of Religion* 24 (September): 253–74.

Bromley, David G. and Phillip E. Hammond, eds., 1987. *The Future of New Religious Movements*. Macon, GA: Mercer University Press.

Bromley, David and Anson D. Shupe, 1980. "Financing the new religions: A resource mobilization approach," *Journal for the Scientific Study of Religion* 19 (September): 227–39.

———, 1979. *"Moonies" in America: Cult, Church, and Crusade*. Beverly Hills, CA: Sage.

Bromley, David G., Anson D. Shupe, and Bruce Busching, 1981. "Repression of religious cults," in Louis Kriesberg, ed., *Research in Social Movements, Conflicts, and Change*, vol. 4, pp. 25–45. Greenwich, CT: JAI Press.

Bromley, David G., Anson D. Shupe, and Donna L. Oliver, 1982. "Perfect families: Visions of the future in a new religious movement," *Marriage and Family Review* 4 (Fall/Winter): 119–29.

Burnett, Virginia Garrard, 1991. "Mid trial and tribulation: Protestantism in modern Guatemala." Paper delivered at the annual meeting of the Latin American Studies Association, Washington D.C., April 5.

Burridge, Kenelm, 1969. *New Heaven, New Earth*. New York: Schocken.

———, 1960. *Mambu*. New York: Harper.

Cardoso, Ruth Correa Leite, 1989. "Popular movements in the context of the consolidation of democracy," Working Paper no. 120. Notre Dame, IN: Kellogg Institute.

Cavanaugh, Michael A., 1987. "One-eyed social movements: Rethinking issues in rationality and society," *Philosophy of Social Science* 17: 147–72.

———, 1983. *A Sociological Account of Scientific Creationism: Science, True Science, Pseudoscience*. Ann Arbor, MI: University Microfilms International: Ph.D. dissertation, University of Pittsburgh.

Chartier, Richard, 1980. "Adolfo Pérez Esquivel: Behind the man and the prize," *Fellowship* 7–9 (December): 23.

Chatfield, Charles, 1971. *For Peace and Justice: Pacifism in America, 1914–1941*. Boston: Beacon Press.

Chaves, Mark, 1989. "Secularization and religious revival: Evidence from U.S. church attendance rates," *Journal for the Scientific Study of Religion* 28 (December): 464–77.

Chilton, David, 1987. *The Days of Vengence*. Fort Worth, TX: Dominion Press.

———, 1985a. *Paradise Restores: A Biblical Theology of Dominion*. Tyler, TX: Reconstruction Press.

———, 1985b. *Productive Christians in an Age of Guilt-Manipulators*, 3rd Edition. Tyler, TX: Institute for Christian Economics.

Chrypinski, Vincent C., 1984. "Church and nationality in postwar Poland," in Pedro Ramet, ed., *Religion and Nationalism in Soviet and East European Politics*. Durham, NC: Duke University Press.

Ciupak, Edward, 1961. *Kultura Religijna Wsi. Szkice Socjologiczne* [The Religious Culture of the Village]. Warsaw: Iskry.

Clark, John G., Jr., Michael D. Langone, Robert E. Schecter, and Roger C.B. Daly. 1981. *Destructive Cult Conversion: Theory, Research, and Treatment*. Boston, MA: Center on Destructive Cultism.

Clegg, Stewart, 1990. *Capitalism in Contrasting Cultures*. New York: DeGruyter.

Cohen, Jean and Andrew Arato, 1982.

Cohn, Norman, 1970. *The Pursuit of the Millennium*, Revised Edition. New York: Oxford University Press.

Coleman, James S., 1990. *Foundations of Social Theory*. Cambridge, MA: Belknap Press.

Colson, Charles and Ellen Santilli Vaughn, 1989. *Against the Night: Living in the New Dark Ages*. Grand Rapids, MI: Zondervan/Morrow.

Cooley, Charles Horton, 1962. *Social Organization: A Study of the Larger Mind*. New York: Schocken.

Cornell, Tom, 1977. "Adolfo Pérez Esquivel," *Fellowship* (September): 6–9.

Cox, Harvey, 1965. *The Secular City*. New York: Macmillan.

Crouch, Colin, 1986. "Sharing public space: States and organized interests in Western Europe," in John Hall, ed., *States in History*, pp. 177–211. London: Basil Blackwell.

Cviic, Christopher, 1983. "The Church," in Abraham Brumberg, ed., *Poland: Genesis of Revolution*, pp. 92–105. New York: Vintage.

D'Amico, Robert, 1990. "Intellectual eclipse," *Telos* 83: 163–67.

Deats, Richard, ed., 1991. *Ambassador of Reconciliation: A Muriel Lester Reader*. Philadelphia: New Society.

DeMar, Gary, 1988. *The Debate over Christian Reconstructionism*. Atlanta, GA: American Vision Press.

———, 1987. *Ruler of the Nations: Biblical Principles for Government*. Ft. Worth, TX: Dominion Press.

——— and Peter Leithart. 1988. *The Reduction of Christianity*. Atlanta, GA: American Vision Press.

Dembowski, Bronislaw, Rev. and Jan Turnau, 1987. "Ruch charyzmatyczny" [The Charismatic Movement], *Wiez* [Bond] 2–3: 30–38.

Deming, Marty, 1978. "What is SERVICIO?" *IFOR Report* (December): 7–8.

Derrida, Jacques, 1990. *Of Grammatology*. Baltimore: Johns Hopkins Press.

Diamond, Sara, 1989. *Spiritual Warfare: The Politics of the Christian Right*. Boston: South End Press.

Dobrowolski, Kazimierz, 1971. "Peasant traditional culture," in Teodor Shanin, ed., *Peasants and Peasant Societies*, pp. 277–88. Harmondsworth: Penguin.

Dodson, Michael, and Laura Nuzzi O'Shaughnessy, 1990. *Nicaragua's Other Revolution*. Chapel Hill: University of North Carolina Press.

Doktor, Tadeusz and Krzysztof Kosela, eds., 1984. *Ruchy Progranicza Religii I Nauki Jako Zjawisko Socjopsychologiczne* [Movements on the Border of Religion and Science as SocioPsychological Phenomena]. Warsaw: University of Warsaw Press.

Dominguez, Enrique, 1984. "The great commission," *NACLA Report on the Americas*, 18, no. 1 (January–February): 12–22.

Dorr, Donal, 1983. *Option for the Poor*. Maryknoll, NY: Orbis.

D'Souza, Dinesh, 1991. *Liberal Education: The Politics of Race and Sex on Campus*. Glencoe, IL: Free Press.

Durkheim, Emile, 1965. *The Elementary Forms of the Religious Life*. Glencoe IL: Free Press. (Original edition: London: Allen and Unwin, 1915.)

Eckstein, Susan, 1989. *Power and Popular Protest: Latin American Social Movements*. Berkeley: University of California Press.

Engels, Frederick, 1950. *The Peasant War in Germany*. Moscow: Progress.

Engleberg, Stephen, 1991. "Polish state keeps its distance from church," *New York Times*, May 26, 1991: E5.

Epstein, Barbara, 1991. *Political Protest and Cultural Revolution: Nonviolent Direct Action in the 1970s and 1980s*. Berkeley: University of California Press.

Eve, Raymond A. and Francis B. Harrold, 1991. *The Creationist Movement in Modern America*. Boston: Twayne Publishers.

———, 1986. "Creationism, cult archaeology, and other pseudoscientific beliefs: A study of college students," *Youth and Society* 17 no. 4: 396–421.

Featherstone, Mike, ed., 1988. Special Volume of *Theory, Culture, and Society* 5 (2/3).

Feher, Ferenc, ed., 1991. *The French Revolution and the Birth of Modernity*. Berkeley: University of California Press.

Festinger, Leon, Henry W. Riecken, and Stanley Schachter, 1956. *When Prophecy Fails*. New York: Harper.

Finklestein, Etian, 1977. "Old hopes and new currents in present-day Lithuania," in Thomas Remeikis, ed., *The Violations of Human Rights in Soviet Occupied Lithuania*, pp. 58–66. Glenside, PA: Lithuanian American Community.

Fireman, Bruce and William Gamson, 1979. "Utilitarian logic in the resource mobilization perspective," in Mayer Zald and John McCarthy, eds., *The Dynamics of Social Movements*, pp. 8–44. Winthrop, MA: Winthrop.

Fiske, Alan P., 1991. *Structures of Social Life*. New York: Free Press.

Freeman, Jo, 1979. "Resource mobilization and strategy: A model for analyzing social movement organization actions," in Mayer Zald and John McCarthy, eds., *The Dynamics of Social Movements*, pp. 167–89. Winthrop, MA: Winthrop.

Frentzel-Zagorska, Janina, 1990. "Civil society in Poland and Hungary," *Soviet Studies* 40(4): 759–77.

Frentzel-Zagorska, Janina and Zagorski Krzysztof, 1989. "East European intellectuals on the road to dissent: The old prophecy of a new class reexamined," *Politics and Society* 17(1) (March): 89–99.

Fuchs, Stephen, 1965. *Rebellious Prophets: A Study of Messianic Movements in Indian Religions.* Bombay: Asia Publishing.

Fundamentals, The. 1988. 4 vols. Grand Rapids, Mich.: Baker Book House. (Original edition: 10 vols. Los Angeles: Bible Institute of Los Angeles, 1910–1915.)

Garfinkel, Harold, 1956. "Conditions of successful degradation ceremonies," *American Journal of Sociology* 61: 420–24.

Garrett, William R., 1988. "Liberation theology and the concept of human rights," in Anson Shupe and Jeffrey K. Hadden, eds., *The Politics of Religion and Social Change*, pp. 128–43. New York: Paragon House.

Garrett, William R. and Roland Robertson, 1991. "Religion and globalization: An introduction," in Roland Robertson and William R. Garrett, eds., *Religion and Global Order*, pp. ix–xxiii. New York: Paragon House.

Giddens, Anthony, 1985. *The Constitution of Society: Outline of the Theory of Structuration.* Berkeley: University of California Press.

Gish, Duane T., 1985. *Evolution: The Challenge of the Fossil Record.* El Cajon, CA: Creation-Life Publishers.

———, 1978. *Evolution? The Fossils Say No!* San Diego, CA: Creation-Life Publishers.

Glazier, Stephen D., 1986. "Prophecy and ecstasy: Religion and politics in the Caribbean," in Jeffrey K. Hadden and Anson Shupe, eds., *Prophetic Religions and Politics*, pp. 430–47. New York: Paragon.

Golebiowski, Bronislaw and Zygmunt Hemmerling, 1982. "Chlopi wobec kryzysow w Polsce Ludowej" [Peasants and the Crises in People; Poland] *Kultura i Spoleczenstwo* [Culture and Society] 1–2: 254–61.

Goodwyn, Lawrence, 1991. *Breaking the Barrier: The Rise of Solidarity in Poland.* New York: Oxford University Press.

Gordon, James S., 1987. *The Gold Guru: The Strange Journey of Bhagwan Shree Rajneesh.* Lexington, MA: Stephen Greene.

Gorlach, Krzysztof, 1989. "On repressive tolerance: State and peasant farm in Poland," *Sociologia Ruralis* 1: xxix.

Goss-Mayr, Jean and Hildegard Goss-Mayr, 1984. "Antecedentes del 'Servicio Paz y Justicia' en America Latina." Rio de Janeiro: SERPAJ-AL.

———, 1971. "Report December 1st to February 15, 1971." Rio de Janeiro: SERPAJ-AL.

———, 1966. "Report on work in Latin America from May to August 1966," November 1966. Rio de Janeiro: SERPAJ-AL.

———, 1962a. "Confidential report on work in Latin America," June 11, 1962. Rio de Janeiro: SERPAJ-AL.

———, 1962b. "News from South America from Jean and Hildegard Goss," April 16, 1962. Rio de Janeiro: SERPAJ: AL.

Gouldner, Alvin W., 1976. *The Dialectic of Ideology and Technology.* New York: Seabury.

Greinacher, Norbert, 1987. "Jeden kosciol a wiele sluzb" [One church and many kinds of service], *Zycie Katolickie* [Catholic Life] 2: 79–92.

Gusfield, Joseph R., 1963. *Symbolic Crusade: Status Politics and the American Temperance Movement.* Urbana: University of Illinois Press.

Habermas, Jurgen, 1990. "What does socialism mean today? The rectifying revolution and the need for new thinking on the left," *New Left Review* 183: 3–21.

——, 1989. *The Structural Transformation of the Public Sphere: An Inquiry into a Category of Bourgeois Society.* Cambridge, MA: MIT Press.

Hadden, Jeffrey K., 1989. "Desacralizing secularization theory," in Jeffrey K. Hadden and Anson Shupe, eds., *Fundamentalism and Secularization Reconsidered*, pp. 3–26. New York: Paragon House.

Hadden, Jeffrey K. and Anson Shupe, 1989. *Fundamentalism and Secularization Reconsidered.* New York: Paragon House.

——, 1988. *Televangelism: Power and Politics on God's Frontier.* New York: Henry Holt.

Halamska, Maria, 1988. "Peasant movements in Poland, 1980–1981," in Louis Kriesberg and Bronislaw Misztal, eds., *Social Movements as a Factor of Change in the Contemporary World*, pp. 189–203: *Research in Social Movements, Conflicts, and Change*, vol. 10. Greenwich, CN: JAI Press.

Hankiss, Elmer, 1988. "The second society: Is there an alternative social model emerging in contemporary Hungary?" *Social Research* 55(1–2) (Spring/ Summer): 13–43.

Harrington, Michael, 1989. *Socialism, Past and Future.* New York: Arcade.

Harrold, Francis B. and Raymond A. Eve, 1987. *Cult Archaeology and Creationism: Understanding Pseudoscientific Beliefs about the Past.* Iowa City: University of Iowa Press.

Harvey, David, 1989. *The Condition of Postmodernity: An Enquiry into the Origins of Cultural Change.* Cambridge, MA: Basil Blackwell.

Held, David, 1987. *Models of Democracy.* London: Basil Blackwell.

Henry, Carl F. 1988. *Twilight of a Great Civilization.* Westchester, IL: Crossway.

Hoffer, Eric, 1951. *The True Believer.* New York: New American Library.

Hofstadter, Richard, 1955. *The Development of Academic Freedom in the United States.* New York: Columbia University Press.

Holsworth, Robert D. 1989. *Let Your Life Speak: A Study of Politics, Religion, and Antinuclear Weapons Activism.* Madison: University of Wisconsin Press.

House, Wayne and Thomas Ice, 1988. *Dominion Theology: Blessing or Curse?* Portland, OR: Multnomah.

Hudson, Winthrop S., 1987. *Religion in America*, 4th Edition. New York: Macmillan.

Hunt, Dave, 1988. *Whatever Happened to Heaven?* Eugene, OR: Harvest House.

Hunter, James Davison, 1987. "The evangelical world view since 1890," in Richard John Neuhaus and Michael Cromartie, eds., *Piety and Politics: Evangelicals and Fundamentalists Confront the World*, pp. 19–54. Washington, D.C.: Ethics and Public Policy Center.

——, 1981. "Operationalizing evangelicalism: A review, critique, and proposal," *Sociological Analysis* 42: 363–72.

Huntington, Deborah, 1984. "God's saving plan," *NACLA Report on the Americas* 18, no. 1 (January–February): 23–33.

Hutcheon, Linda, 1989. *The Politics of Postmodernism*. London: Routledge.

Hvat, Ivan, 1984. *The Catacomb Ukrainian Catholic Church and Pope John Paul II*. Cambridge, MA: Ukrainian Studies Fund.

Jacoby, Russel, 1987. *The Last Intellectuals*. New York: Basic Books.

Jameson, Frederic, 1991. *Postmodernism, of the Cultural Logic of Late Capitalism*. Durham, NC: Duke University Press.

Jasinska, Aleksandra and Renata Siemienska, 1975. *Wzory Osobowe Socializm* [Socialist Patterns of Personality]. Warsaw: Wiedza Powszechna.

Jelin, Elizabeth, 1990. "Introduction," in Elizabeth Jelin, ed., *Women and Social Change in Latin America*, pp. 1–12. Atlantic Highlands, NJ: Zed Books.

———, 1987. "The movement: Eclipsed by democracy?" *NACLA Report on the Americas* 21(4): 28–36, 39.

———, 1986. "Otros silencios, otras voces: El tiempo de la democratización en la Argentina," in Calderon G. Fernando, ed., *Los movimientos sociales antes de la crisis*, pp. 17–44. New York: United Nations University.

———, ed., 1985. *Los nuevos movimientos sociales: 1. Mujeres, rock nacional*. Buenos Aires: Centro Editor de América Latina.

Jenkins, J. Craig, 1983. "Resource mobilization theory and the study of social movements," *Annual Review of Sociology* 9: 527–53.

Johnson, Stephen and Joseph Tamney, 1986. *The Political Role of Religion in the United States*. Boulder, CO: Westview Press.

Johnston, Hank, 1991. *Tales of Nationalism: Catalonia 1939–1979*. New Brunswick, NJ: Rutgers University Press.

———, 1989. "Toward an explanation of church opposition to authoritarian regimes: Religio-oppositional subcultures in Poland and Catalonia," *Journal for the Scientific Study of Religion* 28(4): 493–508.

Johnston, Hank and Jozef Figa, 1988. "The church and political opposition: Comparative perspectives on mobilization against authoritarian regimes," *Journal for the Scientific Study of Religion* 27(1): 32–47.

Kapica, Jack, 1991. "Fifth column: Religion," *The Globe and Mail* (Toronto), September 28: A20.

Klandermans, Bert, 1986. "New social movements and resource mobilization: The European and the American approach," *International Journal of Mass Emergencies and Disasters* 4(2) (August): 13–37.

———, 1984. "Mobilization and participation: Social-psychological expansions of resource mobilization theory," *American Sociological Review* 49:583–600.

Knott, Kim, 1986. *My Sweet Lord: The Hare Krishna Movement*. Wellingborough, Northamptonshire, England: Aquarian Press.

Kosela, Krzysztof, 1991. "The Catholic Church before June elections." unpublished manuscript: Warsaw: University of Warsaw.

Kuhn, Thomas S., 1970. *The Structure of Scientific Revolution*, 2nd Edition. Chicago: University of Chicago Press.

Laba, Raymond, 1991. *The Roots of Solidarity*. Princeton: Princeton University Press.

Larson, Edward J., 1985. *Trial and Error: The American Controversy over Creation and Evolution*. New York: Oxford University Press.

Lasky, Melvin J., 1976. *Utopia and Revolution*. London: Macmillan.

Lechner, Frank J., 1988. "Fundamentalism and sociocultural revitalization: On the logic of dedifferentiation," in Jeffrey C. Alexander and Paul Colomy, eds., *Differentiation Theory and Social Change: Historical and Comparative Perspectives*, pp. 12–30. New York: Columbia University Press.

———, 1985. "Fundamentalism and sociocultural revitalization in America," *Sociological Analysis* 46: 243–60.

Lehmann, David, 1990. *Democracy and Development in Latin America: Economics, Politics, and Religion in the Post-War Period*. Philadelphia: Temple University Press.

Lemert, Charles C., ed., 1991. *Intellectuals and Politics: Social Theory in a Changing World*. Newbury Park, CA: Sage.

Lernoux, Penny, 1988. "The fundamentalist surge in Latin America," *Christian Century*, January 20: 51–54.

Lewy, Gunter, 1974. *Religion and Revolution*. New York: Oxford University Press.

Liebman, Robert C., 1983. "Mobilizing the moral majority," in Robert C. Liebman and Robert Wuthnow, eds., *The New Christian Right: Mobilization and Legitimation*, pp. 50–73. New York: Aldine.

Liebman, Robert C. and Robert Wuthnow, eds., 1983. *The New Christian Right: Mobilization and Legitimation*. New York: Aldine.

Linton, Ralph, 1943. "Nativistic movements," *American Anthropologist* 45: 230–40.

Lipset, Seymour M. and Earl Raab, 1981. "The election and the evangelicals," *Commentary* 71: 25–32.

Livermore, J. D., 1989. "The universal declaration and beyond: Human rights and international action," in Irving Brecher, ed., *Human Rights, Development, and Foreign Policy: Canadian Perspectives*, pp. 145–65. Halifax, Nova Scotia, Canada: Institute for Research on Public Policy.

Maciel, Creuza, 1986. "SERPAJ facing the liberation process. Special: A summary of SERPAJ-AL's history," *Informative Letter* 3 no. 1.

Mainwaring, Scott and E. Viola, 1984. "New social movements, political culture and democracy: Brazil and Argentina in the 1980s," *Telos* (Fall) 61: 17–54.

Manchester, William, 1986. *Disturber of the Peace: The Life of H. L. Mencken*, 2nd Edition. Amherst: University of Massachusetts Press.

Mann, Michael, 1986. "The autonomy of the state power," in John Hall, ed., *States in History*, pp. 111–77. London: Basil Blackwell.

Marianski, Janusz, 1983. "Przemiany religijnosci ludowej w srodowisku wiejskim" [Transformations of popular religiosity in rural environment], in Wladyslaw Piwowarski, ed., *Religijnosc Ludowa* [Popular Religiosity], pp. 27–41. Wroclaw: Wydawnictwo Wroclawskiej Ksiegarni Diecezjalnej.

Marken, Hubert, 1988. *Pat Robertson: Where He Stands*. Old Tappan, NJ: Ravell.

Markus, Vasyl, 1975. "Religion and nationality: The Uniates of the Ukraine," in Bohdan R. Bociurkiw and John W. Strong, eds., *Religion and Atheism in the USSR and Eastern Europe*, pp. 101–22. London: Macmillan.

Marody, Miroslawa, ed., 1991. *Co Nam Zostalo z Tych Lat: Spoleczenstwo Polskie u Progu Zmiany Systemowej* [What is Left of those Years: Polish Society Facing Systemic Change] London: Aneks.

Marsden, George M., 1987. "The Evangelical Denomination," in *Piety and Politics: Evangelicals and Fundamentalists Confront the World*, pp. 55–68. Washington, DC: Ethics and Public Policy Center.

———, 1983. "Creation vs. evolution: No middle way," *Nature* 305: 571–74.

———, 1980. *Fundamentalism and American Culture: The Shaping of Twentieth Century Evangelicalism, 1870–1925*. New York: Oxford University Press.

Martínez, Abelino, 1989. *Las sectas en Nicaragua: Oferta y demanda de salvación* [The Sects in Nicaragua: Appeal and Request of Salvation] San Jose, Costa Rica: Editorial Departmento Ecumenico de Investigaciones.

McAdam, Doug, 1983. "Tactical innovation and the pace of insurgency," *American Sociological Review* 48(6): 735–54.

———, 1982. *Political Process and the Development of Black Insurgency*. Chicago: University of Chicago Press.

McCarthy, John and Mayer N. Zald, 1977. "Resource mobilization in social movements: A partial theory," *American Journal of Sociology* 82 (May): 1212–41.

McLuhan, Marshall and Quentin Fiore, 1967. *The Medium Is the Message*. New York: Bantam.

McManus, Philip, 1991a. "Introduction: In search of the Shalom society," in Philip McManus and Gerald Schlabach, eds., *Relentless Persistence: Nonviolent Action in Latin America*, pp. 1–13. Santa Cruz, CA: New Society Publisher.

———, 1991b. "To discover our humanity: Adolfo Pérez Esquivel [an interview]," in Philip McManus and Gerald Schlabach, eds., *Relentless Persistence: Nonviolent Action in Latin America*, pp. 238–51. Santa Cruz, CA: New Society Publishers.

Melucci, Alberto, 1989. "Nomads of the present," in John Keane and Paul Mier, eds., *Social Movements and Individual Needs in Contemporary Society*, pp. 819–35. London: Hutchinson Radius.

———, 1984. "An end to social movements?" *Social Science Information* 23(4–5): 819–35.

Mencken, Henry L., 1925. *American Mercury*, October.

Mess, Zulkarnaina M. and Barnett Pearce, 1986. "Dakwah Islamiah Islamic politics in the politics of race and religion in Malaysia," in Jeffrey K. Hadden and Anson Shupe, eds., *Prophetic Religions and Politics*, pp. 196–220. New York: Paragon House.

Michel, Patrick, 1990. *Politics and Religion in Eastern Europe*. Cambridge, MA: Polity Press.

Mignone, Emilio, 1988. *Witness to the Truth: The Complicity of Church and Dictatorship in Argentina, 1976–1983*, Phillip Berryman, translator. Maryknoll, NY: Orbis.

Miller, Jon D., 1987. "The scientifically illiterate," *American Demographics* 9(6): 26–31.

Misztal, Bronislaw, 1992. "Between the state and Solidarity: One movement, two interpretations—the Orange Alternative movement in Poland," *British Journal of Sociology* 43(1): 55–78.

———, 1991. "An intellectual vis-à-vis the breakdown of the etatistic order:

Between misunderstanding of the past and misinterpreting the future,"
Litteraria Pragensia 1: 46–49.

————. 1990a. "Alternative social movements in contemporary Poland," in L.
Kriesberg and Bronislaw Misztal, eds., *Research in Social Movements, Conflict,
and Change*, Vol. 12, pp. 67–88. Greenwich, CT: JAI Press.

————, 1990b. "The commodification of housing under the state socialist welfare
policies in Poland," in Willem Van Vliet, ed., *International Handbook of
Housing*, pp. 265–87. Westport, CT: Greenwood Press.

————, 1985. "Barriers to Social Development in Polish Sociological Theory."
British Journal of Sociology 4 (December): 574–85.

————. 1978. *Urban Sociology* [in Polish: Sociologia Viasta.] Warsaw: Iwiez.

Moffett, J., 1988. *Storm in the Mountains*. Carbondale: Southern Illinois University
Press.

Morawska, Ewa, 1984. "Civil religion vs. state power in Poland," *Society* 21, no.
4 (May/June): 29–34.

Morawski, Witold, 1980. "Society and strategy of imposed industrialization,"
Kultura 49 (Dec. 7): 3–4.

Morris, Aldon, 1984. *The Origins of the Civil Rights Movement: Black Communities
Organizing for Change*. New York: Free Press.

Morris, Henry M., 1984. *A History of Modern Creationism*. San Diego, CA: Master
Books.

Munck, Ronaldo, 1989. *Latin America: The Transition to Democracy*. Atlantic Highlands, NJ: Zed Books.

Munoz, Carlos, Creuza Maciel, and Carmen de Souza, 1986. *Resena historica del
SERPAJ-AL. Primer volumen: Una alternativa revolucionaria?* Rio de Janeiro:
SERPAJ-AL.

NACLA Report on the Americas, 1986. 20(2) (April-May): 17–48.

Nagel, Joane and Susan Olzak, 1982. "Ethnic mobilization in new and old states,"
Social Problems 30(2): 127–143.

Nash, Ronald H., 1987. *Evangelicals in America*. Nashville: Abingdon Press.

Navarro, Marysa, 1989. "The personal is political: Las madres de Plaza de Mayo,"
in Susan Eckstein, ed., *Power and Popular Protest: Latin American Social
Movements*, pp. 241–58. Berkeley: University of California Press.

Nelkin, Dorothy, 1982. *The Creation Controversy: Science or Scripture in the Schools*.
New York: Norton.

Nietzsche, Friedrich, 1968. *Twilight of the Idols/The Anti-Christ*. New York: Viking
Penguin.

North, Gary, 1990. *Tools of Dominion: The Case Laws of Exodus*. Tyler, TX: Institute
for Christian Economics.

————, 1988. *Unconditional Surrender: God's Program for Victory*, 3rd Edition. Tyler, TX: Institute for Christian Economics.

————, 1987. *Liberating Planet Earth: An Introduction to Biblical Blueprints*. Ft.
Worth, TX: Dominion Press.

————, 1984. *Backward, Christian Soldiers?* Tyler, TX: Institute for Christian
Economics.

————, 1982. "The intellectual schizophrenia of the new Christian right," in
James Jorden, ed., *The Failure of the American Baptist Culture*, pp. 1–40.
Christianity and Civilization Series 1. Tyler, TX: Geneva Divinity School.

Nosowski, Zbigniew, 1989. "Oazy, drzemiacy olbrzym" [Oases, sleeping giant], *Wiez* [Bond] 4: 31–47.

Nowak, Stefan, 1982. *Spoleczenstwo Polskie Czasu Keyzysu.* [Polish Society at the Time of Crisis]. Warsaw: University of Warsaw Press.

Numbers, Ronald L., 1986. "The creationists," in D. Lindberg and Ronald Numbers, eds., *God and Nature: Historical Essays on the Encounter between Christianity and Science*, pp. 2391–423. Berkeley: University of California Press.

Oberschall, Anthony R., 1984. "Politics and religion: The new Christian right in California," *Social Science News Letter* 69: 20–24.

O'Brien, Connor Cruise, 1987. *God Land: Reflections on Religion and Nationalism.* Cambridge, MA: Harvard University Press.

O'Dea, Thomas F., 1966. *The Sociology of Religion.* Englewood Cliffs, NJ: Prentice-Hall.

Ofshe, Richard, 1980. "The social development of the Synanon cult: The managerial strategy of organizational transformation," *Sociological Analysis* 41 (Summer): 109–27.

Page, Ann L. and Donald A. Clelland, 1978. "The Kanawha County textbook controversy: A study of the politics of lifestyle concern," *Social Forces* 57: 265–81.

Parkman, Patricia, 1990. *Insurrectionary Civic Strikes in Latin America: 1931–1961.* Cambridge, MA: Albert Einstein Institution.

Pasek, Zbigniew, 1989. "Katolicki ruch odnowy w duchu swietym" [The Catholic movement of Renewal in the Holy Spirit], *Chrzescijanin w Swiecie* [A Christian in the World] 186 (March): 31–46.

Pawelczynska, Anna, 1971. "Postawy ludnosci wiejskiej wobec religii" [Attitudes of peasants towards religion] *Roczniki Socjologii Wsi* [Annuals of Rural Sociology] 8: 27–41.

Pawluczuk, Wlodzimierz, 1968. "Swiatopoglad jednostki w okresie rozpadu tradycyjnej spolecznosci terytorialnej [Individual world-view at the time of disintegration of territorial community]" *Studia Socjologiczne* [Sociological Studies] 3–4.

Peretti, Frank, 1989. *Piercing the Darkness.* Westchester, IL: Crossway.

———, 1988. *This Present Darkness.* Westchester, IL: Crossway.

Pérez-Agote, Alfonso, 1986. *La reproducción del nacionalismo vasco.* Madrid: CIS/Siglo XXI Editores.

Pickvance, Chris G., 1988. "Employers, labour markets and redistribution under state socialism: An interpretation of housing policy in Hungary," *Sociology* 22, no. 2: 193–214.

Piwowarski, Wladyslaw, 1984. "Przemiany religijnosci ludowej w srodowisku wiejskim" [Transformation of popular religiosity in the rural environment] *Kultura i Spoleczenstwo* [Culture and Society] 3: 27–41.

Poggi, Gianfranco, 1978. *The Development of Modern State.* London: Hutchinson.

Poloma, Margaret M., 1986. "Pentecostals and politics in North and Central America," in Jeffrey K. Hadden and Anson Shupe, eds., *Prophetic Religions and Politics*, pp. 329–52. New York: Paragon House.

Ramet, Pedro, 1987. *Cross and Commissar: The Politics of Religion in Eastern Europe and the USSR.* Bloomington: Indiana University Press.

Ready, Timothy, Brady Tyson, and Ron Pagnucco, 1985. "The impact of the

Nobel Peace Prize on the work of Adolfo Pérez Esquivel." Paper presented at the International Studies Association Annual Conference, March, Washington, D.C.

Reddaway, Peter, 1975. "The Georgian Orthodox Church: Corruption and renewal," *Religion in Communist Lands* July/October: 14–23.

Redfield, Robert, 1955. *The Little Community.* Chicago: University of Chicago Press.

———, 1953. *The Primitive World and its Transformation.* Ithaca, NY: Cornell University Press.

Reichley, A. James, 1987. "The evangelical and fundamentalist revolt," in Richard John Neuhaus and Michael Cromartie, eds., *Piety and Politics: Evangelicals and Fundamentalists Confront the World*, pp. 69–95. Washington D.C.: Ethics and Public Policy Center.

Reid, P. Nelson and Paul D. Starr, n.d. "Bayou La Batre and the 'Moonies': A multi-national religious corporation enters a Gulf Coast community." Unpublished manuscript funded by the Mississippi-Alabama Sea Grant Consortium.

Richardson, James T., ed., 1988. *Money and Power in the New Religions.* Lewiston, NY: Edwin Mellen Press.

———, 1982. "Financing the new religions: Comparative and theoretical considerations," *Journal for the Scientific Study of Religion* 21 (September): 255–68.

Richardson Nute, Betty, 1974. *Helder Cámara's Latin America.* London: Friends Peace and International Relations Committee.

Rifkin, Jeremy (with Ted Howard). 1979. *The Emerging Order.* New York: Ballantine.

Robbins, Thomas and Dick Anthony, 1982. "Deprogramming, brainwashing and the medicalization of deviant religious groups," *Social Problems* 29 (February): 283–97.

——— 1979. "The sociology of contemporary religious movement," *Annual Review of Sociology* 5: 75–89.

Robertson, Pat, 1991. *Pat Robertson's Perspective*, March-April.

Robertson, Roland, 1991. "Globalization, modernization, and postmodernization," in Roland Robertson and William R. Garrett, *Religion and Global Order*, pp. 281–91. New York: Paragon House.

———, 1987a. "From secularization to globalization," *The Journal of Oriental Studies* 26: 28–32.

———, 1987b. "Globalization and societal modernization: A note on Japan and Japanese religion," *Sociological Analysis* 47: 35–42.

Robertson, Roland and JoAnn Chirico, 1985. "Humanity, globalization, and worldwide religious resurgence: A theoretical exploration," *Sociological Analysis* 46: 219–59.

Rose, Susan D., 1988. *Keeping Them out of the Hands of Satan: Evangelical Schooling in America.* New York: Routledge.

Rushdoony, Rousas John, 1986. *Law and Society: Volume II of the Institutes of Biblical Law.* Vallecito, CA: Ross House Books.

———, 1973. *The Institutes of Biblical Law.* Phillipsburg, NJ: Presbyterian and Reformed Publishing.

————, 1963. *The Messianic Character of American Education*. Nutley, NJ: Craig.

Ruszar, Jozef, 1983. "Duszpasterstwo Akademickie Dominikanow w Krakowie 'beczka' " [College student ministry at the Dominican Church in Cracow— 'the Barrel'], *Wiez* [Bond] 2:67–81.

Rychard, Andrzej and Antoni Sulek, eds., 1988. *Legitymacja: Klasyczne Teorie i Polskie Doswiadczenia* Warsaw. [Legimation, Classical Theories and Polish Experience]. Warsaw: Polish Sociological Association the University of Warsaw.

Salinas, Maximilliano, 1990. "The voices of those who spoke up for the victims," in Leonardo Boff and Virgil Elizondo, eds., *1491–1991: The Voice of the Victims*, pp. 101–110. Concilium Special. London: SCM Press

Sanders, Thomas G., 1987. "Religion in Latin America," in Jack W. Hopkins, ed., *Latin America: Perspectives on a Region*, pp. 102–132. New York: Holmes and Meier.

Sayre, John Nevin, 1961. "The FOR and Latin America: Outline of work carried on 1919–1960." Nyack, NY: Fellowship of Reconciliation.

Schravesande, Joke, 1981. "Servicio Paz y Justicia en América Latina," *Info* 3 (February): 2–9.

SERPAJ-AL, 1987. *Principles, Objectives, and Foundations of SERPAJ-LA*. Rio de Janeiro: SERPAJ-AL.

SERPAJ-Europe, 1984. *SERPAJ-Europe Year Report, 1984*. Leusden, Holland: SERPAJ-Europe.

Sharp, Gene, 1979. *Gandhi as a Political Strategist*. Boston: Porter Sargent.

Shepherd, Gordon and Gary Shepherd, 1984. *A Kingdom Transformed: Themes in the Development of Mormonism*. Salt Lake City: University of Utah Press.

Shinn, Larry D., 1987. *The Dark Lord: Cult Images and the Hare Krishnas in America*. Philadelphia: Westminster Press.

Shipps, Jan, 1985. *Mormonism: The Story of a New Religious Tradition*. Urbana: University of Illinois Press.

Shlapentokh, Vladimir, 1989. *Public and Private Life of the Soviet People*. New York: Oxford University Press.

————, 1984. *Love, Marriage, and Friendship in the Soviet Union*. New York: Praeger.

Shupe, Anson D., 1991. "Globalization versus religious nativism: Japan's *Soka Gakkai* in the world arena," in Roland Robertson and William R. Garrett, eds., *Religion and Global Order*, pp. 183–99. New York: Paragon House.

————, 1990. "Sun Myung Moon's American disappointment," *Christian Century* (August 22–29): 764–66.

————, 1987. "The Unification Church as archetypal heretic: The case of media construction of evil," in Robert N. Bellah and Frederick E. Greenspahn, eds., *Uncivil Religion: Interreligious Hostility in America*, pp. 205–18. New York: Crossroad.

————, 1986. "Militancy and accommodation in the third civilization: The case of Japan's *soka gakkai* movement," in Jeffrey K. Hadden and Anson Shupe, eds., *Prophetic Religions and Politics*, pp. 235–53. New York: Paragon House.

————, 1985. "The routinization of conflict in the modern cult/anticult controversy," *Nebraska Humanist*, 8 (Fall): 26–39.

Shupe, Anson D. and David G. Bromley, 1985. "Social responses to cults," in Phillip E. Hammond, ed., *The Sacred in a Secular Age*, pp. 158–72. Berkeley: University of California Press.

Shupe, Anson D., William A. Stacey, and Lonnie R. Hazlewood, 1987. *Violent Men, Violent Couples: The Dynamics of Family Violence*. Lexington, MA: Lexington Press.

———, 1980. *The New Vigilantes: Deprogrammers, Anti-Cultists, and the New Religions*. Beverly Hills, CA: Sage

Shupe, Anson D., Bert L. Hardin, and David G. Bromley, 1983. "A comparison of anti-cult movements in the United States and West Germany," in Eileen Barker, ed., *Of Gods and Men: New Religious Movements in the West*, pp. 177–93. Macon, GA: Mercer University Press.

Sider, Ron, 1990. *Rich Christians in an Age of Hunger*. Waco, TX: Word Books.

Simpson, John H., 1991. "Globalization and religion: Themes and prospects," in Roland Robertson and William R. Garrett, eds., *Religion and Global Order*, pp. 1–17. New York: Paragon House.

———, 1989. "Toward a theory of America: Religion and structural dualism," in Jeffrey K. Hadden and Anson Shupe, eds., *Secularization and Fundamentalism Reconsidered*, pp. 78–90. New York: Paragon House.

———, 1988. "A reply to 'measuring public support for the new Christian right: The perils of point estimation,'" *Public Opinion Quarterly* 52: 338–42.

———, 1985. "Status inconsistency and moral issues," *Journal for the Social Scientific Study of Religion* 24: 155–62.

———, 1983. "Moral issues and status politics," in Robert C. Liebman and Robert Wuthnow, eds., *The New Christian Right: Mobilization and Legitimation*, pp. 188–205. New York: Aldine.

Simpson, John H. and John Hagan, 1981. "Conventional religiosity: Attitudes toward conflict, crime and income stratification in the United States," *Review of Religious Research* 23: 167–79.

Singer, Margaret T., 1985. "Abuse widespread among nation's cults," *National Association of Social Workers Newsletter* 30 (February): 4, 8.

Skidmore, Thomas and Peter H. Smith, 1989. *Modern Latin America*, 2nd Edition. New York: Oxford University Press.

Slater, David, ed., 1985. *New Social Movements and the State in Latin America*. Amsterdam: Centre for Latin American Research and Documentation.

Slominska, Janina, 1987. "Apostolstwo laikatu—wariant polski" [Apostolship of the laypersons—Polish case], *Wiez* [Bond] 2–3: 12–21.

Smith, Christian, 1991. *The Emergence of Liberation Theology: Radical Religion and Social Movement Theory*. Chicago: University of Chicago Press.

Smith, Donald E., 1974. *Religion and Political Modernization*. New Haven, CT: Yale University Press.

Smith, Tom W., 1990. "Classifying Protestant denominations," *Review of Religious Research* 31: 225–45.

SMOT, 1984. Free Inter-Professional Association of Workers Information Bulletin No. 30, in Ivan Hvat, *The Catacomb Ukrainian Catholic Church and Pope John Paul II*, pp. 273–90. Cambridge, MA: Ukrainian Studies Fund.

South American Committee of the IFOR, 1966. "Christian nonviolence in the Latin American social revolution." Documents of the consultation organized by the Fellowship of Reconciliation and held in Montevideo, Uruguay, May 23–29, 1966.

Staggenborg, Suzanne, 1991. *The Pro-Choice Movement: Organization and Activism in the Abortion Conflict*. New York: Oxford University Press.

Staniszkis, Jadwiga, 1989. *Ontologia Socializmu* [Ontology of Socialism].

——, 1988. "Stabilizacja bez uprawomocnienia," [Stabilization without Legitimation] in Andrzej Rychard and Antoni Sulek, eds., *Legitymacja: Klasyczne Teorie i Polskie Doswiadczenia* [Legitimation: Classical Theories and Polish Experience], pp. 215–39. Warsaw: Polish Sociological Association and the University of Warsaw.

——, 1985–86. "Forms of reasoning as ideology," *Telos* 66 (Winter 1985–86): 151–67.

Stark, David, 1990. "Privatization in Hungary: From plan to market or from plan to clan?" *East European Politics and Society* 4(3): 351–92.

Stark, Rodney, 1987. "How new religions succeed: A theoretical model," in David G. Bromley and Phillip E. Hammond, eds., *The Future of New Religious Movements*, pp. 11–29. Macon, GA: Mercer University Press.

——, 1985. "Europe's receptivity to religious movements," in Rodney Stark, ed., *Religious Movements: Genesis, Exodus, and Numbers*, pp. 301–43. New York: Paragon House.

Stark, Rodney and William Sims Bainbridge, 1985. *The Future of Religion, Secularization, Revival, and Cult Formation*. Berkeley: University of California Press.

Stoll, David, 1990. *Is Latin America Turning Protestant?* Berkeley: University of California Press.

Swatos, William H., Jr., 1989a. "The kingdom of God and the world of man: The problem of religious politics," in William H. Swatos, Jr., *Religious Politics in Global and Comparative Perspective*, pp. 1–9. New York: Greenwood Press.

——, 1989b. "Ultimate values in politics: Problems and prospects for world society," in William H. Swatos, Jr., *Religious Politics in Global and Comparative Perspective*, pp. 55–73. New York: Greenwood Press.

Sywulka, Stephen, 1989. "Evangelicals may become a majority in Guatemala." *Christianity Today*, April 21: 46.

Szatynska, Zofia, Boleslaw Szatynska, and Grzegorz Polak, 1987. "Neokatechumenat" [Neo-catechumenism], *Wiez* [Bond] 2–3: 39–43.

Szelenyi, Ivan, 1990. "Hungary 1989," *East European Politics and Societies* 4 no. 2: 208–11.

——, 1990b. "Alternative futures for Eastern Europe: The case of Hungary," *East European Politics and Societies* 4(2): 231–54.

Tarrow, Sidney, 1988. "National politics and collective action: Recent theory and research in Western Europe and the United States," *Annual Review of Sociology* 14: 421–40.

Taylor, Verta, 1989. "Social movement continuity: The women's movement in abeyance," *American Sociological Review* 54: 761–75.

Teltsch, Kathleen, 1990. "Scholars and descendants uncover hidden legacy of Jews in southwest," *New York Times*, November 11, 1990: 30.

Tillich, Paul, 1967. *Systematic Theology*. Chicago: University of Chicago Press.

Tilly, Charles, 1979. "Repertoires of contention in America and Britain, 1750–1830," in Mayer Zald and John D. McCarthy, eds., *The Dynamics of Social Movements*, pp. 126–55. Cambridge, MA: Winthrop.

Tischner, Jozef, 1991. "Manipulacja religia" [Manipulating with religion], *Relax* 51: 11–12.

Titus, Herbert, 1989. Letter to the Editor, *Christian Century*, November.

Tönnies, Ferdinand, 1957. *Community and Society: Gemeinschaft and Gesellschaft*. East Lansing: Michigan State University Press.

Toumey, Christopher P., 1990. "Social profiles of anti-evolutionism in North Carolina in the 1980s," *Journal of the Elisha Mitchell Scientific Society* 106(4): 93–117.

Touraine, Alain, 1988. *Return of the Actor: Social Theory in Post-Industrial Society*. Minneapolis: University of Minnesota Press.

Troeltsch, Ernst, 1960. *The Social Teaching of the Christian Churches*, trans. by Oliver Wyan. New York: Harper and Row.

Trompf, Garry, 1990. "The cargo and the milliennium on both sides of the Pacific," in Garry Trompf, ed., *Cargo Cults and Millenarian Movements: Transoceanic Comparisons of New Religious Movements*, pp. 34–94. Berlin: Mouton de Gruyter.

———, 1977. "Introduction," in Garry Trompf, ed., *Prophets of Melanesia*, pp. i–ix.

Turner, Frederick, 1991. *Rebirth of Values*. Albany: State University of New York Press.

Tyson, Brady, 1970. "Encounter in Recife," *Christian Century*, June 10: 720–22.

Vallier, Ivan, 1970. *Catholicism, Social Control, and Modernization in Latin America*. Englewood Cliffs, NJ: Prentice-Hall.

Vanden Berg, Frank, 1960. *Abraham Kuyper*. Grand Rapids, MI: Eerdmans.

van Fossen, Anthony B., 1988. "How do movements survive failures of prophecy?" in Louis Kriesberg and Bronislow Misztal, eds., *Social Movements as a Factor of Change in the Contemporary World*, pp. 252–72, *Research in Social Movements, Conflicts, and Change*, vol. 10, Greenwich, CT: JAI Press.

———, 1986. "Priests, aristocrats, and millennialism in Fiji," *Mankind* 16(3): 158–66.

———, 1984. "Prophetic failure and moral hierarchy: The origins of a contemporary French messianic movement," in R. A. Hutch and P. G. Fenner, eds., *Under the Shade of a Coolibah Tree*, pp. 24–35. Australian Studies in Consciousness. New York: University Press of America.

———, 1979. "The problem of evil in a millennial cult: The case of the Vailala Madness," *Social Analysis* 2: 72–88.

Vardys, V. Stanley, 1978. *The Catholic Church, Dissent, and Nationality in Soviet Lithuania*. Boulder, CO: East European Quarterly.

———, ed., 1965. *Lithuania under the Soviets: A Portrait of a Nation, 1940–65*. New York: Praeger.

Varnedoe, Kirk, 1989. *A Fine Disregard: What Makes Modern Art Modern*. New York: Abrams.

Wacker, Grant, 1984. "Heresy in Zion: Evangelicals in postmodern society," in

George Marsden, ed., *Evangelicalism and Modern America*, pp. 17–28. Grand Rapids, MI: Eerdmans.

Wallace, Anthony F. C., 1966. *Religion: An Anthropological View*. New York: Random House.

——, 1956. "Revitalization movements," *American Anthropologist* 58: 264–81.

Wallerstein, Immanuel, 1989. *The Modern World System III: The Second Era of Great Expansion of the Capitalist World-Economy*. New York: Academic Press.

——, 1980. *The Modern World System II: Mercantilism and the Consolidation of the European World-Economy, 1600–1750*. New York: Academic Press.

——, 1979. *The Capitalist World-Economy*. London: Cambridge University Press.

——, 1974. *The Modern World-System I: Capitalist Agriculture and the Origin of the European World-Economy in the Sixteenth Century*. New York: Academic Press.

Wallis, Roy, 1984. *The Elementary Forms of the New Religious Life*. London: Routledge and Kegan Paul.

——, 1977. *The Road to Total Freedom: A Sociological Analysis of Scientology*. New York: Columbia University Press.

Wasilewski, Jacek, 1990. "Bureaucratic elite recruitment in Poland," *Soviet Studies* 42(4): 743–57.

Weber, Max, 1956. *The Sociology of Religion*, trans. by Ephraim Fischoff. Boston: Beacon Press.

Weeks, John, 1986. "An interpretation of the Central American crisis." *Latin American Research Review* 21(3): 31–53.

Weron, Eugeniusz, Rev., 1984. "Wspolczesne koscielne ruchy laikatu" [Contemporary religious movements of the laymen], *Collectanea Theologica* 54: 113–18.

Whitcomb, J. C. and Henry Morris, 1961. *The Genesis Flood: The Biblical Record and Its Scientific Implications*. Grand Rapids, MI: Baker.

Whitehead, Harriet, 1974. "Reasonably fantastic: Some perspectives on scientology, science fiction, and occultism," in Irving I. Zaretsky and Mark P. Leone, eds., *Religious Movements in Contemporary America*, pp. 547–611. Princeton, NJ: Princeton University Press.

Wierzbicki, Zbigniew, 1976. "Rozwoj swiadomosci narodowej chlopow polskich: Zarys problematyki badawczej" [Development of national consciousness among Polish peasants], *Studia Socjologiczne* [Sociological Studies] 2.

Wierzbicki, Zbigniew and Placide Rambaud, 1982. "The emergence of the first agricultural union in socialist Poland," *Sociologia Ruralis* 23: 3–4.

Wilber, Charles K. and James H. Weaver, 1979. "Patterns of dependency: Income distribution and the history of underdevelopment," in Charles K. Wilber, ed., *The Political Economy of Development and Underdevelopment*, 2nd Edition, pp. 114–29. New York: Random House.

Wilkanowicz, Stefan and Jan Turnau, 1987. "Laikat w Watykanie, na calym swiecie i pod Wawelem" [The layperson movements in the Vatican, in the world, and at the Wawel Hill], *Wiez* [Bond] 2–3: 4–11.

Willetts, Peter, 1982. "The impact of promotional pressure groups on global politics," in Peter Willets, ed., *Pressure Groups in the Global System*, pp. 179–200. New York: St. Martin's.

Williams, F. E., 1923. *The Elementary Forms of the New Religious Life*. London: Routledge and Kegan Paul

Williamsburg Charter, 1988. Washington, D.C.: Williamsburg Charter Project.

Wills, Garry, 1990. *Religion and American Politics*. New York: Simon and Schuster.

Wilson, Bryan, 1987a. "Factors in the failure of the new religious movements," in David G. Bromley and Phillip E. Hammond, eds., *The Future of New Religious Movements*, pp. 30–45. Macon, GA: Mercer University Press.

——, 1987b. "Secularization," in M. Eliade, ed., *The Encyclopedia of Religion*, Vol. 13, pp. 159–65. New York: Macmillan.

——, 1982. "Time, generations, and sectarianism," in Bryan Wilson, ed., *The Social Impact of New Religious Movements*, pp. 217–34. New York: Rose of Sharon Press.

——, 1973. *Magic and the Millennium*. London: Heinemann.

Wilson, Everett A., 1988. "The Central American evangelicals: From protest to pragmatism," *International Review of Missions*, 77 (305) (January): 94–106.

Winter, J. Alan, 1991. "Religious belief and managerial ideology: An exploratory study of an extrapolation from the Weber thesis," *Review of Religious Research* 33: 169–75.

Wolf, Eric R., 1966. *Peasants*. Englewood Cliffs, NJ: Prentice-Hall.

Worsley, Peter, 1968. *The Trumpet Shall Sound*, Revised Edition. New York: Schocken.

Wuthnow, Robert, 1989. *Communities of Discourse: Ideology and Social Structure in the Reformation, the Enlightenment, and European Socialism*. Cambridge, MA: Harvard University Press.

——, 1987. *The Restructuring of American Religion*. Princeton, NJ: Princeton University Press.

——, 1982. "World order and religious movements," in Eileen Barker, ed., *New Religious Movements: A Perspective for Understanding Society*, pp. 47–65. Lewiston, NY: Edwin Mellen Press.

Wynia, Gary, 1984. *The Politics of Latin American Development*, 2nd Edition. New York: Cambridge University Press.

Yinger, J. Milton, 1957. *Religion, Society, and the Individual: An Introduction to the Sociology of Religion*. New York: Macmillan.

Zald, Mayer and Roberta Ash, 1973. "Social movement organizations: growth, decay, and change," in R. R. Evan, ed., *Social Movements: A Reader and Source Book*, pp. 80–101. Chicago: Rand McNally.

Zald, Mayer and M. A. Berger, 1978. "Social movements in organizations: Coup d'état, insurgency, and mass movements," *American Journal of Sociology* 83 (January): 823–61.

Zald, Mayer and John McCarthy, eds., 1987. *Social Movements in an Organizational Society: Collected Essays*. New Brunswick, NJ: Transaction Books.

——, eds., 1979. *The Dynamics of Social Movements: Resource Mobilization, Social Control, and Tactics*. Cambridge, MA: Winthrop.

Zawislak, Andrzej M., 1988. "Panstwo kontra gospodarka: Prawidlowosc czy patologia" [The state vs. the economy: Principle or pathology?], in Witold Morawski and Wieslawa Kozek, eds., *Zalamanie Porzadku Etatystycznego*

[The Breakdown of the Etatistic Order]. Warsaw: University of Warsaw Press.

Zulaika, Joseba, 1988. *Basque Violence: Metaphor and Sacrament.* Reno: University of Nevada Press.

Zurcher, Louis A., 1971. "The anti-pornography campaign: A symbolic crusade," *Social Problems* 19: 217–38.

INDEX

ABOUT THE EDITORS AND CONTRIBUTORS

BRUCE BARRON has focused his research on charismatic and evangelical Christians in contemporary America, including their political implications. He holds a Ph.D. in religion from the University of Pittsburgh and has also worked as a congressional aide. His books include *The Health and Wealth Gospel* and a forthcoming volume on the Christian Reconstruction Movement.

MICHAEL DODSON is Professor of Political Science at Texas Christian University. He is coauthor of *Let My People Live* and *Nicaragua's Other Revolution,* and has published numerous research articles on religion and politics in Latin America. In 1985 he was a Fulbright Senior Lecturer in Great Britain.

RAYMOND A. EVE is Associate Professor of Sociology at the University of Texas at Arlington. He teaches and conducts research in the areas of collective behavior and social movements, criminology and deviant behavior, and education (among others). In addition to authoring numerous professional articles, he is coeditor (with Francis B. Harrold) of *Cult Archaeology and Creationism: Explaining Pseudoscientific Beliefs about the Past.*

KRZYSZTOF GORLACH is Assistant Professor of Sociology at Jagiellonian University. His areas of expertise include rural sociology, social movements, and research on social structure. He is the author of *Peasant Question and Polish Sociology* and coauthor of *Peasants in Contemporary Poland: Agents or Outsiders of Social Processes.*

FRANCIS B. HARROLD is Associate Professor of Anthropology at the University of Texas at Arlington. An archaeologist, he has conducted field and museum research in France, Spain, and the United States and has published a number of articles on these projects. His specialty is prehistoric European rock art and stone tools. With Raymond A. Eve he is coeditor of *Cult Archaeology and Creationism: Explaining Pseudoscientific Beliefs about the Past.*

HANK JOHNSTON teaches in the Department of Sociology at San Diego State University. He specializes in the analysis of minority nationalist movements and has published several articles comparing the preconditions of nationalist mobilization, especially under state repression. He has also published articles about religious movements in the United States and religion and politics in Europe and Latin America. His recent book, based on field work in Spain, is entitled *Tales of Nationalism: Catalonia 1939–1979.*

SLAWOMIR JAN MAGALA teaches Cultural Anthropology at Erasmus University in Rotterdam, The Netherlands, specializing in the theory of social change and organizations. He was educated in Poland, West Germany, and the United States. He has published ten books, including *Georg Simmel; Class Struggle in Classless Poland; The Polish Student Theatre as an Element of Counterculture; Business as Unusual: Polish and Hungarian Transitions towards Market Economies*, and over 350 articles.

JOHN D. MCCARTHY is Professor of Sociology and a member of the Life Cycle Institute at the Catholic University of America. He has written extensively on social movements and is the author of the forthcoming *Crashes, Not Accidents: The Citizens' Movement against Drunk Driving.* He is presently studying citizen protest in Washington, D.C.

BRONISLAW MISZTAL is Professor of Sociology at Indiana University–Purdue University at Fort Wayne, specializing in social movements research. Dr. Misztal, who was born and educated in Poland, holds the title of honorary Chair–Jacques Leclercq at Catholic University of Louvain, where he lectured in 1981. In 1981 he received a Senior Fulbright-Hays academic award at the University of Chicago. His articles have been published in *Sociology, British Journal of Sociology, Australian and New Zealand Journal of Sociology, Politics and Society, International Journal of Comparative Sociology, Urban Affairs Quarterly*, and *Récits de vie/Life Stories.* He has also edited and coauthored two volumes: *Poland after Solidarity: Social Movements versus the State* and *Social Movements as a Factor of Change in the Contemporary World.*

JANUSZ L. MUCHA is Associate Professor at Copernicus University in Torun, Poland. He specializes in the history of sociology.

RONALD PAGNUCCO, a doctoral candidate in the Department of Sociology at The Catholic University of America, is currently completing his dissertation on the U.S. peace movement of the late 1980s. He is a longtime member of the Fellowship of Reconciliation (FOR). In 1982 he and FOR member Dr. Brady Tyson founded the Committee in Solidarity with Latin American Nonviolent Movements (CISLANM). From 1982 to 1984 Mr. Pagnucco and Dr. Tyson edited *Solidarity/Solidaridad*, the newsletter of CISLANM and the FOR's Task Force on Latin America.

ANSON SHUPE is Professor of Sociology at Indiana University–Purdue University at Fort Wayne, specializing in the sociology of religion and politics, and has taught at both Alfred University and the University of Texas at Arlington. He is the author, coauthor, or coeditor of over eighteen books and numerous book chapters, journal articles, popular magazine articles, and regional as well as national newspaper editorials.

JOHN H. SIMPSON is Professor of Sociology and Chair of the Department of Sociology at the University of Toronto. He was Director of the University of Toronto's Graduate Centre for Religious Studies from 1981 to 1985.

ANTHONY B. VAN FOSSEN is Lecturer in the social sciences at Griffith University in Australia. His research interests include the comparative sociology and international political economy of radical religious movements. He has published articles on millennialism and messianism in France and the Pacific Islands.

MACIEJ K. ZABA was Assistant Professor at the Institute of Religious Studies, Jagiellonian University, Cracow, Poland, specializing in the sociology of religion. He died in 1991.